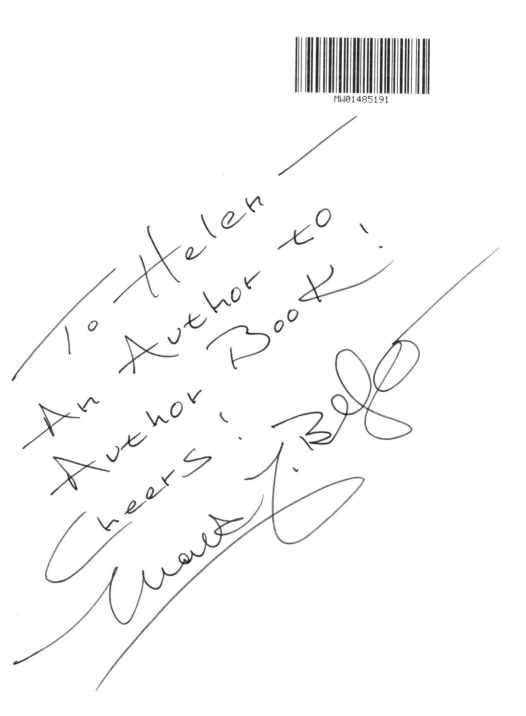

To Helen —

An Author to
Author Book !

Cheers !

JOE COCKER
With a LOT
of Help
from
His Friends

Yorkshire Publishing
TULSA

ISBN: 978-1-960810-17-5
Joe Cocker: With a LOT of Help From My Friends

Yorkshire Publishing
1425 E 41st Pl
Tulsa, OK 74105
www.YorkshirePublishing.com
918.394.2665

Printed in Canada

JOE COCKER

With a LOT of Help

from His Friends

BY MARK BEGO

Contents

Acknowledgements

The author would like to thank the following people for their help, assistance, and encouragement:

—Bob and Mary Bego
—Loren Christenfeld
—Rita Coolidge
—Jesus De Aguiar Porras
—Kent Denmark
—Laura Denmark
—Dave Marken
—Jonathan Moorehead
—Melanie Safka
—David Salidor
—Lisa Saltzman
—Mark Sokoloff
—Linda Solomon
—Special thanks to Mary Wilson as my constant inspiration

Dedication

To Marcy MacDonald:

You were a ray of sunshine and silliness in my life since the 1970s. I miss your kooky little gifts, your late night phone calls, and you—you wild and crazy girl.

Introduction

by *Woodstock* Legend: Melanie

When I think of Joe Cocker, I think of the word "authenticity." The feeling I always got from him was that he was a "true artist," and it was the music that was most important to him. I absolutely loved him. I thought he was so great, and he was so talented as a singer and as a performer, that I got the sense he was from another planet.

Because we were both performers at the original *Woodstock Music Festival* in August of 1969, Joe and I will forever be part of that exclusive club of singers and musicians. There was no experience quite like *Woodstock*, and we were both in awe of the magnitude of the event and the importance of being associated with it.

Throughout his life, Joe was truly "who he was." There was no pretense to him. To me he felt very authentic and real in everything that he did. Not everyone is like that. In the world of rock & roll, there were some "shuck and jive" groups and performers, who were only into making music for the girls, the parties, and the money. However, Cocker was different. He had a genuine passion and a fire within him to sing with his heart and soul. There was no pretense to him.

I have known Mark Bego since the 1970s when he interviewed me for a magazine article, and we have been friends ever since. On these pages, Mark tells Joe's story with the same kind of passion and love of the music that defined Cocker's life and career.

—Melanie

"On The Path Of Self-Destruction"

J oe Cocker is something of an enigma in the rock & roll world. Everyone seems to know his music and his distinctive raspy and world-weary voice, but it seems that very few people know any of the details of his harrowing roller coaster of a story. As you will find on these pages, Cocker racked up several career "highs" in his 70-year life, but he had far more years of "lows" along the way.

In fact, when I first started telling people that I was writing about Joe Cocker, about 75% of the friends I mentioned this to immediately asked me, "Is he still alive?" That was how far "off the radar" Joe had fallen by the time he died in 2014. Everyone knew who Joe was, and they all loved his music, but almost no one seemed to know anything about his life, or the cause of his demise.

I somehow got it into my head that Joe was something of a mystery, and it was my job to understand what "made him tick." It made me want to seek out his friends, his co-workers, and his fans, in an effort to piece this puzzle together.

With regard to his music, if there is one song which he will always be indelibly associated with, it is "With A Little Help From My Friends." He took his distinctive version of this Beatles' classic all the way to Number 1 in England in 1969 when he was only 26 years old. Then when he came across the water to "the states" and performed it in front of half a million people at the famed *Woodstock Music Festival* in August of that year, Cocker instantly cemented his place in rock history.

When he was seen in the filmed version of *Woodstock* and countless millions more people got to see him gyrating spastically on stage in his brightly colored tie-dyed shirt he became permanently welded to and associated with that event. In less than a year Joe was back on the road with the biggest and most famous rock & roll tour of his entire career: *Mad Dogs & Englishmen.*

In so many ways, by the end of 1970, Joe Cocker had already experienced the highest creative peak of his career. In a certain sense, it was all downhill for Joe from that point forward. Yet, on the other hand, there is a lot more to the story beyond that. It was only after years of seeing his life unravel before his eyes that he was able to piece himself back together.

As I did my research, everyone I spoke to who knew Joe had nothing but good things to say about him. Describing him, people most commonly used the words "kind," "innocent," and "naïve." Although I never met him, he seems to have been outwardly "likeable." However, as I delved into Joe's history, I found that throughout his life he had only one enemy to fight against for his survival: himself. Cocker is a textbook case of a life-long battle of career and personal self-destruction. While the rock & roll "side of the road" is littered with the sagas of characters who ruined their lives with drugs, liquor, cigarettes, and depression, it seems that few did it as long and hard as Joe Cocker.

For decade after decade, he seemed to do everything he could to wallow in self-pity and drown himself in a sea of booze, tobacco, and cocaine. And somehow he still survived. Along the way he encountered arrests, deportations, financial disasters, and a battle against the ever-changing landscape of the music scene.

I certainly knew of him from *Woodstock* and *Mad Dogs & Englishmen*, both the films and the hit albums that were released from them. I definitely knew and loved Joe's biggest hits, and I always enjoyed hearing his music, but I was never what can be called "a fan" of his. Until recently, the only album of Joe's I owned was *Mad Dogs*. And for a man who owns thousands of albums, this was really saying something!

My path towards delving into Joe's life and ultimately writing this book came about in a fascinatingly roundabout way. I had written a book with Debby Campbell which was released in 2014 called *Life With My Father Glen Campbell*. It became a Top Ten hit in Nashville and on the Amazon charts, and it garnered some really great reviews. Eventually in 2022 a sharp and aggressive movie producer by the name of Lisa Saltzman phoned me to ask if I had ever written a screenplay.

I told her that I had indeed written a screenplay about Elvis Presley and his friendship with his Memphis Mafia pal, Lamar Fike. Nothing had happened with that 2008 screenplay although it was registered with The Writer's Guild of America. After a couple of discussions, Lisa hired me to write a screenplay about Glen Campbell's life, and I did so. She liked what I did, and I crossed my fingers about its outcome.

After having delivered to Lisa the finished Campbell screenplay I received another phone call from her. She liked what I had done with Campbell, and she asked me if I would be interested in writing another screenplay for her, which I was. According to her, "I either want a screenplay about Gerry Rafferty or about Joe Cocker. Which one would you find to be the better subject?"

I told her I was interested and that I would do a little research and get back with her. I certainly knew who Gerry Rafferty was. He was a member of the group Stealer's Wheel in the 1970s, and they had a big hit called "Stuck In The Middle With You." Then he went solo and had a huge hit in 1978 with "Baker Street." Those were basically the high points of his career. Then, in his personal life, Rafferty spent his years battling the booze bottle, and he died at the age of 62 of liver disease.

Next, I started researching Joe Cocker. He had a bigger career than Rafferty, and Joe had the high point of *Woodstock, Mad Dogs & Englishmen*, and the Number 1 1982 hit "Up Where We Belong" with Jennifer Warnes which won an Academy Award. To put it in the simplest terms: of the two, Rafferty and Cocker, in my mind Joe had the more interesting story. For a full screenplay, I immediately found that there was much more to work with by writing about Cocker.

When I reported back to Lisa Saltzman, I said to her, "Gerry Rafferty was a drunk who eventually drank himself to death and died of liver disease. Joe Cocker was a life-long drunk and a two-packs-a-day cigarette smoker who eventually quit drinking and smoking only to die of lung cancer. I like both subjects, but I find Cocker much more interesting."

With that, I chose to write the Cocker screenplay. After writing two back-to-back screenplays, it was finally time to return to my book writing career. In 2021 I had written a book with singer Freda Payne called *Band of Gold* for Yorkshire Publishing. The book about Freda was a critical hit and won a prize at The Paris Book Festival. It was part of a two-book contract that I signed, and I had to come up with the second subject. To make a long story shorter, I proposed that I write a book about Joe Cocker since I had amassed so much research material about him. Kent and Laura Denmark of Yorkshire Publishing agreed on Joe as a subject, and here is the book!

Writing a screenplay and writing a book, although similar, are completely different in form and structure. In a screenplay, you have to select the key elements that make up a two hour movie. The screenplay writer chooses the scenes and characters that are to be filmed. A biography writer needs to tell about every aspect of the subject's life.

Working on the screenplay re-introduced me to Joe's music and life. But working on this book made me want to do much more research to find the truth and to delve into every aspect of his life.

Come along with me on this journey to discover the facts about Joe Cocker's life, what motivated him, the music that defined his career, and the decisions that he made to live with. So often he made the wrong choices. On these pages are the good parts, the bad parts, and everything in between. You are in for a wild ride. It is a truly wild ride that only Joe Cocker could orchestrate.

—Mark Bego
2023

CHAPTER ONE

"Sheffield Steel"

The city of Sheffield is located in the South Yorkshire section of England. When you hear the name "Sheffield, England" you might think of steel mills, or trains loaded with coal, and smokestacks in the 1800s when it was a steel producing town. Or you might liken the term "Sheffield Steel" to the famous knives made in that town. Or you could think of it as the modern city with acres of trees and greenery. Or perhaps you recall seeing Sheffield in the 1979 movie, *The Full Monty*, as it was filmed there. However, your first thought probably would not be: "What a great and well-known rock & roll town!"

Yet Sheffield is where Joe Cocker was born, grew up, and lived a great part of his adult life. His parents, Edgar and Madge Cocker, were married in 1937 and moved into a Nineteenth Century house located at 38 Tasker Road. Edgar was employed in a nice government job working for The National Assistance Board. He was basically a welfare officer, and he processed people's unemployment claims. Madge was a stay-at-home mother and housewife, and she ran the Cocker household.

Their first child, Victor, was born on October 30, 1940. Then on May 20, 1944, came their second child, John Robert Cocker who was later to rename himself "Joe Cocker" both in his personal life and his professional life. The boys got along great, and they loved to play games together, including one called "Cowboy Joe." Madge was reportedly very interested in having her boys pursue their hobbies and follow their passions, whether it was games, or music, or art.

One of Joe's boyhood friends was John Mitchell who lived across the street at 47 Tasker Road. Apparently, there was a local window washer who worked in the area whose name was Joe. Making fun of the man, as young boys will often do, they began calling each other "Joe" as well. John Mitchell was just poking fun when he repeatedly referred to his friend John Robert Cocker as "Joe Cocker" to his face. And in turn, Cocker would call his friend "Joe Mitchell." For "Joe Mitchell," it was just a childhood phase and an inside joke. However, for "Joe Cocker," it was to become his nickname, his stage name, and his trademark. And it stuck to him for the rest of his life.

While the Cocker boys had their own interests, Edgar Cocker had several hobbies of his own. He loved gardening and was quite a music fan. Edgar had his own record collection, and one of his favorite singers was Mario Lanza.

As Edgar was relishing listening to his own favorite opera and pop standard music, in 1956 there were other musical styles suddenly emanating from both sides of the Atlantic. In the United States, this was the year that Elvis Presley suddenly exploded onto the scene with his first string of Number One international hits, which included: "Heartbreak Hotel," "I Want You, I Need You, I Love You," "Don't Be Cruel," and "Hound Dog." That was also a big year for Little Richard ("Long Tall Sally") and Bill Haley & The Comets ("See You Later, Alligator,") signaling the new wave of rock & roll. Meanwhile, in the United Kingdom the hot new musical star on the scene was Lonnie Donegan and his "skiffle" hit "Rock Island Line."

Like rock & roll, skiffle was guitar-based music that was upbeat and exciting to hear. Born in Glasgow, Scotland, Donegan was originally a member of Chris Barber's Jazz Band, and he eventually became known as "The King of Skiffle." When eleven-year-old Joe Cocker heard Lonnie Donegan on the radio, he was suddenly hooked on the modern music scene.

The strummed and shouted music style that is "skiffle" was an absolute rage in England in the late 1950s and early 1960s. Donegan had two back-to-back British Number 1 hits: "Cumberland Gap" and "Putting On The Style." These records were all a part of young Joe Cocker's growing record collection. He was even a member of the official Lonnie Donegan Fan Club. He had the club badge, and he knew all the lyrics to Lonnie's songs. He would practice singing them in front of the mirror.

Here was Lonnie, a man from Scotland, singing a story song about a train in New Orleans and performing it in a lively and animated fashion. This made thoughts about a music career seem so much more obtainable to young Joe Cocker. To view videos of Lonnie today, you can see the brand of unbridled vocal delivery that Cocker was to later emulate in his own music.

When Donegan performed at The Sheffield Empire at the height of his fame, young Joe was waiting at the stage door for an autograph from his skiffle hero. Lonnie asked Joe, "Well, what do you do?" and Joe replied, "I want to be what you are." (1)

By the time Joe was 14 years old, he had a newspaper route, and it was there that he met another newspaper boy by the name of Phil Crookes. The teenagers would often cross paths and became friendly. They would talk about their mutual love of music, and they would smoke cigarettes. Although he was a young teenager, Joe had already developed the daily habit of smoking tobacco, never realizing the dangers that becoming a life-long smoker would one day yield.

Their mutual love of music would bond Joe and Phil even further. Joe had aspirations to become a singer, and Phil was already displaying his musical talents on his guitar. They both loved American blues performers. And when blues singer Big Bill Broonzy came to Sheffield City Hall, Joe and Phil were in the audience.

Once skiffle music got into his soul, young Joe Cocker had trouble concentrating on school or his studies. He had music on his mind, and it was to become not only a pastime but something of an obsession. It was in the middle of 1956 that a musical performer came out of the Cocker household. It wasn't young "Joe" Cocker, it was his older brother Vic who first entered the fray.

When he was 15 years old, Vic and three friends his age formed their own skiffle band that they christened The Headlanders. Vic played the washboard while another one of his friends, Dave Brooksbank, played the banjo, and the two other members of the group played the guitar. They would occasionally perform at local teenage dances which were often held at youth clubs. Joe was frequently at their rehearsals and their shows.

It was Brooksbank's idea to invite Vic's little brother to sing with the band one night in Fir Street, Walkley. Dave liked Joe's voice and he asked him to get up on stage with the band and sing a song. Even Vic was surprised at how well Joe could sing along with the band. This became the true beginning of the singing career of Joe Cocker. From that point forward Joe knew what he wanted to do with his life.

Although he was just 12 and a half years old, Joe had found his calling. When The Headlanders entered a talent competition that was held at The Sheffield Empire, there was no place on stage with the band for the washboard player's little brother. Recounted Joe, "I remember being at The Empire and thinking, 'God, I wish I could be up there.' I've often wondered if it would have been my claim to fame." (1)

This was the era in which Joe developed the musical taste that would blossom and grow into becoming his musical trademark. He was taken almost simultaneously by both the blues and by the emerging new wave coming across the Atlantic Ocean: rock & roll. As he would later explain, "When I was 13, my brother had a skiffle band,

and I used to sing with them. Lonnie Donegan was the king of skiffle, so he was my first idol. He took his name from Lonnie Johnson, so that was how I found my way back into the blues." (2)

How on Earth did a white boy from England first find "the blues" to be something which resonated with him? According to Joe, "With me, coming from Sheffield and it being a steel town, I had that learning. I've never understood it—what made the war babies in Britain have this obsession for the blues? I've still got a fixation about black music. Something deep down inside me always responds to it. I was into Muddy Waters, Lightnin' Hopkins, and John Lee Hooker. Ray Charles, of course, was my mentor." (2)

Regarding his initiation into the world of rock & roll in 1956, Joe recalls, "All of a sudden 'Be-Bop-A-Lula' came over the air, and I'd never heard anything like that! Gene Vincent blew me away and then a few days later I met Phil [Crookes] and we actually put down a [song on] tape. It was a primitive tape machine that my dad bought me. You attached it to the record player. I remember we did a version of a Big Bill Broonzy tune, and Phil's guitar playing really impressed my brother's skiffle group." (1)

Rock & roll music was indeed exploding all over the world. It was not only on the radio and the television, but it was also blossoming onto the movie screens as well. One of the first rock & roll movies to explode onto the big screen was *Rock Around The Clock* in 1956, starring Bill Haley & The Comets, The Platters, and Freddie Bell & The Bellboys. As Joe recalls, "I took my dad to *Rock Around The Clock* with Bill Haley and he was absolutely horrified. To him it was the start of something new, and he was dead right." (3)

Joe found himself loving all sorts of rock & roll music. Suddenly the airwaves were full of the sounds of Elvis Presley, Eddie Cochran, and Chuck Berry. It was an exciting time for music. At this point, the nightmare that had been World War II was being left behind and replaced by a more hopeful new era of living and of popular music to go along with it.

It was in 1959 that Joe's most important musical influence of all first came to prominence, first on the airwaves and then in Joe's mind. It was the song "What'd I Say" by Ray Charles. Suddenly, Joe's world was shaken in a lasting way. It was bluesy, it was part gospel, and it was all rock & roll at the same time. Although he would always love Lonnie Donegan, he was even more deeply influenced by the sound of Ray Charles.

He first heard the song "What'd I Say" on his little transistor radio which he used to carry around with him. It was his lifeline to the music world. Once he heard this song, the music and singing style of Ray Charles became his main focus and undying passion. Soon his record collection included everything he could get his hands upon. It became something imbedded in him unconsciously.

According to Joe, "When you do that long enough you reach a point where it's all in the back of your head, where the influence becomes a part of you, and you sing a particular way without thinking about it. When I sing now it comes out in the way it does without any conscious effort on my part to sound like Ray Charles." (4)

When Joe used to enthusiastically play Ray Charles' records around the house, his music-loving father didn't care for what he heard. Joe was to explain, "My dad was never too crazy on Ray [Charles] at all. He said he sounded like he had a pin stuck up his arse. Now that's a very English phrase." (2)

It was during the winter of 1959 into 1960 that Joe and his friend Phil Crookes began assembling their first band that they called The Cavaliers. The next member of the band to join was Joe's school friend John Mitchell. When Mitchell was 13 years old, his father had bought him a banjo, and he became quite proficient at it. He and Joe would spend hours singing skiffle songs together. Then there was Bob Everson who had made his own bass guitar in the family cellar.

Since Joe was the natural choice as the lead vocalist of The Cavaliers and because they didn't have a drummer, Cocker handled both tasks.

They added amplifiers to their growing list of equipment, and suddenly it was a band. In need of a rehearsal space and with encouraging parents, the Cocker living room became just that.

As Joe's father was to recall, "We had to retire to the other room. They had drums and amplifiers and all the lot . . . made the place shake it did. It's a wonder our neighbor didn't complain, but she was a widow and she used to go out nearly every night, so she probably never noticed. They used to practice a lot!" (1)

Finally, after much rehearsing, it was time for their first gig in front of a live audience. Their big break was as part of a revue at a local youth club, which was conveniently located right around the corner from the Cocker home. It was not a fancy event where they were paid for their time and talent, in fact, they had to pay the club three pence admission just to be part of the show.

The Cavaliers sang several of their favorite radio hits including:

"Johnny B. Goode"
"Move It"
"Twenty Flight Rock"
"I'm A Man."

Joe sang lead while playing the drums and much to everyone's surprise their most talented musician, Phil Crookes, played the whole set with his back to the audience. They never suspected their most proficient member also had a case of "stage fright."

Meanwhile, Joe had his own confidence issue as well. Although he was instantly riveting as a singer, he was also painfully shy. As he was to later explain it, "I could never just push myself. I've always had a weight problem, ever since I was a kid, and that made me a bit self-conscious over the years, just being tubby. It always made me very shy with girls and all that stuff. It's a reservation . . . a reservation that people wouldn't like me." (1)

Bob Everson had a job as an apprentice for a television rental company, and he worked with a man by the name of Ray Capewell. Ray was four years older than the members of The Cavaliers, and once Bob had bragged about how good they were at making music, Capewell was intrigued. He made arrangements to attend one of the band's rehearsals at the Cocker household. He had a good ear for music, and he also had the use of the company van on the weekends. He loved what he heard, and he became the band's first manager. Ray thought he could get The Cavaliers work, and he could also use the van to drive the lads to their gigs.

It wasn't long before it became obvious that drumming and singing at the same time was one task too many. But instead of finding a drummer and freeing up Joe to be the lead singer of the band, they opted to hire another singer!

Recalled Phil Crookes, "Joe had real difficulty playing the snare drum and keeping the voice going. So—and this is funny, isn't it—we decided to get a singer, a good-looking guy, can't remember his name." (1)

"I was a drummer originally," Joe explained, "but I never thought I was that good; trying to sing and drum was difficult. I remember the band saying, 'You have to do one or the other, and we'd prefer that you drum because we'll never find another drummer.' And we had this horrible kid singer." (5)

The one thing that everyone does remember is that the new singer wore carpet bedroom slippers on stage and was very handsome but could not sing well. After several gigs with the replacement singer, The Cavaliers realized that, even though he had to drum while he sang, having Joe as their lead singer was their best chance at finding any sort of success.

The Ray Capewell era started to unravel when he had a driving accident in his van. Having broken both of his legs in the accident, Ray was hospitalized, and the band came to visit him. He was then forced to convalesce in the home of his wife's parents. To keep him in the loop, for a while, The Cavaliers would come to Ray, and subsequently drive his in-laws crazy with the band's boisterous rehearsals in their home. Particularly irritating to everyone was Joe's constant drumming on everything, including the floor. The band even played at Ray's 21st birthday party, held in a tiny apartment.

Unfortunately, the run of The Cavaliers lasted only a year. Joe was 16 at the time, and after a local school bus strike disrupted his education, he dropped out of Sheffield Central Technical School for good. This was not something that pleased his parents at all, but Joe had completely lost interest in his formal education. He was much more interested in attending the school of rock & roll. He had music on his mind, and there was no stopping him.

CHAPTER TWO

"Vance Arnold & The Avengers"

After The Cavaliers had taken their careers as a local bar band as far as they could it was time for a new incarnation and a more exciting image for teenage Joe Cocker and his friends. From this point forward, Joe and his band re-christened themselves: Vance Arnold & The Avengers.

As Joe was later to explain, "It was just something flash for the times. 'Joe Cocker' wasn't a very acceptable name back then. It was always my big secret that I could never own up to anyone that I called myself 'Vance Arnold.'" (4)

Explaining how he came up with that name, he claimed, "It was self-invented, much to my embarrassment for years. But everyone used to have names in Sheffield like Johnny Tempest & The Cadillacs. We were called The Avengers, and the guys said: 'You'd better come up with a name.' I remember just sitting one day, and I thought of Eddy Arnold, the old country guy, and the 'Vance' was from an Elvis film, I think." (3) It was his idea alright, and it indeed was to gain the new band some desired attention.

The film he was referring to was the famed Elvis Presley cinematic hit, *Jailhouse Rock* (1957), in which Elvis played the starring role as Vince Everett, a jailbird turned rock & roll hero. With a slight spelling alteration, Joe Cocker started the next phase of his career as

Vance Arnold, accompanied by his trusty Avengers. Their trademark on- stage look was matching dark suits worn with matching bow ties.

Joe explained, "I never went to grammar school, and when I was 16 my dad said, 'You've got to get a job. What do you want to do?' I said, 'Be a radio disc jockey.' Everybody laughed. They thought I'd lost my mind. In 1960 it was unheard of for anyone who didn't have education, perfect grammar to get on the BBC." (6)

Being a school drop-out with no experience in radio, Joe's dream of being a disc jockey at the BBC was a real long-shot. Instead, he focused his energies on his new incarnation as Vance Arnold. Their first gig was at a small pub in Sheffield called The Minerva Tavern. Their performance fee was the underwhelming amount of £5. At this point he was still drumming and singing, handling the band's bookings, and paying £2 each way for their transportation to the pub. This gave Vance Arnold & The Avengers a whole £1 to split between themselves for their efforts.

Although Joe was done with school and was actively chasing a career as a rock & roll musician, the music-making was still little more than a hobby which barely paid for itself. As Joe was to recall, "At the time we were called Vance Arnold & The Avengers, and we were playing the pubs, which was a great upbringing. We'd go to these pubs every night after our day jobs and drink a lot of beer and play until the pubs closed. Kept us in 'beer money.' We weren't in a big hurry to be successful." (5)

The task of being the group's drummer, booking agent, roadie, transportation organizer, and lead singer was beginning to wear on Joe. It was too much for the teenager to keep straight on a regular basis. Technical disasters were regular occurrences in those days. One night they took public transportation to The Minerva Tavern, and when they arrived at the club Joe discovered that he had left his snare drum at home.

Recalls guitar player Bob Everson, "He'd hung it out on the washing line to tighten the skin up, and he forgot to take it off! He only had the drum and cymbal to remember, and he forgot the drum." (1)

The crowd at The Minerva Tavern came to hear live bands play cover versions of recent radio hits, and Vince Arnold & The Avengers delivered their faithful renditions of songs including Chubby Checker's "Let's Twist Again" and Jerry Keller's "Here Comes Summer."

Growing restless to move up to more prestigious gigs, from The Minerva Tavern the band graduated to The Fleur De Lys which was located on the edge of town. Recalling The Fleur De Lys, Phil Crookes explained, "That was a top event where all the bands played. When we first played there, we thought, 'Oh, great! This is it!' We were all nervous. The gig was advertised in the [news]paper." (1) For Vance Arnold and The Avengers, this was "the big time" in the Sheffield area.

Unlike The Minerva Tavern where bar fights would break out regularly, The Fleur De Lys was much classier. They were far less likely to be pelted by a hurled beer bottle there. The band's Ray Stuart remembers, "It was at 'The Fleur' around 1961 that Joe really started to get noticed by people . . . [There were] other groups saying, 'Hey have you seen Vance Arnold & The Avengers?' It was him, and it was the material. He was doing numbers by Ray Charles, whom very few people had heard of, and the Chuck Berry stuff was little known in Britain in the very early 1960s. Joe was hooked on that sort of music, but in Sheffield they said, 'Oh that'll never take off.'" (4)

Joe started to stretch out musically while at The Fleur De Lys. He didn't feel bound to play everyone else's pop radio hits; he could delve into some more artsy and obscure material, particularly the blues. The band's set now featured songs like Ray Charles' "Georgia

On My Mind" and Bo Diddley's "Diddy Wah Diddy" and some Chuck Berry tunes as well.

Joe was still attempting to play the drums while singing. However, it was becoming progressively more daunting. According to Cocker, "We did things like Jerry Lee [Lewis]'s 'Move On Down The Line.' It was hard work, singing and playing. I'd always been getting [drum] sticks crossed!" (1)

The time finally came for the band to insist that Joe concentrate on what he did best: singing. At long last they found a friend who could take over the drumming: Steve McKenna. Joe could retire the clip-on microphone and step out front and just be lead singer, Vance Arnold.

It was around this same time that Joe started to adopt his trademark on stage spastic choreography. Was he playing "air guitar?" Was he having a physical breakdown? Was he dancing? Whatever it was, it became his unique signature move during a show. According to Phil Crookes, "Joe never got on with the guitar; he never actually got 'round to playing it, but he always wanted to. So he used to kind of imagine he was playing it. I tried to show him a few things, but he always ended up imagining he was playing and that was probably good enough for him." (1)

The rocky road to success in the music business comes with occasional personnel changes. Vance Arnold & The Avengers were no different. Now that they had a dedicated drummer, Graham Bower came in and replaced rhythm guitar player John Mitchell. Then, after one particularly rough night, Joe walked off and split from the band for several weeks.

As Cocker later explained, "We'd played somewhere near Rotherham and I'd lost my voice which is a pain to any singer, but it doesn't happen to me too often. What happens is that you get over-enthused and tend to blow out too much energy. And they [his bandmates] were going, 'Joe, you're useless,' so I got on the bus and left them! About six weeks later they came 'round, knocking on my door, saying, 'Joe, we can't find anyone else!' So—ALRIGHT! Back in business." (1)

By 1960, when he was 16 years old, his parents finally insisted that Joe get a real "day job" to augment the "beer money" the band was used to earning. To support himself and his growing rock & roll lifestyle, Joe took a job working for the local Gas Board as a pipe fitter. It wasn't as glamorous as being a disc jockey on the BBC, but it paid some bills and got his father off his back.

He was installing and/or repairing people's gas lines for heating and cooking appliances. It was not the most prestigious day job to have, but that was how Joe Cocker supported himself in between his gigs as a rock & roll singer.

Joe was later to laughingly recall his locally famous singing career and his gas fitting career occasionally overlapping: "One of the best things that ever happened was when I was gas fitting. I went to someone's house and the woman said to her husband: 'Oooh, come and look—Vance is putting our fire in!'" (3)

Young Cocker's main job was to fix and/or install the gas lines to kitchen stoves in people's homes, and for a three-month streak, he worked at the Gas Board's showroom as a customer relations representative. Around this time, he became friends with another young boy who worked for the same company, by the name of Pete Jackson. Pete loved to go out drinking which along with cigarette chain-smoking was one of Joe's favorite pastimes. Also Pete owned a Ford Consul with blue flames painted down each side. Together, Joe and Pete would go out on drinking expeditions.

Joe was to recall, "We had some fantastic times together, me and old Pete. We'd go out and terrorize the countryside dressed up in black leather—the Gene Vincent look. We used to wear this night tan. You rubbed it in, and it made you look sunburned. The only trouble was, I'd go to work the next day, and I'd have forgotten to wash it all off. They'd say, 'Eh, what's that brown patch behind the ear?'" (1)

Around this same time Joe was stretching his musical tastes. He was not only listening to his singing hero, Ray Charles, he was now delving deeper into the blues. He would regularly be adding albums by Lightnin' Hopkins, Muddy Waters, Howlin' Wolf, and John Lee Hooker to his record collection.

In September of 1962 a new nightspot called The Esquire Club opened in Sheffield. It was owned by a 30-year-old man by the name of Terry Thornton. Joe and his friends came to the club and instantly thought it was a great place for Vance Arnold & The Avengers to play. So Joe introduced himself to Terry and told him of his vision to play at The Esquire Club. Thornton was to recall, "He said he was a singer and I looked at him and I thought, 'He's never a singer in this wide world.' He was such an unlikely character. We were used to rock & rollers being brash and full of confidence, but Joe was so shy, such a kindly lad. I hedged and finally agreed that he could have a tryout for a fee of £5. He grew ten foot tall!" (1)

One of the reasons that The Esquire Club was less rowdy than several of the other nightclubs in town was the fact that they didn't serve alcohol on the premises. Instead, the patrons actually came to hear the music and not to get into a bar brawl.

It was in 1963 that The Beatles had their first four British Number 1 hit records:

"Please Please Me"
"From Me To You"
"She Loves You"
"I Want To Hold Your Hand."

It was in February of that year that The Beatles made their first concert appearance in Sheffield, and Cocker went to see them.

They played The Azena Ballroom, and they left a lasting impression on 18-year-old Joe. He recalls, "I remember 'I Saw Her Standing There' and thinking how tight they sounded. It was like they had been working at it for years." (1) In reality, they had been working at it for years. It was in the summer of 1962 that Ringo Starr joined the group as their official fourth member, replacing their former drummer Pete Best.

The following year, Beatlemania would sweep America and the rest of the world and along with it the whole British Invasion of the American music charts. Suddenly, British bands were "in," and every record label under the sun wanted to find their own Beatles to sign.

It was also in 1963 that Joe started showing up for his band's gigs with a girlfriend in tow. Eileen Webster had originally met Joe back in the days when he was part of The Cavaliers. In fact, she had met him at The Cavaliers' first gig at The Wesley Hall Youth Club. She was two years younger than him, and she had a job as a clerk working at The National Coal Board.

According to Eileen, "I met Joe when I was 13 and he was 15. We've been good friends for years, but it was nothing more than a good old chat. Then it seemed to happen, and that was it. One of those pathetic old all-American romances." (7)

Pete Jackson was to recall, "The only hang-up Joe had was Eileen Webster. He was always in love with her, and she played him a bit. It was a very on/off relationship because she had two boyfriends: Joe and another lad from Crookes, and she kept switching from one to the other. Every time she went with the other lad, Joe went into a sorrowful state for a considerable time until she came back. Eileen affected him a lot." (1)

Further changes in the band came when Dave Memmott joined The Avengers as their new drummer. As Dave remembers it, "I could see the potential with Joe, so I muscled myself in." (1)

Peter Stringfellow was from Sheffield and was four years older than Joe. He blossomed into becoming a famous nightclub owner, not only in London, but in New York City, and several other cities as well. He started out promoting what he called The Black Cat nightclub. Actually, it took place in The St. Aidan's Churchhall which he rented out on Friday nights.

It was quite a success for Stringfellow, and he continued to stage events in the area. In October of 1963 he rented out The Sheffield City Hall for a night's showcase of Sheffield's and England's up-and-coming rock & roll bands. Stringfellow played host to, amongst other talent, Vance Arnold & The Avengers. He also invited several record company executives for some added excitement. That particular event drew a crowd of 2,000 people which was the biggest audience Joe Cocker had played in front of yet.

At the time, every record label on the planet was busy looking for their own Beatles-like group to sign and record. As Joe was to explain, "After The Beatles, the scouting rush was on. People came north and saw The Avengers and said, 'We don't like your band.'" (5) Well, the tide was due to turn all in good time. Vance Arnold & The Avengers were not quite ready for the recording studio yet, but the stage was definitely set for big things.

Stringfellow's October event was so successful that he staged it again in November of that year and kicked up the stakes by inviting talent who had already been signed to a recording deal, namely, The Rolling Stones. They had released their first single, "Come On," in June which made it up to Number 21 on the British charts. That same month, The Rolling Stones released their second single, "I Want To Be Your Man," in time for the Stringfellow event.

Peter Stringfellow not only booked "The Stones" for that evening, but he also booked Wayne Fontana & The Mindbenders (biggest hit "The Game Of Love" in 1965) and his new local discovery, Vance Arnold & The Avengers, as the opening acts.

Joe took his new girlfriend, Eileen, along with him to this gig. She was known for doing upsetting things, and that night she decided to make a scene with The Rolling Stones. When Joe, Eileen, and The Avengers were introduced to The Stones before the show, Cocker was to recall, "She walked up to Mick Jagger and she said, 'You're rubbish.' I said, 'Leave him alone,' but she said, 'No, I'm gonna tell him, he's rubbish.' And I'm saying, 'Leave the man alone.' I always remember she said to him, 'You're a big head, you!'" (1)

That November night Joe and the band performed amongst other songs, "Hard Headed Woman," "You'd Better Move On," "I'm A Man," and their big showstopper, Ray Charles' "Georgia On My Mind." The Rolling Stones closed the show.

The following day, the local Sheffield newspapers carried rave reviews about the event. *The Sheffield Telegraph* called the evening, "One of the most entertaining and value-for-money shows ever seen in Sheffield."

The reviewer called The Rolling Stones "Five raving beat boys from London who look like Neanderthal Men." (8)

Then the same review glowed about The Avengers' set: "It is doubtful whether even Liverpool can offer a better singer in his class than Vance Arnold. For sheer showmanship and style, Vance Arnold is undoubtedly top of the list. On this showing he must be one of the country's top rhythm & blues artists. Fantastic!" (8) The runway for Joe Cocker was now cleared and ready for the first official take-off for his career.

Vance Arnold & The Avengers had their next big late-1963 gig at The Southern Sporting Club in Manchester. It wasn't that the venue they were about to play in was so important in itself, but it was the added fact that their prime audience was to be Dick Rowe who held the post of Artists & Repertoire representative for Decca Records. Representing the A&R department of Decca gave Rowe the ability to scout and recommend new talent to the label. This was going to be the big "audition" for Joe and the band with one of England's premiere record labels, and it was truly a very big deal.

In fact, this was not a gig with an audience at all, it was strictly staged as an "audition" for Rowe himself. This served to make Joe even more nervous than usual. Liquor acted as the big pre-concert confidence-builder throughout the majority of Joe's life. His ability to consume mass quantities of alcohol before a show was one of the standards of his entire career. It dates back as far as this era. That crucial day in Manchester, Joe reportedly fortified himself with beer and rum to get over his case of nervous tension. This was potentially going to be his and the band's entry into "the big time," and Cocker wanted to be as confident as possible.

When they met Dick Rowe, he was accompanied by another man from the record label, producer Mike Leander. Dick wanted to be able to consult Mike about the degree of talent they were to witness that fateful day. Leander's presence certainly raised "the intimidation factor" in the room that day in Manchester.

Although this was an early point in Leander's career, he was to work with several of the biggest stars in the recording business. This list includes not only The Rolling Stones, but also Marianne Faithful, Van Morrison, Lulu, Dusty Springfield, Peter Frampton, Gene Pitney, and many more.

Finally, Vance Arnold & The Avengers were set up, and they took the stage for their audience of two people. It was somewhat daunting for Joe to perform without a nightclub audience before him, but "on cue," he and The Avengers launched right into it.

The first song they performed was the Tennessee Ernie Ford 1955 hit "Sixteen Tons." It was followed by "You'd Better Move On" and a rollicking version of "Got My Mojo Working." It was a quick audition, and it ended with Joe's favorite song, "Georgia On My Mind."

Both Dick Rowe and Mike Leander showed not a moment of enthusiasm while the band played, while Joe sang his heart out. When they were done with their four songs, Dick and Mike thanked them for their time. Rowe told the band that he would get in touch with them if they were interested in an official recording studio test. That was the end of it. Joe and the lads packed up their equipment and back to Sheffield they went.

Anyone who has done an audition for any sort of performance will tell you how nerve wracking it is waiting for that phone call to come. However, after a couple of weeks, indeed the call came. Dick Rowe and Mike Leander summoned Vance Arnold & The Avengers down to London to Decca's recording studio.

Joe explained, "It was like going to another country. London was so far away in those days, and we never knew if the van was going to collapse. But we got there." (1) The trip, however, wasn't without mishap along the way. The van ran out of gas in London, and Joe and the band had to push it through The West End. But they narrowly made it there on schedule.

By the time the studio audition got underway, Joe and his band mates were nervous wrecks. They so wanted this to work out, they were timid with fright at the possibility of "blowing" their big chance. Almost instantly, the musicians showed off their lack of knowledge of what they were doing.

Mike Leander wanted to get a certain sound and certain beat to the first song they were working on, and he requested that Dave Memmott play the drums in a certain way. Memmott returned the request with a blank look.

Dave later recalled, "He asked me to play something a certain way and I said, 'Oh, I don't know whether I'll be able to do that.' He said, 'Give me the sticks,' and he sat at the kit and did it. We just weren't good enough. In those days we must have looked very raw." (1)

They recorded four tracks that day at Decca Records. The songs included "Got My Mojo Working" and "Georgia On My Mind." Joe and his band members were told that they would get an answer from Decca as to whether or not they would be offered a recording contract. After that they packed up and headed back to Sheffield.

For Vance Arnold & The Avengers, the results were mixed. Decca was indeed impressed with Joe, but they had zero interest in the band. Joe debated for a while whether or not he should step away from his bandmates as a solo recording artist. He soon realized that this was going to be his big break, and he had best take advantage of it.

It was in late January of 1964 that Vance Arnold & The Avengers were booked for another rock & roll show to be held at The Sheffield City Hall. Again, organized by Peter Stringfellow and his younger brother, this particular show not only included Joe and his band, but also on the bill were Wayne Fontana, Dave Berry & The Cruisers, and The Hollies. Not long afterward, Phil Crookes decided to leave The Avengers as he wanted to play music that had more of a country western flavor like Hank Williams tunes not so much blues material. This didn't interest Joe in the least.

According to Phil, "He couldn't get into that at all. I wanted the group to be lighter, but Joe was getting stronger and stronger into the blues. He had this commitment. I think he's followed it all the way down the line. I don't think he's ever strayed from it." (1)

In April of 1964 Joe put his signature on his first management contract. He was signed as "Vance Arnold," a solo artist. His new managers were Terry Thornton and Martin Yale. They were based in Lincolnshire.

Joe returned to Decca Records' London offices in June of 1964 where he recorded a highly orchestrated version of "Georgia On My Mind," his favorite song by his idol Ray Charles. Unlike either Hoagy Carmichael's or Ray Charles' rendition, for this epic recording

Joe was accompanied by a 22 piece orchestra. It was expected to be Joe Cocker's debut recording, but oddly enough it was never publicly released.

Somehow that record was not resonating with the Artists & Repertoire department at Decca, so on July 28, 1964, Joe returned to London, where Mike Leander produced a recording of 20-year-old Cocker singing his version of The Beatles' "I'll Cry Instead" which had originally appeared on the soundtrack for The Beatles' film *A Hard Day's Night.* He was accompanied by a worthy group of professional musicians on the track, including Jimmy Page on guitar. Page would two years later become a member of The Yardbirds and when they broke up, he became a founding member of Led Zeppelin.

Looking back on this era, Joe was to explain, "I remember doing an orchestrated version of 'Georgia On My Mind' which was never released. Then they had me go in and do a cover of The Beatles' 'I'll Cry Instead.'" (5)

The song "I'll Cry Instead" by Joe Cocker was released as a single late in the summer of 1964, and Joe thought this was really going to become his lucky break. No one was hotter than The Beatles that year; surely this could give Joe's career the boost he was hoping for. He was paid the up-front fee of ten shillings for his work on the single in optimistic anticipation of his impending stardom and the demands on his time that it was due to launch. In August of 1964 Joe decided to quit his job at The Gas Board. Realizing how tentative a career in rock & roll was, The Gas Board instead gave him six months' leave, so that he could resume his job as a pipe fitter if everything "went south" at Decca.

His father, Harold, was dead set against this move. Harold was to look back on this era and explain, "His mother used to think, 'Let him do what he wants,' but I had stronger views. I didn't like it at all. I told him to stop and get his final City & Guilds [license] so he would have something to come back to. But he handed in his notice." (1)

Also, in anticipation of the forthcoming hit status of his first single, Joe signed on for a seven-week concert tour, on the road with Manfred Mann, Little Eva ("The Locomotion") and The Merseybeats ("I Think Of You"). It was during this particular tour that Joe started showing off his skills at playing the harmonica on stage. Having dropped the whole "Vance Arnold & The Avengers" label, the Sheffield singer and his band were now called "Joe Cocker's Big Blues."

At this juncture, the last member of Joe's former band, The Cavaliers, exited the Cocker circle. This came with a parting of the way with Bob Everson. Friends since they were both eight-year-old boys, Bob Everson didn't leave voluntarily. Instead, Joe just replaced him, and didn't bother to inform him. When Everson showed up for rehearsal one day he found that his replacement was already there as part of the troupe. This set up another life-long pattern with Joe. When he was done with several of the people in his life, he would just "ghost" them, and they would never hear from him again.

In an upbeat press release that Decca Records issued at the time of "I'll Cry Instead" the company claimed, "Joe looks certain to become a big star on the pop scene, but should anything go wrong, it would seem that Joe is as good a gas fitter as he is a singer." (9)

In a further press statement put out by Martin Yale entitled "IT'S A BIG GAS MAN," he claimed Joe ". . . is either going to become Big Joe Cocker, or Joe Cocker The Great, or go back to fitting Yorkshire gas cookers." Yale described Cocker as possessing "shaggy brown hair and a face like the back of a Sheffield Corporation bus." (10)

Unfortunately, when it was released, Joe's single version of "I'll Cry Instead" didn't "set the charts on fire." The song received a couple of radio plays on the BBC, and disc jockey Jimmy Savile on

Radio Luxembourg claimed on the air, "Joe Cocker is a name you'll be hearing again-and-again." (1)

As Joe was later to explain of his Decca recording debut: "[It was] The Beatles' 'I'll Cry Instead' which died a death. I was still living at home at the time, and my parents said, 'O.K., you had your shot. Now grow up and go out and get a proper job.' My older brother, Victor, turned out to be an economist. He did really well on the straighter side of life." (5)

Indeed, signing to Decca Records didn't do much for his bank account either. According to Cocker, "I got a royalty check for one dollar and 97 cents." (7)

Thanks to his connections, Martin Yale was able to book Joe Cocker's Big Blues on the ITV variety television program called *Stars and Garters*. Although he only sang one song on the television show, Joe and the band were put up in a London hotel with expenses paid. He loved his glamorous newfound status as a recording artist.

Oddly enough, Joe hated his debut single greatly. It was pretty much a faithful version of The Beatles' original recording of "I'll Cry Instead" and did not feature any of his trademark vocal embellishments. To show his dislike for the recording, he refused to sing it on stage when he toured. Here was his one shot at making Decca happy, and in typical "Joe Cocker fashion," if Joe didn't want to do something, there was no way he could be talked into it. Joe held out hope that his version of "Georgia On My Mind" would be released as a single by the company as that much more represented his true singing style.

There was talk about Joe going back into the recording studio to do his rendition of the Chuck Jackson hit "I'll Keep Forgetting," but that never materialized. Instead of releasing "Georgia On My Mind," Decca ultimately and unceremoniously dropped his recording contract, and that was the end of that.

It was back to establishing himself and his circle of musician friends as an up-and-coming bar band. Their concurrent regular gig was at a local Sheffield pub called The Stone House.

The band's bass player, Dave Green was to recall, "The most we every got was £18 / 10 shillings a week each. Joe held the money through the week and on Friday we used to go up to his house, have fish & chips, and get organized. Then we went to the pub." (1)

Playing at The Stone House and other area bars did help to establish the band as a popular local act. According to drummer Dave Memmott, "Everywhere we went the place would be packed and with the same faces. At that time, 1964 to 1965, Joe couldn't put a foot wrong. The crowd might have been waiting since seven o'clock and he might turn up at ten, but they knew him. It was a very easy, laid-back situation. Everybody else tried to please the audience. Joe never did that. Whenever we performed, he always did what he wanted, not what the audience wanted. On a typical night, other groups did the last session with rockers, belting it out, but he never would. They'd be shouting out but he'd say, 'No, later.' The last number on most nights he'd do a song from John Lee Hooker." (1)

As Joe Cocker's Big Blues band would continue to tour and perform at bars throughout 1964, the excessive liquor consumption in the Joe Cocker inner-circle was at a major high point. It was a high point that would be continued for decades to come. It all sounded amusing and innocent in a teenage way, but as time went on, it would reinforce the fact that Joe was grooming himself to become a life-long alcoholic. According to Joe's piano player Vernon Nash, "We'd arrive at opening time, 11:30 a.m., and by 3:00 p.m. when closing time came 'round we'd have had five or six pints [of beer] each, maybe more. Then we'd set off for Cleethropes, or wherever we were playing that night, have a slurp, a transport café fry-up, and have another four or five pints before we set the gear up. Once we'd done that, we'd have another two or three and then we'd have a drink on stage. A lot of people thought we were unprofessional, but it was nothing to do with show business really; we were just playing for ourselves. The instigator was Joe. You can't think of Joe Cocker in the early days without thinking about large amounts of booze." (1)

Without his gas fitter job, Joe was really struggling to make ends meet as a musician. After an especially sparse January of 1965 beginning, Joe had to inform his musicians that he was forced to disband the group. There was simply not enough work to keep the band going.

No sooner had he done that, Terry Thornton of The Esquire club managed to find a gig for Joe Cocker's Big Blues. The gig was to perform at U.S. Army bases in France. The "catch" was that they had to leave the country the very next day. It meant a solid six weeks' work for Joe and the band.

Joe wasted no time getting his musician friends on the telephone and lining them up one-by-one. Dave Memmott, Dave Green, Vernon Nash, and Dave Hopper each signed on for the French booking.

After several crazy challenges along the way, Joe and the band arrived in Orleans, France. They were out of money and only knew the name of the entertainment director of the operation. They were informed that they had better have an ample number of Beatles' songs in their repertoire, or the soldiers would give them a less-than-warm reception.

They did the best they could to entertain the troops, but the bored and horny soldiers mainly wanted nothing to do with an all-male band. Joe was forced to get back in contact with Terry Thornton in Sheffield and tell him to send them a female singer as soon as possible. Somehow Terry complied, and Joe Cocker's Big Blues were suddenly joined by "guest singer" Marie Woodhouse, a busty blonde with a bawdy sense of humor.

Although the military bases were mainly comprised of white soldiers, it wasn't long until Joe and his troupe started gathering a following amongst black soldiers as well. It seemed that they had never heard a white boy who could sing with all of the "soul" and intensity that Joe delivered on stage every night. It gained Joe the nickname of "La Petite Ray Charles" among the servicemen in France.

At the beginning of this tour, it was only supposed to last six weeks maximum. However, by the time it was over, it was a full two months that Joe and his lads were away from Sheffield.

After the high of becoming a hit at the American army bases of France, Joe returned home to face the same problem that he left to solve. He had no steady job, and he had a lack of musical gigs to support himself. He stayed at his parents' house on Tasker Road and did odd jobs. He occupied his time painting the family house and even the house next door. Assuredly, he could have gone back to The Gas Board in Sheffield, but he opted not to do so.

For the next year Joe continued to live at home, and he took a series of odd jobs around town. For a while he worked at a newspaper warehouse. He continued to regularly go out drinking with his friends, and he and Eileen continued to date as well. He had been so driven and determined to establish himself as a singer and performer. It seemed terribly odd for him, for months at a time, to not get up on stage and sing, but that was the reality of his existence for quite some time.

Joe simply walked away from his singing career aspirations for a long period and never looked back. This was something he would tend to do from time-to-time. During this period, he had the uncanny ability to just walk away from it all like he never appeared on stage before. It was a retreat into his own solitude that he would repeat several times whenever things didn't work out the way he expected them to.

Looking back on this era, Joe was later to explain, "After that we just kept rolling along, either getting very little work or else accepting work in pubs where the customers would each have had ten pints by our first break. I got terribly sick of all that, and after the Decca thing collapsed, I just packed it in for a year." (11)

Finally, in the fall of 1966 Joe was inspired to start to force himself out of the solitude of his parents' cozy Sheffield house. Dave Hopper was to recall that one Saturday at lunchtime he was at The Stone House, and Joe shouted out to him from across the room. "He said, 'I've got this gig at the University tonight. I've got to do it, because I promised.'" (1)

Both Hopper and Vernon Nash agreed to play with him, and it ended up with great results. After the show Hopper claimed, "We all went along, no rehearsing, we just did it. And we wiped the floor with the other band that was on. Afterwards I was talking to Eileen and I said it'd be great to get back together. She said, 'Ask him. I'm fed up trying.'" (1)

Joe wasn't instantly convinced that he should again chase his musical aspirations, but eventually he realized that singing was something he was meant to do publicly. As he started to change his mind, he decided that maybe some rehearsal sessions would re-spark his fire and passion to sing with a band. He got together with Dave Hopper, Vernon Nash, and a drummer he found at The Stone House by the name of Freddy Guite. What he needed was a bass player, so he called up another local friend, John Fleet.

Fleet informed him, "It struck me as a nice idea, but I was not long married and looking for a proper job, so in my wisdom I said, 'No. Can you find somebody else?'" (1)

Well, Joe decided to take Fleet's advice, and he cast his net out to find another bass player. The person he ended up discovering was going to be one of the most important and most talented musicians in his entire career. His name was Chris Stainton, and he was to become Joe's best life-long friend.

Stainton was also someone who had been kicking around the Sheffield music clubs since he was a boy. He was known as a member of the local pop singing group who had gone through several name changes, including The Cadillacs, Knives & Forks, and finally The Texans. Oddly parallel to Joe's own recording experience, it was Chris who co-wrote The Texans' one single, "Being With You." Released on Columbia Records in 1964, it had the same reception that Joe's "I'll Cry Instead" garnered. Like Joe, Chris became disillusioned with the music business for a time and went into his own downward spiral.

Joe had originally met Chris at The Locarno Ballroom a couple of years earlier. When word got out that Joe Cocker was looking for a new bass player, Stainton got in touch with him.

As Chris Stainton was to recall, "I was in a local band in Sheffield, and it petered out. I then went to Germany and did a couple of tours there. I then came back home, gave up, and got a job. I was a television engineer and doing quite well, but I was playing in a local Sheffield band at the same time. I was playing at a gig in Sheffield and Joe Cocker suddenly appeared and asked me to join his band. He had a band called Joe Cocker's Big Blues. He asked me to join that. So I joined, playing bass." (12)

When Chris got together with Joe and his new band they were blown away by Chris' talent. He could not only play the bass proficiently, he could also play the drums and was masterful at the piano. It was Chris Stainton's enthusiasm and vast talent that inspired Joe Cocker. Frank Miles replaced Dave Hopper's spot in the band. Dave Mammott eventually rejoined the group as well with Stainton and Joe's current musicians. It was the beginning of The Grease Band, the ensemble that would ultimately take Joe to stardom.

The name "The Grease Band" came from a magazine interview that Joe read. The interview subject was jazz and soul organist Jimmy

Smith. In the story, Smith described a musician as having a lot of "grease" to his playing. The word somehow resonated with Joe, and the core of The Grease Band was born.

The music world had morphed and changed since Joe had gone into seclusion circa 1965 to 1966. Yes, The Beatles were still THE driving force in the music world, but they were joined by lots of new voices. While "The British Invasion" was taking place in the U.S. music charts, Britain had discovered and embraced "The Motown Sound." That influential record company, known as "Tamla/Motown" in the U.K., introduced the world to such hit-makers as The Temptations, The Supremes, Marvin Gaye, Martha & The Vandellas, and The Four Tops.

To keep the new audiences happy, Joe started opening his set with The Four Tops' hit "It's The Same Old Song," and closing it with that Detroit quartet's "Can't Help Myself." Both turned out to be huge crowd-pleasers for what was currently billed as "Joe Cocker's Blues Band."

Soon they were playing at several local pubs. One favorite booking was at The Borrow Hill Hotel, close to Chesterfield. They also had an ongoing gig at The Shirecliffe Hotel that had them playing several sets throughout the evening.

Vernon Nash recalls of Stainton, "There was something weird going on all the time with Chris. He was a very strange, eccentric fellow, what you might call 'laid back.' When he first joined, he was a TV repairman . . . Drove around in an old Ford car. One day he was driving to The Barrow Hill Hotel and a wheel dropped off. He said, 'We'll have to walk,' got out the car and he never mentioned it again. Just left it and that was that." (1)

Stainton might have left his crippled car in the dust, but at the same time it became clear that with him as part of the group, "Joe Cocker's Blues Band" was going places. This was also the beginning of Chris inspiring Joe to start composing some of his own music to sing.

According to Nash, "They started smoking dope and composing together. Joe had certain ideas. He didn't know anything about chords, so he used to sing it and Chris arranged it. Chris knew that he was onto something with Joe and that they could sell it. Chris was ambitious and without that pull from him, Joe would never have made it." (1)

Indeed, in 1967, at the age of 23, Joe Cocker had the vocal talent and unique performing persona to really do something with his life in the music business. But without the spark of talent and drive that Chris Stainton had, Joe Cocker may never have successfully gone from being a local bar band singer, to becoming an international singing star.

Chris wasn't the only musician in the fledgling Grease Band to be able to compose songs. Frank Miles was writing material as well with a friend of his by the name of Tom Rattigan. Miles and Rattigan were friendly with a record industry figure by the name of Len Black. They had gotten Stainton involved in the creation of a song called "March Of The Mysterons." It was an instrumental number, and it was intended to be used for a children's puppet show.

Len Black loaned Miles and Rattigan a recorder to put down the song on tape. When Joe heard the song, he was inspired to come up with some lyrics for it. As a result, it was transformed into the song "Marjorine" which was destined to become Joe's second single.

Inspired by the way "Marjorine" came out on tape, Chris and Joe composed two further songs of their own, "Sandpaper Cadillac" and "The New Age Of Lily." Joe and Chris additionally recorded those two songs, with Stainton playing all of the instruments on it.

Chris always thought that Joe was on the threshold of breaking through at any moment, and he wanted to do what he could to be part of it and help it happen. According to him, "He was destined to be somebody." (12)

What they needed was a demo tape to show off what they could accomplish musically. They ended up borrowing a tape recorder and capturing the best version of "Marjorine" they could on the little machine.

There was a local Chesterfield disc jockey by the name of David McPhie. After Chris and Joe brought the tape and the borrowed tape recorder to his flat to give him a listen, McPhie was instantly impressed.

It was McPhie's idea to take the demo tape that Joe and Chris had made, drive down to London, and play the three songs for another radio D.J. by the name of Tony Hall. One of things that Hall was best known for was discovering new talent and giving up-and-coming singers and bands a chance to be heard by a wider audience. Hall was known as the first person to play Otis Redding's music in England and to turn him into a star in the U.K.

McPhie took the demo tape to Hall's house early one morning. When Hall heard what Joe and Chris had put together, he was blown away by the songs. He instantly knew what he had to do with it. Hall took the tape to a London music publisher, David Paltz. At the time Paltz was working with a record producer he knew by the name of Denny Cordell.

Denny Cordell had gained quite a reputation as an independent record producer in London. He had produced songs for Georgie Fame, The Move, The Moody Blues, and the huge Procol Harum smash "A Whiter Shade Of Pale." When Tony Hall gave Denny a listen to the Joe Cocker/Chris Stainton recordings he was likewise impressed by what he heard.

As Joe was to later recall, "I sent a tape to producer Denny Cordell because I'd seen what he'd done for other people. I thought he'd be the person to know if it was any good. I thought to myself, 'If he says the tape is rubbish, we'll pack it in.'" (7)

Ironically, it was the way Joe was recorded and the music that accompanied him that initially got Denny's attention. It was "Marjorine" which really triggered his imagination. According to Cordell, "Whoever had produced the record had some great little ideas. That's what caught my attention—the structure rather than the singing, which was echoey and varied. Obviously, the singing worked, but I had no idea that this was a great voice. None at all." (1)

Whatever the hook was that intrigued Cordell—the song, the singing, the arrangement, or just the overall sound—it had that magical quality that made him want to listen to it again and again. Now the machinery was all falling into place. After Denny Cordell heard the demo tape made by the lads in Sheffield, he had to meet the duo who produced it. Joe Cocker and Chris Stainton were summoned to London to meet with Cordell, and suddenly they were on their way to the next plateau of their budding careers.

CHAPTER THREE

"With A Little Help From My Friends"

Something very significant happened in 1967 when Joe met record producer Denny Cordell. Both he and Chris left an indelible impression on Cordell. In fact, Denny never quite forgot it. It was the creative duo's chance at a truly big break in their fledgling careers, and they contrastingly dressed for the meeting. Chris had an outlandishly colorful outfit on, and Joe dressed like a total slob. Together they showed off the contrasts of the era.

Joe was to recall, "Chris had this outrageous suit on—it had fur cuffs! We charged into the office, and it was all very official. I remember the girl, Janice, saying, 'Mr. Cordell will see you in ten minutes,' and we just sat there screwing our knuckles. Then Denny came out and he looked at Chris and said, 'I expected you,' and he turned to me and said, 'But I didn't expect him!'" (1)

According to Cordell, "Chris sort of fitted in with the image of what was happening. His suit was made of curtain material or something you'd cover a sofa in, with tassels, the sort you'd see around the bottom of furniture, down the sleeves and round the cuffs. And it was pink! I mean, hippies were hippies and there was a lot of outrageous expression, sartorially. But this was obviously one made up on a shoestring budget. And he looked great! But Joe . . . he didn't look like any part of the pop scene at all. He was right chubby, and he was wearing a donkey jacket, totally nondescript. Not someone who was making any effort at all to slot into the visuals of what was going down at the time. He could have been doing anything in life, a blacksmith's assistant, road sweeper, anything. He just looked a real old scruff." (1) That was Joe to a tee: scruffy and come-as-you-are.

As crazy as this duo from Sheffield looked, within minutes Cordell realized that they were onto some sort of creative streak that he would have to see live on stage to appreciate and understand the whole picture. Arrangements were made for Denny to venture north to one of their upcoming Saturday night gigs in Sheffield. In fact, Cordell was also invited to the Cocker family's Tasker Road home where he met and had tea with Harold and Madge and their madcap son Joe.

When Cordell and one of his mates, Simon Miller Mundy, saw and heard Joe Cocker's Big Blues in action, they were bowled over. They were expecting a really good rock & roll bar band. What they saw instead was an excellent blues band who could play rock.

To take things to the next level, Cordell made arrangements for Joe and his band to play a gig as the opening act for the group Traffic at The Speakeasy nightclub in London. Denny called his friend and business associate, Chris Blackwell, to come see the show as well. Both together and separately they were to become two more of the ten most important men in Joe Cocker's musical career.

Chris Blackwell distinctly recalls the first time he saw Joe in full swing with his insanely kinetic choreography. "I remember thinking, 'Why does he do that on stage?'" Was it just an insane part of his act? Then Blackwell saw Joe in the recording studio, and all of the trademark spastic moves were still solidly in place. "Wow, this is incredible. It's just coming out of him like this. It wasn't show business. It was like the way you'd see a conductor in classical music." (13)

Everyone who saw Joe performing wondered what was the motivation or inspiration for the jerky, almost seizure-like choreography he did with his arms and hands while singing. It was beyond unique, and it became one of his trademarks.

Analyzing where it came from, Joe explained, "I used to play drums and when I started singing there was this terrible thing about, 'What do I do with my hands?' Most people feel rhythm in their feet." With regard to expelling on stage "tension," he claimed, "I feel mine in my arms, and waving them about helps me relax." (14)

Laughing it off he claimed, "I never played organ or piano or guitar, so it was more out of frustration and me just trying to impersonate in a way. I did it subconsciously. People mistook for me being ill, like I had palsy." (15)

After Joe and the band's London showcase opening for Traffic, Denny Cordell decided that he wanted the chance to capture Joe's singing and Chris' musical ideas in the recording studio. However, after this gig he was also convinced that their performing band was not good enough for what he was looking to record.

Cordell explained of the evening in London, "It was a huge success, but somewhere along the line I came to the conclusion, rightly or wrongly, that we couldn't record this band." (1)

The decision was made to record their song "Marjorine" using Chris on bass and piano and a group of session musicians to play the music. The added musicians included Clem Cattini on drums and guitars by Albert Lee and Jimmy Page. Albert is a renowned British guitarist who worked with Eric Clapton, The Everly Brothers, and in the 2000s he has toured with The Rolling Stones' former member, Bill Wyman & His Rhythm Kings.

March 22, 1968, marked the date of the release of the Joe Cocker single, "Marjorine," on the Regal Zonophone label in England. A light ballad, the "Marjorine" single included another Cocker/Stainton composition, "New Age Of The Lily," as it's B-side. Since the song "Marjorine" had started out as an instrumental composition by Chris Stainton and a couple of the other members of Joe Cocker's

Grease Band, both guitarist Frank Myles and Tommy Rattigan were credited as songwriters as well. When Cordell decided to use studio musicians instead of them they knew their time as Joe's performing band would soon be coming to an end.

Echoing Myles and Rattigan's sense of doom, Grease Band drummer Dave Memmott was to recall, "After 'Marjorine' was recorded, we were excluded. It became a Joe/Chris sort of thing. They were writing and recording; we were playing the gigs. It was like an incestuous relationship; they would go into huddles or record, and we wouldn't be told about it. It was never nasty, but towards the end it got rather sly and secretive. Joe was listening to everything that Chris said. He was right. Chris was sticking him in the right direction." (1) Vernon Nash likewise sensed that he was soon to be replaced in Joe's inner-circle as well, and he was right.

In an interview with *Melody Maker* magazine in 1968, Joe proclaimed, "Chris Stainton is very important to me because he can communicate my ideas musically to the band. We work out the arrangements together." (14)

Two days after the single's release, the original Grease Band played their last gig with Joe. Interviewed by *Top Stars Special*, Joe explained of his band's firing, "It had been coming for three weeks, and things were a bit tense. Finally last night we split up." (16)

Unfortunately, the song "Marjorine" only made it to Number 48 in the U.K., then it promptly dropped off the charts. Still, Denny Cordell was convinced that he had a creative gold mine with Cocker and Stainton, and he was determined to go back into the recording studio with the duo from Sheffield.

Joe was later to explain of this whole process, "Well, you're going back to about '67 and '68, and the record deal I got, Denny Cordell was the producer. And imagine just a simple Sheffield guy coming into London, and we had a single, Chris Stainton and I, called 'Marjorine,' And Denny says, 'Let's make an album. Who do you want to play on it?' And he's mentioning all these names: Jimmy Page, Mike Kelly from Spooky Tooth, my God, all these people I admired. And I said, 'If you can get 'em, that would be wonderful.' So a lot of different sessions evolved just from Denny calling 'round London to see who wasn't working at the time. And that first album I still treasure to this day because you don't have the kind of time to make that kind of record anymore. We had over a year to produce it." (17)

Explaining their songwriting process, Joe said, "The way we do it now is to just go in and bash at a piano for hours, trying to get riffs together to form a melody. Chris does most of this bit and then I add the lyrics when he's finished. I had a mental block about writing words for a while there. I got to thinking that my lyrics really weren't very good; in fact, I was very skeptical about my own songs, very uncertain as to whether I can write something that I can make come over really heavy when I sing it. What I really want to do now is to write simply, to communicate the way that the very simple stuff communicated to me when I was a kid." (11)

Convinced they were on their way to the "big time," within a couple of weeks Joe Cocker and his creative mate, Chris Stainton, moved down to London to immerse themselves in the creation of the first Joe Cocker album. They were joined by one of their buddies from Sheffield, keyboard player Tommy Eyre. The next incarnation of The Grease Band came about in London as they were joined by drummer Tommy Reilly and guitar player Micky Gee.

When Chris originally started playing with Joe, he was the bass guitar player. But then he switched to being the keyboard player. According to Stainton, "That happened in England in 1968 because The Grease Band line-up changed quite a lot. It went from the Sheffield one when I was playing the bass and we had Tommy Eyre who went on to play with George Michael. We had him on organ and I was on bass. He was a great, great player. We changed bands and Joe decided he liked my piano playing since I played piano on a few tracks on the first album as well as bass. He wanted me on piano and was like, 'Well, get a bass player and drummer.' We got Bruce Rowland and Alan Spenner from another band and they came in. That's how it started. It was because he liked my piano playing so much and I was thrust onto piano." (12)

It was Denny Cordell's buddy, Chris Blackwell, who provided the newest version of The Grease Band with their rehearsal space which was a renovated theater in Westbourne Grove. Meanwhile, Joe, Chris, and Tommy's living accommodations were a one room flat in Sussex Gardens.

With Cordell at the helm, in between gigs on the college circuit and in small nightclubs, Joe and Chris started recording songs to be used as album tracks and B-sides to singles. These included "Something's Coming On," "Sandpaper Cadillac," and "Bye Bye Blackbird." Amongst the other famous musicians who were to appear on Joe's first album were Steve Winwood of Traffic and stellar British soul singer, Madeline Bell.

During this era, it was Joe Cocker's preference to take the songs of other stars and musicians, have them played in 3/4 time, and make them sound unique. This fascination with the classic 3/4 beat turned every song into something that sounded like a waltz.

According to Joe, he had begun to feel his passion for music on the wane until The Beatles' most famous single album, *Sgt. Pepper's Lonely Hearts Club Band*, was released in June of 1967. Known for its brilliant audio experiments, like music tracks played backwards, it turned the music world on its ear. It was also revolutionary for having The Beatles quirkiest member, Ringo Starr, open the album with one of his trademark songs, "With A Little Help From My Friends." It was Ringo's jaunty tune that greeted the listener to the kaleidoscope of sound that the rest of the album featured.

For some reason, Joe was fascinated with this song and wanted to do something different with it. According to him, the concept he had for recording his own version of this song came while seated in the outdoor toilet at his family's Tasker Road home. That was Joe: do something unconventional and perform it even more unconventionally.

Chris Stainton laughingly recalls, "That was Joe. He thought of it at home in Sheffield. Apparently, according to legend, he was on the toilet. In those days, we had outside toilets in Sheffield. There's now a plaque on this toilet to the effect of, 'That's where it was conceived.' But I don't know if that's true or not." (12)

Stainton explains, "It was Joe. He was always a fan of Ray Charles and Aretha [Franklin] and that kind of soul, the Atlantic Records stuff. He loved the 6/8 swing beat, the way the girls sang. He envisioned it. I don't know how he came across it, but he said to me, 'Why don't we try this way?' We had a band, and we ran through it, and it came together. It was a combination. I thought of a few bits, but it was Joe's idea, mainly." (12)

Tommy Eyre was to recall, "He'd become obsessed with 3/4, but it's a weird tempo to be able to play comfortably, for it to swing as good as a 4/4 thing. So when he said, 'Hey, you know that Beatles' song you did with Glen [Dale & The Candies]? I wonder what that'd sound like as a waltz?' Everybody went, 'Urgh! Not another *effing* waltz!' But I said, 'Hang on a bit, it could work.'" (1)

Joe then said to 18-year-old Eyre, "Can you give us a Bach intro and then change the chords in the verse so that it sounds more classical?" (1)

Fortunately for him, Tommy was classically trained, so he took this goal as a musical challenge. According to Eyre, "So I did the opening and I had to rework the chord line in the verse because Joe said, 'Let's make it heavier.' And Chris came in with a bass line, which he suggested would also work nice on guitar. And all the drum fills—they just sort of happened." (1)

Joe liked the new arrangement of "With A Little Help From My Friends," and he and the current incarnation of The Grease Band started featuring the song in its live act. By this time The Grease Band was to become a revolving door of members, and Tommy Eyre and Mickey Gee were about to be on their way out.

When Cocker and Stainton went into Olympic Studios in June of 1968 to record the classic Beatles' tune, they did so without inviting Eyre and Gee. Producer Denny Cordell loved the way this song sounded, and he was itching to get the track recorded as it was earmarked as Joe's next single release, and he was under a lot of pressure to create it the way Joe envisioned it. He booked the studio time and lined up two of the members of the band Traffic to perform the music, Steve Winwood and drummer Jim Cipaldi. Unfortunately, although Cipaldi was a seasoned musician, he too was perplexed by the 3/4 tempo. The waltz beat to the song proved problematic, and there was a reported 35 "takes" at recording the song. According to Denny Cordell, he was so frustrated with the results they had in this recording session, when he went home, he literally cried. His wife told him that he had best get a good night's sleep and return to the studio the next day and have another crack at it.

That was exactly what he did, but this time around he replaced the guitar player and the drummer. He enlisted Jimmy Page on guitar and Procol Harum's B.J. Wilson on drums. It wasn't an easy session, but finally on "take 13" they got it right. Somehow, after two days, once "version 43" song was finished, everyone instinctively felt that was the rendition of the song that was destined to become a hit, and they were right.

With that song finally finished, it was time for Joe and Chris to hit the road again, this time with some new members in The Grease Band. After a round of auditions in London, they discovered an Irishman by the name of Henry McCullough. And as their new drummer they hired a character by the name of Kenny Slade whom they knew from Sheffield.

Joe and his refreshed band had plenty of work during the summer of 1968. They not only had regular gigs at several London clubs including Revolution, Blaises, The Marquee, and Scotch of St. James, they also got to play in front of their largest, to date, gig, *The Windsor Festival*, which was staged at Kempton Park racecourse. They were on the bill along with Jethro Tull, Deep Purple, Jeff Beck, and one of Joe's favorite inspirations, Jerry Lee Lewis.

According to Tommy Eyre, "It was a lovely day, a lovely setting, a huge expanse where all the kids sat, and then it rose up about 15 feet to like a natural stage. It was all hippie, lots of dope, peace and love and all that." (1) At this stage of his career, Joe liked to open with the Ray Charles song, "Let's Go Get Stoned." The song, written by the American hit-making team of Nicholas Ashford & Valerie Simpson, was perfectly tailored for Joe's audience.

Regarding his stage act at the time, Joe was to explain, "We're not an underground group, but we are doing very well in the Universities. I think it's because we're such a solid band and people know we are trying to put on a good performance for them. We play with soul, but not in the 'gotta gotta' vein which has really had its day. It ended up with every group sounding the same. I'm funny about the material I use. I like good lyrics with a blues flavor. We're writing ourselves, but none of it is good enough to perform yet." (14)

After Joe had moved down to London, he ended up getting a place of his own, and his longtime on-again/off-again girlfriend, Eileen, moved in with him. According to her at the time, "At first, we had to be very careful what we said in interviews." Eileen confessed, none-too-sheepishly, "because our parents didn't know we were living together. Joe and I aren't married, but that's fine. We stick together because we have mutual interests. I wouldn't feel any more secure just because of a piece of paper. Joe's a great fella. He's a terrible driver though, and really, he's not together at all. And he hasn't got any image yet, so I can't say, 'Yes he is like that, or no, that's all rubbish.' He's simply a guy who started off as a blues singer and progressed from there." (7)

Denny Cordell had a trip to Los Angeles booked for September of 1968. A deal had been struck with the American music label, A&M Records, to release Joe Cocker's recordings in "the states." A revolutionary record label, helmed by trumpet player Herb Alpert and his business partner Jerry Moss, A&M Records had become quite cutting edge during this era. In the next few years, it would also become the home of Styx, Peter Frampton, Rita Coolidge, The Carpenters, Peter Allen, Leslie Gore, Richie Havens, and a host of new up-and-coming talent. Joe Cocker was a perfect addition to that label's growing roster.

One of the most impressive aspects of working and recording at A&M Records was the fact that their entire operation was housed in what had formerly been the movie studio owned by Charlie Chaplin. Located on North La Brea Avenue in Hollywood, it not only had a lot of history, but it also had giant sound studios and was an inspiring setting for creating music and films. It has since been sold and is now called Jim Henson Studios.

It was Cordell's idea to take Joe along with him, introduce him to Jerry Moss, and even record a song or two while there. This was to be Cocker's debut visit to Los Angeles, California, and he was eager to see it and experience it.

Likewise, Moss was anxious to meet Joe. He was a big fan of the song "Marjorine," and he was very enthused to see and hear what Cocker could accomplish with his forthcoming debut album on A&M. Jerry Moss recalled, "Obviously, we were into Joe from the very beginning. We really liked him. You know, some artists come in and they are hard to speak with, or to get to, but he was very relaxed.

We were able to have a conversation right away. It was an immediate rapport. Everybody embraced; we had a great time." (1)

Denny Cordell had recently listened to the new self-titled *Traffic* album and was intrigued by the song "Feelin' Alright." He thought it would be perfect for Cocker. When Joe heard it, he immediately agreed it would be great for him. He lined up several LA musicians to play on the track, including Artie Butler on piano and Paul Humphries on drums. Since Joe was such a devoted fan of Ray Charles, who better to sing back-up vocals on this track than Ray's own female singing trio, The Raelettes? Ray's revolving trio of gals at the time included Merry Clayton, Brenda Holloway, and her sister Patrice Holloway. Merry is famous for her singing on The Rolling Stones' song "Gimme Shelter" (singing its chorus, "It's just a shout away"). And Brenda Holloway is famous for being a 1960s Motown solo singer, responsible for several hits, including "Every Little Bit Hurts."

There was also a percussionist from Brazil by the name of Laudir who was in the next studio working on a Herb Alpert album, and Cordell enlisted him to play on "Feelin' Alright" as well. Denny had hoped to come up with more than one Joe Cocker song that day, but he was so happy with the way "Feelin' Alright" came out; he was more than satisfied.

Coming to America for the first time left a lasting impression on Joe. According to him, "I arrived in '68, in the flower power time and the hippie days. It all seemed very blissful for a brief moment there." (2)

When he got back to London, Joe explained this by saying, "I've been singing since I was ten years old. I've worked in tough Sheffield pubs which is really a strange scene. There were so many pubs I was working seven nights a week for £10. I used to drink incredible quantities of beer, about ten pints a night. I don't anymore, because you can't get Sheffield beer anywhere else. We haven't really made that much impact on London yet, to be honest. I suppose we don't get through because I'm from the north or something. But we've never had a bum night and when I came back from America and found the record was happening suddenly, everywhere was packed and we were getting great reactions." (14)

On October 2, 1968, the British single version of "With A Little Help From My Friends" was released and began to cause a stir immediately. It rose up the charts at a meteoric pace going all the way to Number 1. All totaled, it spent 13 weeks on the charts, and suddenly it was official: Cocker had finally arrived in the middle of the "big time" in Europe. The song also reached Number 1 in Belgium and Switzerland. The next goal was to cross over that same success to America. It was the week of December 14 that the song peaked on the U.S. charts at Number 69. For Joe Cocker, it would take some more work for America to notice him and his unconventional style.

Joe's breakthrough in Europe came where he was making headlines and television performances. While in England he was seen on the TV programs *Dee Time*, and *Top Of The Pops*.

Chris Welch in *Melody Maker* in October of 1968 asked the musical question, "Which pop star uses the Mario Lanzo method? You're wrong—it's not Tiny Tim. It's our old blues shouting, Beatle bellowing mate Joe Cocker! His powerful voice is even now tearing the nation's television sets apart as he perforates his hit rendition of 'With A Little Help From My Friends' on *Top Of The Pops*." (14)

According to Joe, "I sing from the stomach and not from the throat. It's the Mario Lanza method." (14) Apparently, hearing his dad's old Mario Lanza records back in Sheffield must have paid off.

There were a couple of glitches along the way, however. Joe was at Heathrow Airport on his way to Amsterdam for a promotional trip when he was searched by customs officers. They found him to have a detectable amount of cannabis resin on him, and three days later he was to appear at the Uxbridge Magistrate's court. He was fined £55 for this infraction.

From the perspective of 1988 Joe was to recall this incident and his drug use at the time. "I never smoked pot when I was young. I was a very late bloomer in that. I made up for it after. I always swore I'd be a drinker to the end. But then, when someone turned me on to some black hash, musically speaking, it was such an opening to the eyes and senses. When I got popped, busted, in 1968, it was an incredible sensation to find yourself on the evening news busted for pot. It was almost like the fuss they made about Boy George, the kind of fuss now over heroin that smoking a joint was then." (5)

This era was to be Joe's first taste of commercial success and his first taste of fame. His trademark "non-rock star" wardrobe and his distinctive face made him instantly recognizable. Going through some photos of himself from this time period, Joe was to recall, "I had a little flat with a girlfriend from Sheffield when we first moved to London. 'Little Help' was Number 1 and I went to Sloane Square to get a newspaper and there were a bunch of schoolgirls on a day out. There's me with my long hair and my tie-dyed T-shirt, and they saw me from across the road and came running. It was in my hash-smoking days. And I remember the horror in my heart as these teenyboppers came running towards me. We weren't into the old autograph thing." (3)

Working with Dee Anthony as his booking agent, it was Dee's goal to get the American market to open up for Joe. Dee Anthony had been in the music business for years and, in fact, spent 17 years working for jazz singing legend Tony Bennett. By the time Dee and his Bandana Management company started working with Joe Cocker, he was already the manager of such stellar early '70s rock groups as Traffic, The J. Giles Band, Ten Years After, Humble Pie, and Emerson, Lake & Palmer.

At the time, the best way to "break" an act in the U.S. was to book them on the famed Sunday night television program, *The Ed Sullivan Show*. The following letter, written by Chris Blackwell, was sent to facilitate this:

25th November 1968
Mr. Ron Sunshine
Premier Talent Associates, Inc.
New York, New York 10019
USA

Dear Ron:

Thank you very much for your recent letters, telephone calls, and cables regarding JOE COCKER.

I have decided that the way I want to go with JOE COCKER in America is, that I do not want him to go over to the States until there is a big demand for him. I feel that for him to work the underground scene would not be the best way to break him in the States, but rather to wait until there was a really big demand then bring him in when, and if you got an *Ed Sullivan Show* or a show of that status followed by a good college tour for good money.

He is really a phenomenal act on television and the stage, and even with the lousy presentation that *The [Ed] Sullivan Show* seems to provide, I am quite sure that he will project very well.

I will be working with Dee Anthony on the management side and have told him of your interest and enthusiasm regarding JOE, but as I said, I would want to be quite sure of getting some sort of TV exposure for him, before firmly committing myself to one particular agency.

Yours sincerely,
Christopher Blackwell
cc: Dee Anthony
(18)

It is ironic that Joe started his recording career by covering The Beatles' song "I'll Cry Instead" and the fact that it was another Beatles tune that ultimately made him a star in his home country. This was not wasted on The Beatles. The two writers of the song, John Lennon and Paul McCartney, sent Cocker a telegram which read: "THANKS—YOU ARE FAR TOO MUCH. JOHN AND PAUL." (1)

This was not the last time during Joe's six decade recording career that he covered the songs of The Beatles. In fact, he was to do it several times in his career, right up to the end.

Just after "With A Little Help From My Friends" hit Number 1 he was actually asked to come to meet with The Beatles where he was to be presented with two more of their compositions to cover.

Joe was later to recall, "If you could imagine towards the end of the '60s, living in London, you know those guys were almost gods by that time. Well, just ahead of *Abbey Road*, Denny says to me, 'Joe, you know, The Beatles want to give you some songs.' So I went down to Apple Records one afternoon to talk with George and Paul, and George picks up a guitar and starts playing 'Something (In The Way She Moves)' and he says, 'You're welcome to take that one.' And he was offering me all these acetate demos, and when I look back on it, I maybe should have jumped on more of them than I did. There was 'Old Brown Shoe' and some other stuff he didn't record until his solo days. But then Paul played me 'Golden Slumbers,' and I said, 'Can I have that one?' and Paul said, 'No, I was just playing that one for you.' But then Paul says, 'I've got another one.' And he plays me 'She Came In Through The Bathroom Window' and I released it on the second album before they put *Abbey Road* out." (17)

After the success of "With A Little Help From My Friends," there was a big rush to get the debut album, *Joe Cocker* (British album title), together and ready for release. It was admittedly cobbled together with a year's worth of tracks that he had "in the can." This was to include his first hit single, "Marjorine," "Bye Bye Blackbird," another Cocker/Stainton composition called "Change In Louise," and a couple of favorite Bob Dylan songs, "I Shall Be Released," and "Just Like A Woman."

Joe was later to explain of the long and harrowing recording process of that album, "Like we must have done 'I Shall Be Released' ten different ways with Al Kooper and Aynsley Dunbar before deciding in the end to use a take featuring completely different people." (11)

Fully aware that his debut album was "cobbled together," Joe was happy to have it out, but he admitted there were several drawbacks. As he was to explain, "Our first LP is the problem, because as far as I'm concerned, putting out an album with a million old B-sides is a waste of time. A lot of LPs don't have good continuity." (14)

When A&M Records released the debut album, the song "With A Little Help From My Friends" was already a hit in America, so that became the title of the U.S. version of the album. It made it to Number 35 on the U.S. charts and Number 29 in the U.K. Any way you looked at it, or listened to it, Joe was now considered to be a hot and rising rock star on the scene.

The cover of the *Joe Cocker / With A Little Help From My Friends* album was quite attention-getting in itself. It features a less-than-glamorous close-up shot of him mid-song, by photographer Martin Keeley. Regarding it, John Mendelssohn in *The Los Angeles Times* proclaimed, "It's apparently not in his nature to be distressed by the gruesomely unflattering picture A&M emblazoned on his album cover. In it he looks rather like a blubbery fish with a nest of worms for hair. Truth be known, he's quite amused by everyone's efforts to capitalize on his ill-founded ugly-fat-boy-with-a-soul-of-gold mystique." (11) Indeed, Joe knew he was not a classic "pretty boy" at all, and he was happy for his distinctive look.

To celebrate Joe's newfound international fame, the publication *Top Stars Special* interviewed several people in his inner circle, including his father. According to Harold Cocker, "I'm glad he's got to the top. He's tried long and hard enough. He really feels his music." (19)

Indeed, it had been a long hard climb for Joe Cocker. He had been working away at establishing himself as one of the most soulful and unique singers to come out of England in the 1960s. Now, what was he going to do with his new-found fame?

CHAPTER FOUR

"By The Time I Got To *Woodstock*"

For Joe Cocker, the year 1969 was to be the biggest, most exciting one yet. It was full of new music, massive rock festivals, and a sea of drugs and liquor. After the huge success of "With A Little Help From My Friends," the executives at A&M Records were anxious for follow-up music from Joe. When they released "Feelin' Alright" as his next, North America only, single it made it to Number 69 in the U.S. and Number 49 in Canada. This put further pressure on Joe and on Denny Cordell to come up with his next album to capture his career momentum.

Unlike his debut LP the second one was well plotted out by Cordell. Known for his ability to put teams of musicians and singers together in a recording studio to make wonderful music, this time around he really "pulled out the stops." During this era, he had run into an incredibly creative and expressive singer-songwriter by the name of Leon Russell and his girlfriend, Rita Coolidge. They were notable at the time because of their involvement with the ever-evolving musical act, Delaney & Bonnie & Friends.

Over the next two years, some of the most important characters in Joe Cocker's career and life were to include Leon Russell, Rita Coolidge, and various members of Delaney & Bonnie & Friends. Joe was to sing and perform with all these creative characters in various combinations on his next two albums and on the most famous tour of his career, 1970s *Mad Dogs & English Men* mega-rock show.

Musician and songwriter Delaney Bramlett was originally from Pontotoc, Mississippi, and he moved out to Los Angeles in 1959. He worked as a session musician, and from 1964 to 1966 he was a guitar player in the house band for the highly successful American rock and pop television show, *Shindig!* on ABC-TV. The keyboard player in the band was Leon Russell with whom he instantly became friends.

Bonnie Lynn O'Farrell was born in Granite City, Illinois, and was an aspiring singer. Her soulful style landed her one of the most unique singing gigs in the business as the only white "Ikette" in The Ike & Tina Turner Revue in the mid-1960s. When she moved out to Los Angeles in 1967, she met and married Delaney Bramlett.

Leon Russell, who came from Lawton, Oklahoma, started his musical career in Tulsa, Oklahoma, when he was 14 years old. He played in a band with a friend of his, David Gates who later became famous for being the head of the musical quartet David Gates & Bread. Leon moved to Los Angeles in 1958, and in the 1960s, along with Gates, guitar player Glen Campbell, and several others, became part of the famed "studio group," The Wrecking Crew.

Leon was great as a songwriter. His songs were often quirky, but always fascinating. He once explained of their creation, "I'm sort of an 'automatic' writer. I'm not much for chiseling away at songs or working at them for days trying to make them perfect. If I can sit down and write something in five minutes, then that's great. And if that doesn't happen then either it doesn't get finished or else it's usually not any good." (20)

Rita Coolidge is originally from Lafayette, Tennessee, and went to high school in Nashville, alongside singer Brenda Lee. During the late 1950s and early 1960s Brenda achieved hit after hit on the pop charts, including "I'm Sorry" and the perennial "Rockin' Around The Christmas Tree." Rita could instantly see from Brenda's musical success what was possible to be achieved in the music business. She moved to Los Angeles where she began her career singing background vocals for the albums of others, including Leon Russell. All of these people were about to become intermingled with Joe Cocker as he began work on his second album, which in America was ultimately entitled *Joe Cocker!*

Meanwhile, Joe had all sorts of concert dates set up in the United States, so Joe, Cordell, and The Grease Band all came to Los Angeles. That was where the *Joe Cocker!* album was to be recorded in the late spring, early summer of 1969, in between concert dates.

Denny Cordell became familiar with Leon Russell's keyboard work, having heard him on the first Bonnie & Delaney & Friends album, *Accept No Substitutes* (1969), and he invited Russell to come to one of his recording sessions. Cordell found Leon to be a quirky but creative character and asked him to play on this new album he was recording for Joe Cocker at Sunset Sound recording studios.

According to Cordell, "About two or three days into the session the unmistakable figure of Leon—grey hair right down his back and completely dressed in white appears with Rita Coolidge on his arm. And she was stunningly beautiful—the Cherokee Indian deal. It was all terribly low-key. We did the platitudes, 'Like a cup of coffee?' And they sat on a sofa in front of the speakers underneath the desk. They didn't move, didn't say anything to anybody for three hours. Then about two o'clock in the morning they got up and said, 'Thank you very much, very nice,' and left. So we thought, 'Oh well, that was a bit strange. Wasn't it a bit weird?' And then, the next day, we got a message from [A&M employee] Michael Vossey saying, 'Leon really liked what you guys were doing last night, and he's got a tune that he thinks Joe might like.'" (1)

Interestingly enough, Leon was later to recall that evening from a different perspective. It was he who was more stunned by all the drugs and wasted time he witnessed. Russell explained, "When I first dropped by Sunset Sound where the Cocker sessions were to take place, I found much sitting around going on, the studio liberally sprinkled with ganja and prime hash in huge blocks, sporting the seal of the government of Morocco. After I had been there for about two hours, the situation maintaining absolute continuity, I started to get a little nervous. I was from the Hollywood school of union record-making where you were expected to cut three songs in the allotted three-hour session, no matter what. All I could see was the $200 per hour studio tab, plus the $1,500, or more, three-hour bill for the musicians." (21)

Chris Stainton, Joe Cocker, and Denny Cordell all went up to meet Leon Russell at his house where he had created an 8-track recording studio in his garage. He proceeded to play four of his songs for the trio, including "Delta Lady" and "Hello Little Friend." Not long afterward they were in the studio recording both songs.

Along the way to creating Joe's second album, Cordell found that he had run out of studio time. He recalls, "We took the 16-tracks and went up to Leon's pad to his funky little studio. [Eric] Clapton came up there that night and then we had Rita Coolidge, Merry Clayton, and Bonnie Bramlett. Leon finished it off by putting the guitar down on it, and I always remember Eric saying, 'Oh man, this is a hit, this is a real hit!'" (1)

According to Leon Russell, he re-mixed the *Joe Cocker!* album for them in his own studio. As he was to explain, "I was used to dealing with tape under a microscope, overdubbing and inserting parts and generally repairing anything that might have been a mistake or something ill-conceived in the recording. At first, the process was difficult on this particular project because Denny and Joe kept up a constant commentary about how this or that didn't sound quite right or this part seemed wrong. I explained I was dealing with component parts of the sound and that it was premature to judge at this point. Asking them to please let me finish the whole process, I told them the time would come when their commentary would be timely and, if they didn't like something, I could fix it then. After the work was done everyone seemed to be happy, and Cordell later told me he had never seen any plastic surgery more successfully accomplished." (21)

Recalls Rita Coolidge, "When Joe recorded his second album for A&M Records in 1969, *Joe Cocker!*, Leon was credited as the co-producer, and through him I was called in to record background vocals on several of the cuts. That's how the business was back then in California. I would pick up some of the greatest gigs from friends calling me up to sing on the sessions and during their stage performances." (22)

Rita also fondly remembers, "During rehearsals at Leon's for the Cocker album, I sang background vocals with Bonnie Bramlett, which was a flat-out thrill. I met Jim Gordon. Jim was the most in-demand session drummer in the world at the moment. He was 'the guy' on both coasts. He would do a session in the morning in New York and fly to LA to do a session in the afternoon. On top of that, my God, he was gorgeous." (23) Jim Gordon was to become part of the Cocker circle soon too.

In reality, Rita Coolidge is the "delta lady" in the song "Delta Lady." She was someone who inspired and/or had a hand in the creation of two of the greatest Cocker songs. Not only was she the lady of the delta, she was also the heartbroken subject of the song "Superstar" which is about her love for Eric Clapton who she became acquainted with through her work with Delaney & Bonnie & Friends. Is this tale of Cocker and his friends getting incestuous enough?

At the time Joe was enthusiastically looking forward to the release of his second album. In anticipation of it he said, "It amazes me how someone like Paul McCartney comes up with his lyrics. We do this song he gave us called 'She Came in Through the Bathroom Window.' It has a line in it, 'And so I quit the police department to find a steady job.' It turns out he got that when he was riding in a cab in New York." (11)

While the recording of tracks for the *Joe Cocker!* album was underway, Joe, Chris and the rest of The Grease Band (Alan Spenner, Bruce Rowlands, Henry McCullough) were busily touring the countryside.

Joe had come to Los Angeles with Denny Cordell in 1968, but Chris Stainton had never traveled across the Atlantic. He was later to recall his first U.S. visit. "That was early 1969. It was an eye-opener for me. I'd never been to America. We landed up in New York and there was all the craziness and yellow cabs everywhere. It was just a complete shock to me. We stayed at a place called Loews Midtown on Eighth Avenue and 48th [Street]. Joe and I stayed in a room together." (12)

One of the first things they did in New York City was to perform on *The Ed Sullivan Show* in April of 1969. Performing his latest single, Joe Cocker was more than the staid Sullivan producers were used to. When he began flailing his arms in the middle of the song "Feelin' Alright," the camera men about went berserk trying to disguise his jerky and spastic choreography. Alan Spenner was to recall, "It caused quite a stir. The older generation thought he was a lunatic and should be sent home, and the youngsters thought he was 'the bee's knees.' It was the perfect start." (1)

Meanwhile, the 1969 American concert tour opened at The Fillmore East in East Greenwich Village with Cocker and his Grease Band playing opening act for Jeff Beck. According to Chris Stainton, "We did good straight from the start. We had a hit with 'With A Little Help From My Friends.' The audience rushed the stage. They went berserk. I don't think they'd ever seen anything like Cocker." (12)

Describing his stage act circa 1969, Joe was to explain, "Well, I've got my own version of 'Let's Go Get Stoned' which always goes down well. And I do Dylan's 'I Shall Be Released' and Moby Grape's 'Can't Be So Bad.' We also get into a lot of impromptu blues things." (7)

Other notable performances took place in Boston, and in Detroit they were the opening act for The Who. They played all up and down the Atlantic coast playing gigs in New Jersey and some New York City club dates at The Scene and Ungaro's. It was during their stay in Chicago that Chris Stainton met the love of his life, his wife Gail, and they are still married to this day. When they got to San Francisco, Cocker and crew opened for The Byrds at the famed Fillmore West.

Amongst the high-profile gigs for Cocker and troupe included appearances at *The Denver Pop Festival* and *The Newport Rock Festival*. However, no matter where else they played during 1969, the one big thing that was going to set Joe Cocker apart from the crowd was his appearance at the *Woodstock Music Festival* in August of 1969.

There was no other music festival in history bigger, more famous, or more insane than *Woodstock* which attracted half a million stoned hippies and music mavens. Michael Lang and Artie Kornfeld were two of the principal producers of 1969's impossibly huge *Woodstock Music Festival* which was held in Bethel, New York. Lang was the Executive Producer of the whole event, and Artie Kornfeld was in charge of Publicity and Subsidiary Rights.

In the 1979 book *Barefoot In Babylon, The Creation Of The Woodstock Music Festival, 1969*, author Robert Stephen Spitz wrote, "One chance that Lang *had* decided to take was with a virtually unknown performer whom Artie had brought to his attention a month before the staff's move to [the city of] Wallkill. Artie had disappeared for a few days without telling anyone where he could be contacted. When he resurfaced, he casually told Lang that he had 'gone to the [Caribbean] Islands to do a little gambling' and had met a 'real tough cat' named Denny Cordell at one of the casinos. Cordell was a rock manager who insisted that Kornfeld listen to a new act he was producing. 'Send me the record,' Artie said, a typical record-executive response. 'I'll do better than that, man. I'll give you the single we've just done, and you can tell me right away what you think.' Artie feigned enthusiasm and half-heartedly accepted Cordell's invitation. He soon made a complete about-face. The record was called 'Feelin' Alright,' and Artie thought the singer, a growling Englishman named Joe Cocker, was just about the most exciting new voice he had ever heard. 'You gotta get into this guy, Michael,' Artie insisted. 'We gotta grab him to do the festival before he gets hot.'" (24)

According to Spitz, "Within a few days, Joe Cocker had signed to open Sunday afternoon's show at a mutually acceptable price of $2,750. It was perhaps the first bargain, other than Santana, they had gotten since putting the show together." (24)

What started out as a music festival in the small, artsy, upstate New York town of Woodstock, failed to get the permits necessary for such an event. So its organizers had to move it to the only place they could find that was large enough to support such an event: a plot of farmland in near-by Bethel, New York. As Joni Mitchell immortalized the event in her tribute song, "Woodstock," by the time it was over, it drew "half a million strong" attendees, spurned a hit album, a hit documentary, and magnified the careers of everyone involved in it.

Boasting such established headliners as The Jefferson Airplane, Sly & The Family Stone, and Janis Joplin, *Woodstock* also launched the careers of several lesser-known performers like Melanie [Safka], ShaNaNa, Richie Havens, Country Joe & The Fish, and Joe Cocker. Several of the acts, including Melanie and Joe Cocker, had to be transported to the event by helicopter.

Decades later, Chris Stainton spoke of the rock festival to end them all: "*Woodstock.* Yeah. I didn't really pay much attention at the time. But we all went up there by helicopter. They couldn't get us in any other way. They flew us back out with a helicopter. It was ridiculous. I had some acid just before I went into the helicopter. I just remember it being so noisy and everything. It [the festival crowd] was colossal. It was a colossal experience to see the crowd, but it was a good feeling. There wasn't any bad vibes or anything. It was all good. Everybody was being really great." (12)

The other thing that Chris Stainton remembers about the acid and the helicopter ride was the fact that he was so high he vomited. Said Stainton, "I'd taken two tablets of Orange Sunshine and I started feeling a bit sick. The guy opened the hatch, and I threw up out the helicopter over the crowd. I vomited over *Woodstock*!" (1) That does not make for a pretty picture of the festival.

For once the members of The Grease Band were all stoned on drugs, and Joe was not. According to him, "I was furious because all the band had taken acid and they didn't tell me. I was the only one straight. I have been offered brown acid in my time, though. Even black acid. I took that. That was very weird. It was a very dark trip." (3)

Interestingly enough, there had been an announcement over the P.A. system at the festival to avoid the brown acid that some people were tripping on and having a bad reaction. Cocker was to clarify, "To get back to the warning that I received. You may take it with however many grains of salt that you wish. That the brown acid that is circulating around us isn't too good. It is suggested that you stay away from that. Of course, it's your own trip. So be my guest, but please be advised that there is a warning on that one, O.K.?" (3)

To fill out the three days of *Woodstock* they needed a lot of musicians, and Michael Lang and his associates were booking any legitimate performers that they could find to fill the stage with music. That is why there were so many performers there who were not yet huge stars. This list included Richie Havens, Melanie, and Joe Cocker.

They were not household names before *Woodstock*, but because of their performances at *Woodstock* that is what they became.

What was it like to be transported by helicopter and to see the sea of people that was the crowd of 500,000 waiting to be entertained? Melanie distinctly recalls how intimidating it was to get into a helicopter for the first time and to be taken to the backstage area of *Woodstock*. She recalls, "I was just there, and I realized this was big and I'm not and 'What am I doing here?' I had so many people coming up to me and recognizing me saying, 'Melanie! Melanie! You've got to go to the helicopter!' I said, 'What are you talking about? What helicopter?' Here I had driven up to Bethel, New York, with my mother in a Chevy Impala. Someone said to me, 'O.K., let's go.' And we were running and running toward the helicopter. I felt like I had gotten scooped up into this big thing that was happening and now I had to get on a helicopter." (25)

Melanie was in awe seeing what the crowd looked like while hovering above it all. "I was on the helicopter with the pilot and some other people I didn't know," she explains. "We went up, and I looked down, and I see these little colorful dots, and I said to the pilot, 'What is that?' And, he says, 'People.' I said, 'Oh, no, I mean all those little colored dots right down there.' And he said, 'Yeah. That's people.' I said, 'How can that been a field of people? It looks like some sort of colorful crop of something.' And he said, 'No, it's people.' Then he points to the stage, and it looked like it was the size of five football fields. I had never been on a stage bigger than a little platform. I was thinking, 'Oh, my God. I'm gonna die. How am I gonna get out of here?'" (25)

It was anything but glamorous. After the helicopter landed, Melanie was taken to a tent to wait for hours. According to Melanie, "I spent the afternoon in that tent with the dirt floor all day. Every once in a while, they would say, 'You're on next.' And I would panic and throw up. It was absolutely horrible. At one point, Joan Baez sent me over a cup of tea for my throat." (25)

In other words, there were a couple of different scenarios going on with the performers at *Woodstock*. Melanie was given a cup of tea by Joan Baez. In contrast, the members of The Grease Band were given tabs of LSD.

Finally, they brought Melanie out on stage where she performed her recent songs including the "peace and love" anthem, "Beautiful People." She recalls, "I thought people were gonna throw things at me. I didn't have a band. Imagine not having any band or anyone or anything out there on stage with me. At least Joe Cocker had his band up there, so it seemed somewhat normal in comparison to being all alone on that stage." (25) Based on her *Woodstock* experience, Melanie wrote her song "Candles In The Rain," and several months later it became her first Top Ten hit record. Not everyone had the same experience.

Joe remembers, "When we landed by the side of the stage my band was already there and wired up and ready to go. It was pretty early in the day, as I recall, and the crowd was all doing other things until we did 'Let's All Get Stoned,' the old Ray Charles number, and that kind of woke everybody up a bit. If you look at the film, we did a pretty good job with 'A Little Help From My Friends.' People say, 'Well, you look a bit *gazongo*,' but it was like a gospel thing where you'd get so caught up in it; it's like swooning in the church." (15)

Fortunately, through his eyes, everything went quite smoothly for Joe. Although he was performing in front of 500,000 people, by now he was used to large crowds. Cocker was to recall, "We were kind of lucky because we got on stage real early. It took about half the set just to get through to everybody, to that kind of consciousness. You're in a sea of humanity and people aren't necessarily looking to entertain you. We did 'Let's Go Get Stoned' by Ray Charles, which kind of turned everybody around a bit, and we came off looking pretty good that day. A lot of other artists didn't enjoy themselves at all." (3)

Indeed, Joe Cocker was one of the big surprises of *Woodstock*. His August 17, 1969, set with The Grease Band was something unexpected for the audience, who for the most part, had no idea who he was before this performance. Their 11-song set started around 2:00 on Sunday afternoon. It included:

> "Dear Landlord"
> "Something's Coming On"
> "Do I Still Figure In Your Life"
> "Feelin' Alright"
> "Just Like a Woman"
> "Let's Go Get Stoned"
> "I Don't Need No Doctor"
> "I Shall Be Released"
> "Hitchcock Railway"
> "Something To Say"
> "With A Little Help From My Friends"

When the massively successful Number 1 ranking three-disc *Woodstock* album was released and the documentary of the festival was released, it was only Joe's performance of "With A Little Help From My Friends" that was included in either. It wasn't until the year 2009 that A&M Records released the CD *Joe Cocker Live At Woodstock*, that his entire set was made public. Sporting a colorful tie-dyed shirt, blue striped jeans, and boots emblazoned with big white stars on them, Joe Cocker gave his all to this performance.

It made for a memorable impression. Unfortunately, Chris Stainton remembered very little of it. According to him, "I don't know how I played because I was out of my brains on acid. I stopped thinking and just went along with it and everything was fine." (12)

In his 1979 book, *Barefoot In Babylon, The Creation Of The Woodstock Music Festival, 1969*, author Robert Stephen Spitz claimed that the awe struck on-lookers were ". . . startled by the singer's striking similarity to Ray Charles' style of blues, breathlessly squeezing out the last few syllables of a refrain while sliding right into the next line with a surging, yet short-winded, growl. But while Cocker's vocal inflections paid tribute to his American mentor, the visual show was an invention all his own. Cocker arched his shoulders and pumped the microphone with his chest in time to the bass runs. Occasionally he stumbled backward, dipped, then sprang toward the mic to deliver the next swell of sound with an almost animalistic intensity. Cocker's own inimitable trademark, however, was the way he accompanied his back-up group, The Grease Band, on an imaginary guitar. He would spasmodically slap at its invisible strings while twisting his pretzel-like body into rhythmically responsive contortions. Each song seemed to be a totally enervating experience for the tortured Cocker, yet he bounced back with the resilience of a prizefighter conditioned to go the distance." (24)

It had been threatening to rain all day, and suddenly the premonition was about to become a reality. According to Spitz, "Joe Cocker grabbed the bottle of beer at his feet, tucked it under his arm, and fled to safety. There was no time for apologies or long drawn-out 'goodbyes.' He disappeared into the service elevator with the rest of The Grease Band close on his heels. 'Hit the power!' someone screamed from behind a bunker of amplifiers. The storm-troopers, armed with their balled-up plastic slipcovers and cans of surface shield, galloped across the stage for the second time that weekend." (24)

Woodstock organizer Michael Lang recalls being blown away by Joe that day. He claimed, "It was the first time anybody I knew had seen him, and he had so much soul power. It was one of those magical moments." (13)

The weather that weekend in Bethel was alternately rainy and dry. Not long after Joe's set at *Woodstock*, the skies opened up and turned the farmland into a sea of mud. Joe remembers, "We were on before it turned into a mud festival. The rains hadn't started coming down yet. I vividly remember looking into this sea of people, and it was beyond calculation. I had already played to 50,000 people earlier that year at *The Atlanta Pop Festival*, so I had some idea what it was like to play to a huge crowd. I flew in on a helicopter, and I remember saying to the pilot, 'What's all that stuff on the horizon?' And he said, 'That's where you're going to play.' It was an ocean of people." (15)

Looking back on it, Joe proclaimed, "Those early tours of the States were the greatest. Like the gig at The Atlanta Raceway with Spirit, and Janis Joplin, and [Jimi] Hendrix. I remember going on at, like, six in the morning, and all these kids acid-blazed. It was a very warm occasion. And the hotel, too. One of the floors caught on fire, four days' wait for room service. But they were great times, hippie times." (5)

Throughout his career, Joe was able to look back at the *Woodstock* festival with fondness. According to Jerry Moss, "We had a conversation once and he said, 'Well, performing in front of a half a million people—that was something!' He always remembered that, not just as a breakthrough but as an incredible experience." (13)

Although Joe and The Grease Band were only paid somewhere in the vicinity of $2,750 for appearing at *Woodstock,* it bumped his asking price up to $6,500 per show. Adjusting that price to today's economy, that was a significant jump in income.

It was the era of the huge rock & roll outdoor music festivals, and in 1969 Joe established his career at several more of them in addition to *Woodstock*. On September 1, 2, and 3 of that year, Atlantic City, New Jersey, played host to one of the biggest ones. Held at The Atlantic City Race Track, in addition to Cocker, this one also featured Joni Mitchell, Janis Joplin, The Byrds, Frank Zappa, Booker T. & The M.G.'s, The Chamber Brothers, Canned Heat, Procol Harum, The Buddy Miles Express, and closing with one of Joe's early idols, Little Richard.

In his review of the festival, John Lombardi wrote in *Rolling Stone* about the huge turning stage that everyone appeared on. As soon as one set was over, the stage would turn to reveal the next performers. He wrote, "When the revolving stage turned at the end of the [Canned Heat] set to reveal Joe Cocker and The Grease Band, it was like watching some fabulous jukebox turntable. Cocker, replete with jutting gut and exaggerated finger motions, was a vast improvement. He needed very little help from his friends. [Janis] Joplin had been hanging around backstage during Cocker's act, alternately sucking on an orange and pulling at a bottle of Gavilan Tequila." (26)

One of the things that impressed Joe the most was the fact that he was playing on the same stage as some of the biggest rock acts in the world. The one who made the most indelible impression on him was guitar playing legend, Jimi Hendrix. According to Cocker, "Oh, God. In the late '60s, all musicians were awed by Jimi. Eric Clapton, everybody. You couldn't get much of a conversation out of Jimi. I once went down to his house in one of the canyons in LA, and he played it great. I sat around his house until he woke up at two in the afternoon. He'd already heard me sing, so he just got up and played the guitar for four hours. It was like nothing I had ever heard in my life. He was really fantastic, a genius." (2)

When his sophomore album, *Joe Cocker!,* was released by A&M Records in the U.S., it hit Number 11 and Number 10 in Canada. Joe turned "Delta Lady" into a Top Ten hit in the U.K., Number 34 in Australia, and Number 15 in the Netherlands. In addition, "She Came In Through The Bathroom Window" hit Number 30 in the U.S., and Number 31 in Canada.

Although, at the time he was performing on stages of all sizes, large and small, it was his performance at *Woodstock* that was to be remembered by everyone as his most significant of all. He had finally arrived at a career peak. He was looking forward to the release of his second album, and he was on the threshold of still another year of milestone performances. Joe Cocker was truly getting by with A LOT of help from his friends.

CHAPTER FIVE

"Mad Dogs & Englishmen"

If you were to list the two biggest and most significant things that ever happened in Joe Cocker's life and career they are his August 1969 performance at *Woodstock* and his massively famous 1970 concert tour of America operating under the title *Mad Dogs & Englishmen*. It provided Joe with the biggest-selling album of his career, several of his biggest hits, and his second hugely successful rock & roll documentary. With rare exception, everything that directly followed those two events was to be either a career depth, a temporary comeback, or a headline-grabbing disaster.

From the outside, the *Mad Dogs & Englishmen* tour was a brilliantly conceived, excellently executed rock & roll vaudeville revue of a show which gave Joe his Top Ten hits "Cry Me A River" and "The Letter." And the double-disc album that came from that tour hit the Top Ten in the U.S. (Number 2), Australia (Number 3), the Netherlands (Number 9), and Canada (Number 2).

The tour itself was born out of desperation, chaos, and the threat of lawsuits. It sounded like a horrifying list of circumstances to launch this uniquely magical mystery tour. They had to book all of the talent within a single seven-day week and take it on the road. At one point Joe really loved it and loved the new music that was featured in it. It became an incredible showcase for his expressive vocals and his dynamic on stage energy. It also brilliantly capitalized on the career trajectory that his *Woodstock* performance had promised. However, on a personal level, by the time *Mad Dogs & Englishmen* had finished its hectic three-month run, Joe Cocker found himself burned out, exhausted, and completely disgusted with the music business in general.

On one side of the coin, *Mad Dogs & Englishmen* showed off Joe as one of the most unique hit-making forces in the early-1970s rock scene. On the other side of the coin it magnified his occasional lack of drive, and it underscored his lifelong lack of self-confidence which left him an unhappy drug and alcohol-addicted mess.

When someone becomes a big star in the music business there are two equally important aspects to it: the music and the business. If you are able to make appealing and passionate music, you have the requisite talent to become a rock star. But if you don't have the business part of your life together, it is not going to end well.

The odd thing is that, circa 1969-1970, Joe Cocker had his business seemingly in order, organized, and moving along perfectly. He had Denny Cordell as his record producer, and that was incredibly solid, at least for his first three albums. He had Dee Anthony as his manager and booking agent. Joe definitely had differences of opinion with Dee along the way, but Dee was making sound business decisions for Joe. Cocker also had, through Dee, Frank Barselona as his booking agent presenting Joe and The Grease Band in some of the best venues to progress his career.

Right after *Woodstock*, Cocker and his band played the massive *Isle Of Wight Festival* and returned to the U.S. for more dates. As of October, they were back in Sheffield. Joe ended the 1969 holiday season with gigs in England, and in January they played at the industry gala, MIDEM, in Cannes, France. After that, Joe and the band expected a little vacation. That was not to happen for long.

Dee Anthony contacted Joe in early 1970 to tell him that he had his next tour about to start in March in Detroit. Joe informed

Anthony that he had disbanded The Grease Band and wasn't interested in going back to work so soon.

Rita Coolidge remembers, "On March 12, Dee flew to Los Angeles and informed Joe that he had been signed to do all these concert dates in the United States, a lot of them, all over the country. Joe was completely clueless. He just kind of showed up in Los Angeles the week before he was supposed to leave, and NOTHING had been put together. There was no band; there was no anything. On top of that, A&M Records wanted to film the tour in its entirety to make a feature film out of it. It was the first truly big tour in his career, and nothing was even in place for it. According to what I was told, Joe's whole attitude was something to the effect of, 'Well, I'll just blow it off.'" (22)

Coolidge further explains, "Dee Anthony and the representatives from A&M Records sat him down and said to him, 'Joe, you GOTTA do this! This is the big time, a BIG TIME tour! You can't maybe do it or not do it. This is all carved into stone, and promoters all over this country are expecting big shows.' Not only would he be sued by the promoters, be deported back to England, and be denied any further work permits, he would probably lose the use of both of his legs! Some of these promoters *really* mean business. I mean, it was real serious stuff. That was about the point where I came into the picture. The following day, March 13, I was just at home minding my own business, when I got a frantic call from Leon Russell. He told me the whole story and informed me that he and Joe had gotten together some of their musician friends and were stringing together a hot rock band for Joe to front. Joe at this point was still thinking that this was going to be the kind of situation where he could just kind of float onto and off of the stage with sort of a 'If I feel like doing it, I'll do it' and 'I don't feel like doing it' kind of attitude." (22)

Cordell was to recall that Joe had gone down to Jamaica for a little vacation when Dee found him. According to Denny, "The same day that Joe arrived in Los Angeles, so did Dee Anthony and Frank Barsalona, saying, 'Look here, Son, you've got to play this tour; otherwise, you'll never be allowed into America again.' I think that the first time Joe mistrusted Anthony and Barsalona was when they forced him to do the *Mad Dogs*." (27)

Denny was to later explain of this pressurized situation, "It was never a question of Leon or me offering to help Joe out. It was a question of Joe and I meeting with Dee Anthony and walking away convinced that we had to do the tour. Joe was desperate. He certainly wasn't coerced by me. He had an inherent fear that Dee was a gangster. He didn't want to do the tour, and for two days we went through tears and pleadings, sitting in hotel rooms for hours while Joe pleaded not to do it. He just wasn't ready for it. If any of my artists didn't want to do a tour, there's nothing I wouldn't do to cancel it clean." (18)

It was Cordell who instantly called Leon Russell for help. According to Dee Anthony, "You don't put a band like that together overnight. They'd been rehearsing and we knew it. They used Joe's tour to launch Shelter Records. Look at the promotion they did on Leon Russell. But they wanted to take their time. Because we expedited the tour and made sure it took place when it was supposed to, they had to take their finger outta their ass and get everything together. There was no reason for Joe not to go out; he had contracts and he had to fulfill them." (27)

Leon Russell claimed, "Joe didn't want to do the tour in the first place. Then about ten days before we set off on the road, he changed his mind and decided to go along." (28) Once the green light was switched on, the music making machinery went into action.

According to Denny, "The *Mad Dogs* tour was a salvage job. Joe had no idea a tour had been planned when he arrived in LA. He'd got rid of The Grease Band for whatever reasons he had, but he was followed into LA by Dee and Frank who told him he had to do a tour or he'd never play in the country again. They also told him that the Musician's Union would disown him and that the promoters would sue, so he was pressured into it. The band for the *Mad Dogs* tour just came about. It had to be done in a hurry and when you've got that many people, it's obviously going to run to a certain amount of expense." (18)

One of the main events that happened to bolster the Cocker project was the fact that Leon Russell found out that Bonnie & Delaney & Friends had just let their band go, so he started calling the musicians they had used on their last tour.

Leon Russell recalled, "I originally wanted two drummers, but for every person we asked to play, two more asked to play with us. There were about 21 people playing and singing on most of the dates, and the other 25 were family and friends." (28)

Denny Cordell was in awe watching Leon pull this all together. According to him, he told Leon, "This is great . . . It's going to work . . . We've pulled it out of the frying pan. But, Leon, we can't have three drummers."

Leon said to him, "Well, which one are we gonna have? Who's gonna tell the other two they can't come?" (1) They ended up with a trio of drummers on stage. Sometimes, as in the case of this tour, excess is best!

As Rita Coolidge explains, "It really came around to Joe and Leon and Denny Cordell getting on the phone and just calling people, trying to put together what they considered to be their Number 1 band. They really needed to find a troupe of people they could depend upon and people who would be able to get the material together quickly. Not only was I asked to sing background vocals in the act, which I quickly agreed to, but it was also my job to put together 'The Choir,' to be in charge of it, and to make sure that all of the singers had their parts and knew all of their cues. We had exactly four days of rehearsing at the A&M lot to pull it all together.

We would rehearse 10, 12, or 14 hours a day—sometimes 16 hours a day. We had to get all this material down before we left." (22)

Joe watched in awe as an entire rock & roll revue, centered around him and his music, could be constructed so quickly. According to him, "We really weren't going for the big band that it turned out to be. It was my intention of just making it a small group. But Leon said the only way he would do it was if he could put the band together, so we ended up with brass and choirs." (1) Naturally, Joe contacted Chris Stainton and asked him to join the tour that was gaining steam by the moment. This was definitely a time when he needed his best mate and music co-conspirator by his side.

Chris Stainton recalls, "I was in New York, and I drove over there with our roadie, Pete Nichols. We hired a van and drove from New York to LA. It took us about seven days. We arrived at Leon's house, and everyone was there, like [bass player] Carl Radle and [drummer] Jim Gordon and [trumpeter] Jim Price. It was a whole lot of them." (12)

Rita Coolidge explains, "When 'The Choir' was finally in place, there were ten superb voices that could blend beautifully behind Joe. They included Nicky Barclay, Bobby Jones, Claudia Linnear, Daniel Moore, Matthew Moore, Pamela Polland, Don Preston, Donna Washburn, Donna Weiss, and myself." (22)

Material? What all was Joe going to sing? Surely his most recent and biggest hit singles had to be performed, including "Feelin' Alright," "She Came In Through The Bathroom Window," and "Delta Lady." Instantly stepping into the role as Musical Director for the project, Leon Russell began suggesting other songs for Joe to sing, including The Rolling Stones' "Honky Tonk Woman." It was also Leon's idea for Joe to do "Cry Me A River" and the recent hit by The Box Tops, "The Letter." They even worked up a blues medley of "I'll Drown In My Own Tears," "When Something Is Wrong With My Baby," and Otis Redding and Jerry Butler's "I've Been Loving

You Too Long." This also marked the recorded debut of the song "Let's Go Get Stoned," which was so perfectly 1970!

According to Rita Coolidge, "Ultimately, the show itself was constructed like a classic 'musical revue.' I had a solo spot, Leon and Joe had a duet, and there were several different solo spots of several of the performers. Over those four frantic days it all just evolved and grew. As we went along we decided that we wanted more singers, and it just got bigger and bigger. It was so big, in fact, that we had three drummers on stage, Jim Gordon, Jim Keltner, and Chuck Blackwell. Chuck also played percussion, along with Sandy Konikoff." (22)

Rita remembers, "We rehearsed March 14, 15, and 16. On the 17th, the rehearsal was recorded in its entirety, and a single was released from those tapes with 'The Letter' on one side and 'Space Captain' on the B-side. It was a four-day marathon, and we just rehearsed and rehearsed, and somehow, we pulled our ragged asses together. It was on the 18th that the idea of filming the tour was first proposed, and like the rest of the tour, a camera crew was assembled at the last minute as well. The resulting film was more of a documentary. Or as they say in *Spinal Tap*, 'It's a Rockumentary!'" (22)

When Jerry Moss came to see Cocker and the band rehearse on the A&M lot, he was blown away. According to him, "Joe was able to sing on top of it with power and strength. In those days he couldn't sing out of time. He was the greatest white blues singer." (13)

It was actually Jerry Moss' idea to film Cocker's *Mad Dogs & Englishmen* tour. This way they could release the documentary and promote it along with the album. It was to end up a win/win project for the company. With regard to the film and the title of the tour, Joe Cocker explained that the title was Denny's idea. "It's from Noel Coward, you know. Denny was a bit like that." (1)

Rita Coolidge explains, "On March 19th we left the A&M lot with 55 people, men, women, and kids, due to the fact that Denny Cordell's kids were along with us for the ride. Pamela Polland, who was one of the singers, brought along her dog, Caterina. Then there were all of the *extra* people, all of Leon's friends like Big Emily who was just in charge of good times and keeping the parties going. She was just fabulous. Big Em is featured prominently all over the film. In addition to this whole troupe, Leon also invited all of these great people from Oklahoma just to round out the traveling party atmosphere that the tour assumed. We all climbed into a new Super Constellation plane and flew to Detroit for the opening night of the tour, the very next day." (22)

Joe Cocker recalls, "You know, we flew around on one of those big prop Constellations, and I used to swear it would be tilting back because there were so many people on board. We had a choir of 20 people, and everybody had their girlfriends, and wives, and dogs. It seemed very hectic at the time, but it was really kind of low key, no big money. We stayed in regular hotels, but it was an experience, all right!" (17)

March 20, 1970, Joe Cocker starring in the stage-show *Mad Dogs & Englishmen* had its debut in Detroit, Michigan. Somehow, with all of the rehearsing and the overall feeling of camaraderie that the first part of the tour carried, it worked! Next stop, New York City and The Fillmore East. The two nights that they played there made up the bulk of the released recording from the tour.

Denny Cordell recalls, "Many of the supporting cast had never left California before and, consequently their vibe was extremely intense. It made the tour a very heavy weight to carry, but having started with all these people you can't just throw some of them off. I didn't know what was happening until it happened. Every time. I got the band only five or six days before the first date. We rehearsed it, and the band kind of grew until it was perfect, and we went out on tour. Obviously, the band soon became much tighter and about half the people became redundant. They could have been dropped, but the general feeling was that this wouldn't have been a very nice

Joe Cocker: With a LOT of Help From My Friends

thing to do. After all, many of these people had musical pursuits and careers. They'd dropped everything they'd been doing. To have thrown them off the tour would have been unfair." (18)

Through March, April, and May of 1970, Joe, Chris Stainton, and the troupe wound their way through the United States, ending up back in California. Rita Coolidge remembers that this insanely large tour wasn't all sunshine and roses. According to her, "Although the tour seemed like it went on for about three years, it was just a seven-week tour, only a couple of months in duration. It changed and evolved along the way, and I think that the personalities in the group went full circle. People who left home as best friends, came back absolute killing-each-other enemies. There were power struggles; there were a lot of drugs and just a whole lot of incestuous stuff going on. It was especially incestuous considering that we had just left home as one big happy family. Sometimes it was just ridiculous." (22)

Chris Stainton was to echo that sentiment by explaining, "It wasn't as great as it seemed. It was a lot of drugs. TOO many! There were too many drugs floating around and people were giving Joe drugs all over the place and messing him up big time. I don't have too many good memories of it, but we had some great gigs. We did The Fillmore East a couple of nights and that was really great. I don't know how people managed to stay together, but it wasn't everybody. I know Joe and I did quite a few [drugs], but there were people that didn't. Carl Radle was Mr. Clean. Jim Keltner was with us for a while, and he didn't do anything. Quite a few people were clean and healthy, but we made up for that!" (12)

Speaking of drugs, Rita Coolidge remembers that Cocker was often a bit withdrawn on the tour. According to her, "Joe was not much of a social butterfly. He was very withdrawn, and it took a lot of drugs to be able to walk out and do it every night. It was amazing that he could remember lyrics and stay on his feet." (13)

Joe was kind of in awe as to how this whole tour came about and how it unfolded. According to him, "Leon came up with the idea for *Mad Dogs*. We all lived up at Leon's house. We all ran around in the nude and had some pretty wild times. But it was strange. Leon was into this revivalist sort of thing. He'd always have to have a [group] meal before a show. We'd all sit down, and he would say a little prayer." (5) Leon seemed to set the tone for much of what unfolded.

Although this was clearly Joe Cocker's chance to shine as the star of the show, *Mad Dogs & Englishmen* also promoted the hell out of Leon Russell. Not only was he the master of ceremonies, he also had two solos of his own in the show, "Hummingbird" and "Dixie Lullaby." Background singer Claudia Linnear performed The Beatles' "Let It Be," and Don Preston did "Further On Up The Road." However, the biggest non-Cocker moment belonged to Rita Coolidge who had a featured solo song with "Superstar."

The prevailing backstage controversy to come out of the *Mad Dogs & Englishmen* tour was that somewhere along the line, Joe's admiration for Leon Russell's talent was overshadowed by his growing resentment that Leon was stealing too much of the spotlight. Did Leon Russell construct Joe's show to best show himself off? Was Joe Cocker somehow used to promote Russell? Cordell explained, "I don't feel that Joe was used; that would be an unfair thing to say. I told Leon after the first rehearsal, 'Do you realize you're going to be accused of career profiteering just because of the way it looks?' He said, 'I don't care, man, this is going to be great fun anyway.' About a year after the tour Leon said to me that he remembered my warning distinctly and had never thought that it mattered, but now he often wished he'd never gone on the tour with all the negative feedback." (18)

In the 1990s, looking back at the *Mad Dogs & Englishmen* tour, Joe described his relationship with Leon Russell. According to him,

"I knew he was an incredible talent, and it started like he was a big brother to me. As the tour progressed and all the attention was on me, he got a little envious. He was very conscious too of a limp he got from a motorbike accident, which meant he was in pain a lot of the time. But he took over the whole show, became like a slave master, though it wasn't quite as bad as that. It just ended up bitterly, which is a shame." (29)

According to legend, on this particular tour, Joe Cocker would take whatever drug was given to him. And he was given a lot of drugs. The other thing that was rampant on this tour was the sexual freedom and the orgies back at the hotels in each city. After all, it was 1970 and The Sexual Revolution was in full swing.

Jerry Moss was to explain, "There were a lot of drugs on that tour, and Joe was just starting to become very evasive and not very communicative. Joe was a guy that, especially during that tour, would never say 'no' to anybody about anything." (1)

Rita Coolidge recalls, "I was fairly naïve about a lot of the orgies and other stuff that went on amid this tour, because I was not that long out of college at this time. I had been on the road with Delaney & Bonnie, but this was something bigger than life. I remember in one of the cities I went down to the lobby one day to take a walk, and everybody in the band was lined up. It looked like everyone was getting ready for some sort of a group outing. I walked over to one of the guys in the band, and with a big smile on my face, thinking they were embarking on some sort of site-seeing expedition, and I asked him, 'Where are you guys going?' He leaned over and told me very privately in my ear, 'We all have to go to the hospital. We all have to get shots, because we ALL have VD!' Now, that's what I call 'incestuous.' It was one of those late night orgies that got the whole band!" (22)

Behind the scenes there was a lot of drama as well, with Dee Anthony and Denny Cordell trying to control what was going on while *Mad Dogs & Englishmen* was on the road. According to Anthony, the tour was bleeding money all along the way.

In a letter dated May 3, 1970, that Dee Anthony wrote to Denny Cordell, Dee explained, "The other day, when I was giving you my opinions concerning the skyrocketing expenses being tacked onto Joe's tour, I didn't have any figures in front of me. However, I just got the ledger in from the road, and it contains a few numbers that I want to pass on to you quickly. I don't know whether it is already too late, but perhaps even at this stage, it will save a lot of money to put the brakes on. For example, you will recall that we estimated a salary payroll each week for performers of about $3,200.00. According to the ledger, that is now running about $4,740.00 a week. More important, the expenses for the group traveling with Joe started out at $3,467.82 per week. As the tour picked up more and more people, however, it started to race wildly upwards to a point where the latest weekly figure is $8,297.02. That includes the amazingly vast expenses of the communal suppers, the additional hotel expenses that we never planned to pay for people we never expected to have along, and the additional transportation costs. You know how shocked I was when the original Super Constellation turned out to be too small for all the additional hangers-on! Then when we expanded into extra commercial flights, I could not do a thing but stand back and pray for the best." (18) That was just the beginning.

While the tour raged on, Dee Anthony tried to rein in the expenses. Amidst the tour, Dee kept writing to Denny Cordell about his concerns. However, they apparently fell on deaf ears.

In one of his letters to Cordell, Anthony wrote, "Denny, I am writing this very late at night after I have just seen the figures off the road and have been sitting here mulling over the whole situation. Maybe it is coming out like I am only interested in the money. I think, however, that you know me well enough to realize that money doesn't balance out against Joe's artistic and creative integrity and the kind of atmosphere he needs to work in. That does, and always will, come first. But somehow we can't lose sight of the fact that Joe still has to live, and pay his rent, and do the things he wants to do AFTER the tour is over, and that is up to us, you, as his Producer, and me, as his Manager, to do everything (within the limits set by his own artistic needs) to see that there is something better than zero on the balance sheet when he is all finished with the tour. It could have been so great, and it still can be great, if we can cooperate these next few weeks." (18)

Looking ahead, Dee suggested to Cordell, "Just in case you really can't slow down the expenses as much as you or I would like, I do want to say that we will have at least had the most extraordinarily successful artistic and creative tour that Joe might have had, and certainly a perfect base from which to launch the next series of concerts and show, hopefully with a permanent back-up band we talked about two weeks ago in Los Angeles. I still think that that is going to be a tremendous saving grace out of this whole thing. It ought to let us avoid strenuous drawn-out tours in the future, and permit us instead to pick our dates, and place Joe and the back-up band in lucrative concert situations spread out with enough room for Joe to breathe in between." (18)

Danny Cordell was later to complain, "As for Dee Anthony sending me any letters, he's full of shit. How could he have sent me any letters? I was on the fucking tour every day. Where would he have sent them? To the next address on the line? Anyway, I spoke to Dee almost every day. He didn't tell us that the tour was running expensive until there was only a week and a half of the tour left to run. He insisted on doing six extra dates, which he said would recoup the money. But they didn't. We ran parallel with all the other expenses." (18)

In addition to the costs and the craziness, one of the other things that made Joe's *Mad Dogs & Englishmen* tour so famous was the documentary of the same name that was made from it. Rita remembers that it was more than disconcerting, to say the least. "We had a camera crew with us, and they shot from the time we left until the time we got home. There was a camera in your face all the time. It was unbelievable. I was so used to it that it was one of those experiments that they do on TV where they follow you around, put people in a situation, and kind of study people. Filming real life was really what it was. It was like a cross between a documentary and a NYU Film School cinema project. They all but went to the bathroom with us. Had we let them, they probably would have filmed that too! I don't remember how many hours of film they ultimately had when they were finished, but it was something insane like 150 hours of film to edit down into an hour-and-a-half feature film." (22) Through 40-some shows, via Chicago, Minneapolis, Tulsa, San Antonio, and San Francisco, the *Mad Dogs* mega show and traveling orgy made its way across the country.

Rita Coolidge not only ended up with her own solo song, "Superstar," on the *Mad Dogs & Englishmen* album, but on the last night of the tour she was offered her own recording deal. It would ultimately interpret into a series of 1970s hits and Grammy Awards of her own.

She recalls, "That night after the show at The Santa Monica Civic Auditorium in Los Angeles, Chuck Kagen, who was one of the A&R [Artists & Repertoire] guys at A&M, came backstage and said, 'We want to sign you to A&M. And we'd like to do it tonight.' I was like, 'Cool!' I pretty much had a feeling that that was going to happen. I had a feeling that A&M was interested, which was great." (22)

Putting the resulting *Mad Dogs & Englishmen* album together had one acoustic problem: the background vocals by the choir were out of tune. Rita Coolidge and several of the other singers were brought into A&M recording studios to rerecord some of them. When the two-disc album was released in August of 1970, it made it to Number 2 in the U.S., Number 3 in Australia, Number 2 in Canada, Number 9 in the Netherlands, and Number 16 in the U.K. In America it was Certified *Gold* for selling more than half a million copies.

While Joe was on tour with *Mad Dogs & Englishmen*, the original big screen documentary version of *Woodstock* was released. Although the only Joe Cocker performance to appear in the film was his singing of "With A Little Help From My Friends," it was so revolutionary and impressive that it was an instant star-making big screen turn for him. Millions more would now have the chance to witness Joe Cocker in his prime.

CHAPTER SIX

"It All Falls Apart"

It would seem that Joe Cocker should be sitting on top of the world in 1970 having just exploded on the top of the charts and having completed two of the most hectic and exciting tours in rock & roll history. *Woodstock, The Isle of Wight, Mad Dogs & Englishmen*, one performance a bigger hit than the next. And yet Cocker found himself feeling burned out and cast aside.

Hit tour, hit albums, chart hits! That was Joe Cocker circa 1970. So what was the problem? The problem was Joe and how he personally chose to fit himself into the picture. The first part of the problem was the self-destructive nature Joe had developed. For the first three decades of his musical career his way to cope with conflict and stress was to chain-smoke two packs of tobacco cigarettes a day, drink liquor from morning to night, and do every hallucinogenic drug that was offered to him, including marijuana, hashish, cocaine, and eventually, even heroin.

The other problem was a financial one. Joe was expecting to emerge from the *Mad Dogs & Englishmen* tour with at least $10,000 in his pocket. Unfortunately, the tour wound up being so expensive to produce that there was almost no money left at the end. Reportedly, Joe walked away with a paltry $862.

How could that have possibly happened? According to Dee Anthony, "I had informed Joe what the economics of the situation would be. He took nearly 50 people out on the road. I was confronted with a tour that was economically impossible. It wasn't even earning much money because we were playing only small halls that had already been booked in anticipation of The Grease Band. On *Mad Dogs* there were sometimes 60 or 70 people sitting down to dinner. I even had to throw some people off the tour because they were just hanging on. Did Joe know this? Yes, he did. But he would say, 'That's O.K., no problem.' I never got a straight answer on anything." (18)

The concert halls that were booked were in the 3,000 person capacity level, so that a sold out house would gross at best $15,000. Then there was the added expense of a second Constellation chartered airplane for the equipment. There were 43 people on salary, plus food, lodging, ground transportation, and the list goes on-and-on.

At the *Mad Dogs & Englishmen* shows and on the album there were three compositions by Leon Russell and several other songwriters — Otis Redding, Bob Dylan, John Lennon, Paul McCartney, and several more. According to Dee Anthony, "If you want to find out who's making bread from the film and the album, just look at who owns the publishing for most of those songs. I've known Leon Russell for a long time. That long hair doesn't fool me." (18) Clearly, everyone wanted their piece of the pie.

An unnamed musician who was described as "one of Joe's band" was quoted in *Crawdaddy* magazine as saying, "Joe felt that he'd been used as a freak who would propel everyone else into the limelight." (18)

On the other hand, Joe was the first to admit that he was bad with money from the very start. According to him, "Denny Cordell gave me a copy of Kahlil Gibran's *The Prophet*, so we all got into the spiritual thing of saying we should give everything away. And people would take it. Ten grand here, ten grand there. Anything business-like I didn't want to know. So in many ways it was my own fault.

But there were the men with big cigars and the sharks. We fell for them, not just me, but many artists." (3)

Joe finished the *Mad Dogs & Englishmen* tour not only financially strapped, but completely exhausted as well. Denny Cordell told Joe that he could stay at his house as long as he wanted. According to Cordell, "Joe just hung around the house and did nothing. Joe had become good friends with my children, but they left, and from then on, the house was completely empty in the daytime." (27)

Rita Coolidge remembers going to Denny Cordell's to visit Joe during this period. She was appalled at what she discovered. "He was sleeping on a doormat in the foyer of Denny Cordell's house. It just broke my heart after what he'd been through on that tour, to be sleeping on a mat like a dog—and taking drugs. At the time I was living with my sister, Priscilla, and Booker T., and I'd take Joe over. He'd stay with us for two or three days. He would sober up, dry out, and I would cook soul food, which he liked. I'd get him sober and straight and then the next thing I knew, he would be back on the floor again." (1)

Denny was to explain the situation, "My main concern was to get Joe working. There was obviously some personality something-or-other that made it hard for Joe and Leon to form a band together. Joe was despondent and didn't want to do much, but I persuaded him to play a pop festival in Japan. I thought he'd got over *Mad Dogs* and we could form a band with Jim Keltner on drums, and Chris Stainton, Allen Spenner, and some guitarist and just take it from there. But Dee thought I was trying to make some managerial power play, I think, and he just put the blocks on it. Anyway, the irony was that the pop festival never materialized. But if Anthony had said, 'Great, go ahead,' we'd have been in rehearsal for two weeks, we'd have had the basic unit, and we could have done something else. Joe knew then that Dee didn't have his best interests at heart." (27) Ultimately, the festival deal fizzled, so it was no longer an issue.

The one totally constructive career task that Cordell was to convince Joe to do was to fly to Alabama to Muscle Shoals Studio to record the single, "High Time We Went." Written by Joe Cocker and Chris Stainton, it went on to become an international 1971 Top 40 hit, peaking at Number 22 in the U.S., Number 21 in Canada, Number 25 in Australia, Number 16 in the Netherlands, Number 13 in France, and Number 8 in Belgium. It was in fact, the most successful song that Joe and Chris wrote together.

Meanwhile, Delaney & Bonnie & Friends had a recording deal for ATCO/Atlantic Records, and in 1971 they released an album called *Motel Shot*. Joe Cocker sang background on two of the tracks on the album, "Where The Soul Never Dies" and "Talkin' About Jesus." That was at least one more attempt at getting "back in the saddle again." It was a short-lived burst of creative energy.

Finally, Joe decided to get off the door mat and to go home. According to Denny Cordell, "Chris Stainton was going back to England, and Joe decided to go too. Then he went back to England and just slumped out." (27)

Once Joe was back in England, Cordell went to great efforts to get Joe to go in the recording studio. He claimed, "I went over there on two separate occasions to record with him, and when we got to the studio he just sat there and didn't really get into it. We had a good band—Ringo [Starr], Chris [Stainton], [Allen] Spenner, and Alvin Lee on guitar. Joe would say, 'No, no, let them jam, I'm not hearing it right yet.' So I had to say, 'O.K., fellows, let's go home.'" (27)

Explaining his post-*Mad Dogs & Englishmen* depression, Joe claimed, "I went back home after *Mad Dogs* and did nothing really for two years. I was fed up and I stayed in Sheffield most of the time. It was good to be back around Scotland for a while and the south of England, but I did nothing else really. I tried to do some recording at Island [Records Studio] about a year back, but we didn't come out with anything we could use." (18)

Alan Spenner remembered seeing Joe in his post-*Mad Dogs* depression era. According to him, "He was like a different person— talking to himself. He could be talking about something and then in a second, he'd change subjects and be talking about something completely different. He seemed very depressed, very unhappy, very alone and it looked to me as if he'd suffered a lot. I know he did the tour under protest, and I think he just downed as many anesthetics as he could. He was totally shattered and disillusioned by the whole business." (1)

In the November 1970 issue of *Circus* magazine, Phil Ardery wrote an article called "Joe Cocker: The Road Which Lies Ahead." In it he interviewed Joe and found him to be burned out, energy wise, and bitching about A&M Records at every chance he could. The article was painted in a way that presented one of two scenarios: either Joe was (A) being overworked or (B) Joe was the most ungrateful and perpetually whining rock star on the charts. In Phil Ardery's mind, at this point Joe clearly fell into the latter category.

According to Ardery's essay, "One complicating factor is the way A&M, Joe's record company, has been handling him, their first genuine rock star. He has been hustled through an almost continuous tour to promote three albums in a single year—*With A Little Help From My Friends*, *Joe Cocker!*, and *Mad Dogs & Englishmen*. Many of us think that Joe needs time to rest, time to reflect. 'The Mad Dogs'—Leon Russell, Chris Stainton of the erstwhile Grease Band, some Delaney & Bonnie Friends, and about 20 other assorted musicians—were scrambled together at the 'eleventh hour' because somebody had scheduled a Joe Cocker tour without telling Joe. Their performances were highly erratic (all things considered, that's a high compliment), but A&M insisted on a live album anyway. The tapes for *Mad Dogs & Englishmen*—which feature, besides Joe's songs, numbers by Leon, Rita Coolidge, Claudia of The Ikettes, and Don

Preston—came from scattered gigs in Detroit, Santa Monica, Dallas, and New York." (30)

With regard to Joe himself, Ardery claimed, "If Joe himself were really getting behind these ventures, then criticizing A&M would be grossly unfair, but from the evidence we have, the man seems confused. When asked what direction he's headed in musically, Joe answers, 'Well, I'm not quite sure. I'm living day-to-day, and whichever way it goes, it *goes.*' But aren't you trying to give your music some direction? 'I've got no idea, man. I don't really think about it, man. I've got no idea.'" (30) No wonder Joe's life and newly-minted career was in a state of sheer confusion following the *Mad Dogs & Englishmen* tour.

Ray Stewart worked for BBC Radio's show *Scene & Heard*, and during this era he interviewed a depressed Joe Cocker. According to Stewart, "He was very disappointed with what had happened on the *Mad Dogs* tour. He said, 'It started out as "love and peace, man," and ended up chaotic.' He was disillusioned. He seemed to be thinking, 'That's it—I've done it now, and I don't want to do it anymore.' He just wasn't bothered about rock & roll music. I don't think he wanted to be mixed up with music people." (1)

Kenny Slade, who was in-and-out of The Grease Band, recalled Joe showing up one day in front of his house with a Rolls Royce and a driver, wanting to know if Kenny wanted to go out for a drink. He agreed and bid his wife and child "goodbye" for a couple of hours. As he was to recall, he was gone with Cocker on this partying binge about five days. Slade remembers ". . . getting drunk and just being outrageous . . . chauffeur driving us everywhere. Plenty of pills, plenty of acid, and plenty of booze . . . We were usually stoned. He used to do all the paying, I'll give him his due. He never talked about *Mad Dogs*, but I know he didn't like Leon Russell at all. Hated him." (1)

In the time that Joe had been centering his confused attention on his career his brother Vic had taken a totally different path. He had continued his education and worked as an economist for the North West Gas company doing research and planning. Then at some point in 1968, Vic had changed jobs and started to work for West Midlands Gas as a deputy planning manager.

Vic explained of this era, "Eileen got hold of me and suggested that I ought to contact Joe. She was living with some guy who Joe had known previously, but she'd heard stories about drugs, and she told me to get in touch with him and make sure he was all right. I met him, and he came up to our house and stayed a couple of nights. He chatted, but it was difficult to know what was going on." (1)

Even Joe's father, Harold Cocker, remembered, "He was like a zombie. He just sat here all day, staring into space. He never said anything; he just ate his meals and sat here. He seemed played out entirely." (1)

On February 27, 1971, Leon Russell and his new band played Sheffield, England. Leon went so far as to telephone Joe to see if he would make a guest appearance. According to Joe, "I'd dropped a bunch of acid and said, 'No.' We'd fallen out pretty badly." (1)

Later that spring, Rita Coolidge was in Sheffield as part of a tour with The Byrds. According to her, "I called him when we got in, just said I wanted to see him. So Joe showed up that night; he came backstage, and we decided that he'd come out and sing with me. I remember he was on stage, and we were having the time of our lives. I know Joe had taken a lot of acid that night. I said, 'Joe, how can you do that? How can you take ten tabs of acid and function at all?' He said, 'Rita, the only difference in one tab of acid and ten tabs of acid is the pain in the back of me neck!'" (1) That was Joe during this dark era of his life: a dysfunctional mess.

Joe remembers putting himself in some pretty sketchy situations. According to him, "When I came back from [the *Mad Dog*] tour in '71, I'd made a lot of money, and I parked myself in Shepherd's Bush and met all these dealers who happened [to] find me, as they do. I would walk around with an ounce bag of cocaine, and I could never give the stuff away. Then I got into heroin, and anybody who's been there knows you can feel it get its grip on you so fast, though I never fixed up; I just used to snort the stuff. It's such a placid kind of drug that any musician would fall for it. It's only the horror of not being able to get access to it . . . I realized then that those guys had got me by the balls. They suddenly wanted all this money to score for me—a thousand quid for a few grams of stuff. But I was never a serious junkie because I felt what was happening to me in time. After that, I tended to hit the booze pretty heavily too, to compensate for the smack." (29)

Looking back at this era from the vantage point some 20 years later, Joe explained, "I used to get really black moods and totally wound up about things that were irrelevant. But no longer. I was a beer drinker when I started, and I've resorted back to it now. Back then we started smoking hash, and in the States in the late '60s every substance in the world was about. I just got sidetracked" (29)

It was such a shame that Joe had arrived at this point of wallowing in his own misery. He had every reason to bolster himself up, put his energy into picking up the pieces of his career, and concentrate on moving forward. Sadly, that was not the case.

On September 23, 1971, the filmed version of *Mad Dogs & Englishmen* was due to debut in London at The Ritz Cinema. Representatives from the film company, MGM, were dying to get hold of Joe so that he could attend the premiere. Joe was, after all, the star of the film. And Cocker was nowhere to be found. He was quickly cementing his reputation as the most reluctant rock star in the show business world.

Throughout the year and a half that followed the *Mad Dogs & Englishmen* tour, Dee Anthony did everything he could to convince Joe to get back to work. Unfortunately, Joe simply didn't want anything to do with Dee and told Dee so several times.

According to Cordell, "Dee's reply was to send Joe a letter showing that Joe was signed up to him for another four years, and Joe didn't know anything about that. I'll never forget the look on Joe's face when he came in and he threw the papers on the bed and said, 'Look at what I got in the post. I never signed these.'" (27)

Dee Anthony was to argue, "That's ridiculous. Joe knew damn well that he was signed. If that were their basis for a defense, then they should have taken it. I went to the [West] Coast three times, went over to England three times, made various attempts to see Joe. He was supposed to meet me one afternoon. He never showed up. I waited nine hours. Let Cordell produce one letter of dissatisfaction from Joe Cocker; let him show one time that Joe Cocker sat with me and told me he wanted out. They sent a lot of flakes in, trying to make deals all the time for their own benefit, but never Joe. The last thing Joe said to my brother Bill, who put him on the plane back in England in 1970, was 'Tell Dee I'll be seein' him soon and we'll be rocking and rolling.' I spoke to Joe on the phone: 'Ya happy, anything wrong?' He said, 'No, Man, I just want to get my head together.' The first time Joe said he wanted out was when I had an injunction against him, and he was sitting around the settlement table. And they had to force him to say it." (27)

It was Frank Barsalona who had to step in to negotiate a truce between all of the warring parties. According to Barsalona, "It took ten minutes for Joe to tell Dee, 'I don't want you as my manager.' Everyone was saying, 'Say it, Joe!' Even Dee was saying, 'Say it, Joe!' And he finally spit it out." (27)

In August of 1971, Denny Cordell went to see Dee Anthony to inform him that it was Dee who was preventing Joe from getting back to work. Recalls Cordell, "He said, 'Well, if that's the case, I'll get out of the picture, and you won't have to pay me any money, and I'll take five percent, and you manage him.' I said, 'Fine,' and I went to England specifically to set this whole thing up with Joe, and the day I arrived there I got a letter from Dee Anthony stating, 'On reflection, I think you're cheating me, and I renege on my deal.' And I was left in a high state of embarrassment." (27)

Dee Anthony was to recall, "Cordell came in and he wanted to work a deal with me. He wanted a piece of the action. He's a money grabber, and he knows it, and everybody else in the business knows it, and if he doesn't watch out I'll really go after his ass, 'cause I'm tired of his nonsense. I sat there and just listened to him. Then I spoke to my attorneys, and they just had me send him a letter." (27)

Rolling Stone magazine estimated that at Joe's 1972 stature in the business, he could be making $50,000 a night. According to Frank Barsalona, "If he'd come back and played the big houses, he'd be a multi-millionaire." (27) Instead, Joe sat on his ass and felt sorry for himself for a year and half.

It all dated back to *Mad Dogs & Englishmen*. It ended up costing more money to stage than anyone could have predicted. According to Cordell, "See, Dee wasn't paying Joe. And he kept saying, 'Cordell and Leon are ordering vintage wine every night, so there's no money left to pay Joe.' But when the accounts came to light, Dee owed Joe $32,000. Just after the tour, we went through the records with Dee Anthony and his accountant and saw all the things that were wrong and [they] said, 'We'll have to look back and adjust this,' and they never did." (27)

Claimed Anthony, "Once again he's a liar. In fact, Joe said it was the most meticulous accounting he ever saw. He said it in front of four witnesses. They didn't object to one thing. Every penny spent on that tour, every receipt was signed by Denny Cordell and Joe Cocker. Jesus Christ, this was in the court case and won the injunction because I had documents." (27)

Dee Anthony further claimed that Joe Cocker whining about money was ridiculous. According to him, "Joe had a *Gold* album from the tour, his price tripled and there was a movie. Joe can't kid no one. He took out close to half a million dollars in A&M royalties." (27)

Anthony did make several points about the excesses of the *Mad Dogs & Englishmen* tour. He explained, "They also played Tulsa—Leon's hometown! And Cocker lost $12,000 'cause we had to fly the planes from Seattle back to Tulsa for a picnic and then back to Seattle at Joe's expense. We sent Joe a letter before it happened telling him it was a bad move. And we threatened—Frank was threatened and was threatened by them—that if we didn't play Tulsa, Leon would quit the tour." (27)

Further explained Dee: "The court decided that there were no grounds to suppose that I'd mismanaged any funds. I was glad that my honesty had been vindicated, there had been a lot of vicious things said about me. Although I wouldn't call myself 'St. Anthony,' I'm glad my track record spoke for itself. Eventually, we settled out of court. I'm to be paid $250,000. I was given a certified check by Nigel Thomas Management for $100,000 in advance. That's fair. I broke my ass to develop an artist who flaked out on me for two years." (18)

Throughout 1971, there was a concentrated effort to get Joe Cocker back on the road. Dee Anthony repeatedly tried to get Joe off of his parents' sofa and back to work. He wrote the following letter to Joe:

9th June 1971

Mr. Joe Cocker
Sheffield 10, Yorkshire
England

Dear Joe:

Just a few words to keep you abreast of things.

I trust this letter finds you in good health and that things are going right for you there in England.

Frank [Barselona] and I had a meeting with Jerry Moss two weeks ago prior to Jerry's going to England. He seemed very excited about the reaction on the new single ["It's High Time We Went"], and I can report to you that it is doing rather well.

As you well know, without your presence here on personal appearances, it is rather difficult to keep a solid momentum going. We are doing everything we possibly can and I hope that by the time you receive this letter, you will have undoubtedly spoken to Jerry Moss and perhaps started the ball rolling in that direction.

I have been informed that you will be recording either this week or next, which delights me to no end. I think the time is now appropriate for you and to really activate yourself. As you know, this is a fickle business we are in.

I am coming over to London on the 18ᵗʰ of June and would appreciate it if you can make yourself available on either the 18ᵗʰ or 19ᵗʰ, so that we can sit down and rap about different things.

I will be staying at The Churchill Hotel for a couple of days and you are welcome to stay there with me if you wish, should you come down from Sheffield. It will be a gas seeing you again.

There are numerous other things that I would like to discuss with you. Rather than put them in a letter form, I think it would be a hell of a lot better if you and I can sit down and have a nice chat. I really would appreciate it, Joe, if you would block out a day.

Valerie is feeling fine and sends you her very best, and the little baby is a cosmic beauty.

If you find a chance between now and the 18th, I would appreciate a call from you. I can be reached at the office during the day or at home in the evening.

Hoping to see or hear from you soon.

Warmest Personal Regards
BANDANA ENTERPRISES
Dee Anthony
(18)

Clearly, there was work and a demand for Joe. In a letter from promoter Howard Stein to Dee Anthony he claimed that the desire for a Joe Cocker tour was high. He wrote the following letter to try to persuade Dee into getting Joe back on the road:

8 December 1971
Mr. Dee Anthony

Bandana Enterprises, Inc.
New York, New York

Dear Dee:

Pursuant to our conversation, I am formalizing offers to you for Joe Cocker in the following cities:

NEW YORK
Madison Square Garden. Guarantee $50,000 against a percentage.

CHICAGO, ILLINOIS
Chicago Amphitheatre. Guarantee $35,000 against a percentage.

MIAMI, FLORIDA
Miami Convention Center. Guarantee $35,000 against a percentage.

ATLANTA, GEORGIA
Atlanta Municipal Auditorium. Guarantee $15,000 against a percentage.

ST. PAUL, MINNESOTA
Metropolitan Sports Arena. Guarantee $50,000 against a percentage.

Specific dates in mid-winter can be worked out to your touring convenience.

With best regards as always, I remain
Sincerely,

Howard Stein (18)

Joe claimed that the money was the least of his concerns. According to him, "Having come out of the *Mad Dogs* tour with no money never really bothered me. Back then, the feeling was [that] it was a crime to have money anyway. We were into this trip of stripping off our worldly goods. I remember giving money to various people—$70,000 here, $40,000 there to people that I had known for years who wanted houses. I said, 'If you ever make it back, you can pay it back.' Of course, I never heard from them. But five years later I did hear from the tax people who demanded I come up with all the money I thought I could give away like *The Magic Christian*." (5)

In conclusion, the results of The Commercial Arbitration Tribunal, which was issued on February 14, 1972, essentially settled the dispute in favor of Dee Anthony and upheld his claim to be recognized as Joe Cocker's sole personal manager. "Petitioner, Bandana Enterprises, Limited, (hereinafter referred to as "Bandana") seeks an order restraining respondent, Joe Cocker, pending conclusion of arbitration between the parties, from interfering with Bandana's right to act as Cocker's personal manager and restraining Cocker or others acting on his behalf from contracting or offering to contract for the performance of services by Cocker. Specifically, Bandana seeks to preliminarily enjoin Cocker from continuing with the planning and performance of a series of concerts in which Cocker will participate absent Bandana's consent and participation or from applying the monies therefrom in a manner inconsistent with provisions of the agreement between the parties . . ." (18) and so on.

Denny Cordell was to explain, "The proof of the situation is now evident from the outcome. Joe's people have gone to great lengths to raise huge sums of money to get Dee Anthony out of the way. He's no longer involved now, but I'm producing a live album for Joe while he's on tour. We've already recorded at two concerts, one in Tuscaloosa, another in New Orleans, enough material for a double album." (18)

Since *Mad Dogs & Englishmen* had ended, Denny Cordell started his own record label, Shelter Records, with Leon Russell as its first artist. According to Denny, "As for Joe, the experience he gained from that tour will be invaluable for the rest of his life; the same goes for Chris Stainton. For my money, Leon and Shelter Records would have made it without that tour. O.K., so maybe the tour helped bring the focus on Leon faster, but I refute any suggestion which Dee Anthony constantly makes, that Leon wouldn't be anywhere today if he hadn't ridden on Joe's coattails. We'd already made a successful album. It was well reviewed and was selling very well, and Leon gave up his pursuits to help somebody whom he admired and respected." (18)

After all disgruntled parties figured out all of the paperwork, slowly things began to fall into place for Joe to return to work. It was Chris Stainton who finally got the ball moving. However, it was not a direct return to work for Cocker. In fact, Chris had to start his own band and forget about Joe for Cocker to ultimately come back to work.

As Denny Cordell was to explain it, "This winter, Chris had kinda got a bit pissed off with Joe. 'Cause Chris had been rehearsing the band over there [in England] and Joe had been to see it, but he wouldn't get up and sing with it. So Chris said, 'Fuck it, let's go to America and rehearse there and we'll find a singer over there.' So they tried the singers out and they weren't any good, and so Chris phoned Joe up and said, 'Look, we need a fucking singer, would you come over?' and Joe said, 'Yeah, why not?' And that's just the way the man moves. Then Nigel phoned me up and said, 'The problem seems to be Dee Anthony and Joe doesn't want to work until Dee's out of the picture.' I said, 'It sounds like what should have been done months ago, and that's a good idea.'" (27)

It had been two years since the last *Mad Dogs & Englishmen* tour date, and finally Joe Cocker decided to come out of his parents' house in Sheffield and return to his musical career. Would anyone notice Joe after such a hiatus? It remained to be seen.

Chris Stainton's new band called themselves The Concert and had their own manager, Nigel Thomas. After Chris got hold of Joe and invited him down to their rehearsals, something started to happen, and suddenly reluctant Cocker was interested in music again.

Nigel was no stranger to show business. He had been a club performer, working as a "satirist." He segued into managing groups including Juicy Lucy, The Grease Band, and singer Gerry Lockran. He also coordinated the European concert dates for Leon Russell.

As Chris Stainton was later to explain, "I was looning around, and Nigel said, 'What are you doing? Glenn Campbell's doing nothing.' So we brought in [drummer] Conrad Isadore and started rehearsing in January [1972]. We auditioned one singer from the West Coast, Paul Frank, a good looking version of Rod Stewart, but he wasn't up to it. So in the end I thought, 'Fuck it, I'll call Joe.'" (18)

Sometimes the direct approach was the best way to get through to Joe. According to Chris, "I just got drunk one night and called him. He said, 'Yes,' right away. He'd do it, and he came over on the next plane. Nigel had brought the band together." (18)

According to Joe, "Chris said, 'How would I fancy coming out and singing with the band?' And I was, ya know, real pleased to just step into another road show." (27)

Speaking of his re-entry to the music business, in 1972 Cocker claimed, "I feel a bit strange now. You know, I'm 28 now and I still feel a bit like I'm pioneering, but it was even stranger being away for two years. I did just two live gigs. Rita Coolidge did a concert in

Sheffield, and I just got swamped in there when I went down to see her. I got up on stage and did some blues. About a week later, I went to a club in Leeds, and I got roped in again. I sang with a band called The Gingerbread Men, amazin' little band really, I don't know what happened to them." (18)

Chris and the band had been rehearsing in Connecticut with a U.S. tour in his sights. Finally, Joe had relented, and he came to see what was transpiring. Suddenly, Cocker was back in the picture.

As Chris Stainton explains, "We did a tour with Joe in 1972, and we rehearsed in Westport, Connecticut. It was just my band, all English musicians. We were rehearsing and trying out singers and nothing was working out. And so I give Joe a call, and he came out and joined us, and we had a good band." (12)

As with so many of Joe's business dealings, this particular U.S. tour was somewhat done "on the fly," and there were a lot of loose ends. The tour was due to kick off at Madison Square Garden on May 25, 1972. It was definitely a high-profile spot for what turned out to be more of a dress rehearsal than a fully developed concert.

Just prior to Joe's big return to concert performing and his opening night at Madison Square Garden, Timothy Crouse of *Rolling Stone* magazine went up to the Westport Playhouse in Westport, Connecticut, to see Joe and Chris and the newly cobbled-together band where they were rehearsing. However, what he found was a lot of alcohol consumption and a lot of monkey-business.

They say in business that "the tone is set at the top," so what Crouse reported was that Joe's new manager, Nigel Thomas, had readily adopted Joe Cocker's drinking habits. His drink of choice: vintage 1964 Dom Perignon champagne. Was that perhaps a bit prematurely precipitous to be drinking expensive booze by the bottle like "cost is no object."

When asked about it, Nigel replied, "Well, yes, it's precipitous, but it's not fun if it's not precipitous, is it? The band has been rather loose, and we hope that going in there will, ah, bring out the best in them. 'Course, it could bring out the worst." (27) Unfortunately, it was to prove that the latter was closer to the truth. Joe and company were already over-confidently burning money before the tour even started.

The night before the first gig, Joe and the band were at The Westport Theater trying to patch together a growing group of musicians, most of whom had never worked together. In addition to this, Joe absolutely forbid the inclusion of several of the crowd-pleasing songs from *The Mad Dogs & Englishmen* tour, like "The Letter." The troupe had yet to roll into New York City, and already it had all of the ear-markings of a sheer disaster.

A horn section as well as conga player Felix Falcon were all hired within 48 hours of the show's debut at Madison Square Garden. As the musical director, this sent Chris Stainton into a frenzy trying to teach this "patchwork quilt" of a band the songs in the eleventh hour.

While Chris and the cobbled-together band worked on the music, Joe was in the theater smoking joint after joint with a group of local hippies. After they got him and Eileen high, they were supposedly working out a deal to purchase a pound of marijuana.

Eileen was quoted in *Rolling Stone* as pointing out, "You know, on the road you need the booze and the drugs and what-not just to cope with all the creeps that push themselves at you." (27)

When the band was solidified, it consisted of Chris Stainton and Allen Spenner of the original Grease Band, slide guitar player Glenn Campbell (not to be confused with country guitarist Glen Campbell), lead guitarist Neil Hubbord, as well as Conrad Isidore, Felix Falcon, horn players Rick Alphonso and Fred Sherbo, and the singing trio, The Dips.

There had been an astonishing seven weeks of rehearsals, and after that seven weeks the band still could not work successfully as a musical unit.

Opening night of the tour at Madison Square Garden was a reported disaster. Music critic Timothy Crouse wrote in *Rolling Stone* magazine, "Joe Cocker and The Concert bombed at The Garden. Twenty-odd thousand kids (less than a full house) had come out with *Mad Dogs* still echoing in their rears, hoping to hear more of the same. What they got was a raggedy and badly uncoordinated band that was struggling to keep together and a performance by Joe that had all of his usual gravel and very little of his subtle and beautiful phrasing." (27)

The opening numbers that disastrous night were:

"Love The One You're With"
"St. James Infirmary"
"Midnight Rider"
"Black-Eyed Blues"
and the new composition "Woman To Woman."

The bulk of the show consisted of an hour and a half of uninspired blues music. In between numbers, the band reportedly took "long breaks" getting ready for the next song. While this was going on, members of the audience were shouting out requests for the songs they had bought tickets to hear, like "She Came In Through The Bathroom Window" and "Space Captain." Their requests fell on deaf ears right up to the end when Joe and band played their latest hit single, "High Time We Went."

Famed rock & roll critic Lillian Roxon was in the audience that night and wrote, "His biggest mistake was to choose to perform unfamiliar material when the audience was dying to hear old favorites." (31)

When Allen Spenner was asked what went wrong that very first night he was later to explain, "You mean, Madison Square Nightmare? Everyone was very calm, cool, having a good time and all. And we walked on stage to do the gig. Everybody's feeling good. We did the first number, and that was good. Did the second number— 'O.K.' And then, then the rot set in. The numbers broke down, people broke down. I just stood there and heard myself playing like shit. We all staggered off and said, 'My God, what happened?' I'm afraid there's no logical explanation for it." (27)

If there was an explanation for the disaster, Allen could only say, "Some mixed signals but mostly just people fluffin' up notes. It only takes two or three people in the band to sort of fluff up at the same time and the whole thing goes," with that he used his hand to mimic an airplane spiraling downward into a crash. (27)

Unquestioningly, Joe did everything wrong on this tour. It was an almost unheard of music industry *faux pas* for Cocker not to have a new album on the market to promote. To his credit, *Mad Dogs & Englishmen* and the film that was made of it became huge hits, and people showed up wanting to hear that music and feel that kind of excitement. Instead, Joe delivered a show devoid of his hits and dominated by a bunch of half-hearted and ill-rehearsed obscure blues numbers and a sub-par vocal performance from an out-of-shape star.

It would seem that as the tour continued things on stage would improve. However, two weeks after the disastrous Madison Square Garden, the group's Boston engagement with Edgar Winter as the opening act, was another "hot mess." Finally, things began to improve. Jim Keltner was brought in as a second drummer, and The Dips were fired and replaced by some more professional singers.

According to Joe, "It was strange to be rockin' again after two years. At Madison Square [Garden] I had a sore throat, and my voice wasn't relaxed, though it's getting along. Fortunately, we've not been too strained. We've had a couple of days off every now and then. We should be recording a live album on tour. We had it scheduled for Chicago, but it didn't come off. I think we forgot to phone each other up." (18)

JOE /COCKER

JOE COCKER

Joe Cocker was never a "pretty boy" in the world of rock, but in the
beginning of his career, he was fresh-faced and fun-loving.
(Photo: Premier Talent / MJB Archives)

Joe's first exploded onto the music scene with his 1968 Number One hit in the U.K., "With A Little Help From My Friends." (Photo: A&M Records / MJB Archives)

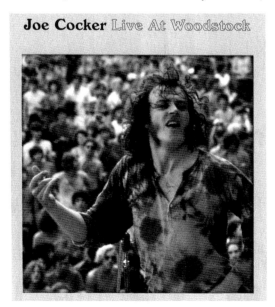

Joe's entire *Live At Woodstock* set from 1969 was released in 2009 to commemorate the 40th Anniversary of the music festival that launched Cocker in the U.S. (Photo: A&M Records)

According to Joe, "I used to get really black moods and totally wound up about things that were irrelevant." (Photo: A&M Records / MJB Archives)

The Beatles loved Cocker from the minute they met him. Ringo Starr, George Harrison, John Lennon, and Paul McCartney below. Paul and George gave him songs, and Ringo played drums on one of Joe's recording sessions. (Photo: Capitol Records / MJB Archives)

Joe never really wanted to do the 1970 *Mad Dogs & Englishmen* tour in the first place, but as soon as he signed on, it grew to be an event. (Photo: MGM Pictures / A&M Records / MJB Archives)

It was Leon Russell who really got the ball rolling, and put the whole *Mad Dogs* band together. (Photo: MGM Pictures / A&M Records / MJB Archives)

What started out as a simple rock tour grew to be a "love in" on wheels, known as *Mad Dogs & Englishmen*. Rita Coolidge is in the Afro wig, second from the left, in the back. Joe is on the floor, in the front, second from the left. Leon is in the top hat. (Photo: MGM Pictures / A&M Records / MJB Archives)

The tour was so huge that they had to charter a plane to keep the show on schedule. Here is the crew boarding the *Mad Dogs* aircraft. (Photo: MGM Pictures / A&M Records / MJB Archives)

For the biggest album of his career, Joe Cocker's *Mad Dogs & Englishmen*, the singer found himself by two of the strongest musicians in the business: Leon Russell (left) and Chris Stainton (right). (Photo: A&M Records / MJB Archives)

Every night for *Mad Dogs & Englishmen,* the troupe included over 40 people on-stage. It was a rock & roll circus at its finest. (Photo: MGM Pictures / A&M Records / MJB Archives)

Rita Coolidge was the singer of the song "Superstar" on the *Mad Dogs* tour, and A&M Records loved her so much, they gave her a record contract of her own. (Photo: A&M Records / MJB Archives)

Melanie was one of the stars of the *Woodstock Music Festival* along with Joe. Unlike Joe's band, Melanie's *Woodstock* experience did not include an acid trip. (Photo: MJB Archives)

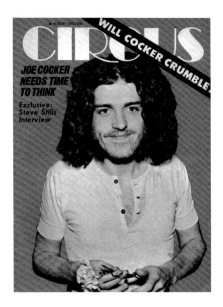

Since Joe literally dropped out of the music business for two years following *Mad Dogs & Englishmen,* the rock press started to worry about him. (Photo: Circus magazine / MJB Archives)

JOE COCKER TOUR Left to right: Gordon Edwards, Patti Punch, Marrianne Lindsay, Richard Tee, Steve Gadd, Phyllis Lindsay, Joe Cocker, Eric Gale, Cornell Dupree.

Joe Cocker and his band on tour in the mid-1970s. He was touring with the studio session group who called themselves Stuff, but as his career fell apart, they proved too expensive for him to afford. (Photo: A&M Records / MJB Archives)

After splitting from A&M Records, Joe signed with Elektra Records, and it looked like he was off to a fresh start. The fresh start was short-lived. (Photo: Elektra Records / MJB Archives)

In the 1980s and into the 1990s Joe signed a contract with Capitol Records, and he had a great run with them. (Photo: Capitol Records / MJB Archives)

Robert Palmer, Aretha Franklin, James Brown, Wilson Pickett, Joe Cocker, and Billy Vera, at a TV taping in the 1980s: *James Brown & Friends.* (Photo: Linda Solomon)

So much of Joe's career was sidetracked or sabotaged by
his depression issues, and his excessive drinking problem.
(Photo: Paul Cox / Capitol Records / MJB Archives)

Joe suffered from self-confidence issues, was a chain smoker
for most of his life, as he struggled to keep his career on track.
(Photo: Paul Cox / Capitol Records / MJB Archives)

It wasn't until after he met and married Pam Baker that he finally came to terms with his crazy life, and gave up liquor. (Photo: Linda Barcojo / Sony Records / MJB Archives)

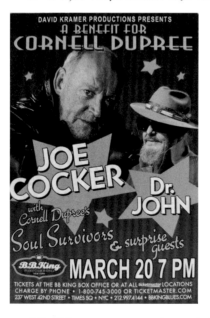

Joe Cocker and Dr. John were amongst the music industry luminaries who donated their time to raise money in benefit of Cornell Dupree, in 2011. (Photo: Jonathan Moorehead)

At the 2011 benefit for Cornell Dupree of the group Stuff, Cocker was in good spirits, and finally off of the liquor and cigarettes. (Photo: Jonathan Moorehead)

Eventually, Joe moved to Colorado where he lived a cleaner lifestyle, and seemed to enjoy his career more than ever before. (Photos: Jonathan Moorehead)

Joe Cocker will always be remembered as one of the most talented and unique
singers of the Twentieth Century.
(Photo: Greg Gorman / Capitol Records / MJB Archives)

Cocker claimed at the time, "I still have this feel for live music. I prefer it as opposed to makin' records, and I still like the touring scene in America. It's very loose, and somehow it all seems to hang together. I've a feeling it'll go right this time." (18)

When he was asked if he was now a calmer version of himself, Joe explained, "Well, I still get sloshed you know. I mean I like a taste of everything. And I still have a good time. It's a good feeling when you look out in the audience and see all those people. Sometimes I wonder where they all come from. I'll probably feel like a rest again after this tour though we may be doing some recording either in Jamaica or New Orleans." (18)

Crawdaddy magazine quoted an un-named representative of A&M Records as explaining of the Toronto gig on the tour, "I'm sure they'll want to hear all the old favorites, and Joe's dropped a lot of those from his repertoire. The audience reaction's been very mixed so far. I heard Madison Square Garden was a disaster, but in Montreal we only had a week's notice after the injunction was lifted, and the place was jammed with 15,000 raving kids. They really dug him there. I don't know what it will be like tonight. This is a very conservative city. People here follow the regulations. Nobody comes to Toronto because they like it; people come here to make a buck." (18)

There weren't any dogs or children on this tour. The personnel were just 21 people which included the musicians and their girl-friends, including Eileen. And they were playing much bigger venues than the little 3,000 capacity places that *Mad Dogs* troupe had played in 1970.

According to Nigel Thomas, "There was a lot of apprehension on many people's part because Joe didn't work for two years. Everyone assumed it was for some dark, evil reason which is totally untrue. Relations broke down with Dee Anthony and [Denny] Cordell for a while, but it's not true to say that Joe didn't work because of Dee

Anthony, and Leon certainly did not climb on Joe's back. Relations are fine with Leon. Leon's running his own band." (18)

Nigel Thomas further explained, "Joe went home last time with $800, but this time he will earn money, minus commissions of course which will go to vicious business ogres like myself," he laughed. (18)

Joe was feeling good, and his high-volume drinking was in full swing during this tour. Reportedly, the night before their 1972 Toronto concert at Maple Leaf Gardens, Joe and the troupe dined at the city's finest French restaurant. They consumed so much wine that they were accused of nearly drinking the entire establishment's cellar dry.

On one hand, the tour of "The Concert, featuring Joe Cocker" was doing smooth business. Joe was busy cementing his reputation for lateness, unprofessionalism, and what can be best described as "rock star arrogance." Hours before the Toronto concert, Joe was booked at one of the top rock & roll FM radio stations for an in-studio interview. He was due at the studio at 3:00 p.m. Joe didn't wander in until after 5:00, and he mumbled his way through his brief radio appearance.

For the show that evening, a singer-songwriter by the name of Gerry Lockran was the warm-up act. Since Joe consistently threw off the planned schedule he was on, it became evident that he wouldn't be making it to the Toronto concert on time.

Nigel Thomas was heard on the phone yelling at one manager, "I don't care if Gerry Lockran has to hold the audience for two hours. He can go on at 8:20, do two sets if necessary. Lockran is the perfect guy to tell an audience that the star's going to be an hour or two late." (18)

Regarding the state of disarray in Joe's career, Nigel was to explain, "Nobody else knew what anybody was supposed to be doing before I took over. A lot of evil things have been said about Cordell, but he was the only person there at the time. I don't feel anybody is really to blame for *Mad Dogs*. It was an incredibly hard tour, and I just don't think the finances were particularly well handled." (18)

According to his critique of the Toronto show, Peter McCabe in *Crawdaddy* magazine wrote, "That night at the concert in Maple Leaf Gardens, some of the old Joe Cocker magic seems to have been trimmed away. The band was tight, but Chris Stainton, though more than competent on piano, is no Leon Russell, and there were times when Cocker wasn't being reinforced. The lack of unity. Most of Toronto's reviewers still proclaimed Cocker's performance 'magnificent' which it was except that a certain vibrance was missing, a vibrance that may have burned out along the course of the *Mad Dogs* tour. And the Toronto kids seemed to notice it." (18)

Peter McCabe also claimed, "Off stage Joe Cocker is as shy as he is raucous on stage as if everything is bottled up inside him until the spotlights glare and Chris Stainton hits the piano keys. Then it all comes out. But getting Joe Cocker to talk is like blowing into a balloon in which somebody had pierced a hole." (18)

Many of the critics of Joe's current stage show complained that Cocker had stuffed the show with a lot of obscure blues tunes that rock & roll fans had no interest in, whatsoever. When pressed about this, Joe defensively claimed, "I'm not really doing any obscure blues. I never really listened to obscure blues. Sonny Boy Williamson was the most obscure I ever got. You know the people I followed were Lonnie Donegan, Barber, Patterson, Gene Vincent, Eddie Cochran. I saw both Vincent and Cochran when they first came to England. But it's true the blues stuff has been running right through all along. I'd like to write more songs, but there's a difference between what I call writing songs and makin' them up." (18)

Joe was never the type of performer who would, or could, just sit and write himself new songs to record. Instead, he now had a solid reputation as a unique interpreter of other people's material and in turn making the songs uniquely all his own. According to Cocker,

"I've never been much of a songwriter, so there are keystone songs that have become very special for me. People would always say, 'Joe, you're doing too many covers.' But when you don't write, you don't have any choice. Still, I did get a bit of fame for doing it. It all came about with a little help from my friends." (15)

Denny Cordell was encouraged by what he heard on stage and set about to record several of Joe's concerts. Since he couldn't seem to get Joe to go back in the recording studio he made several of the tracks into live recordings for the next A&M album: *Joe Cocker.* Those two tracks were "St. James Infirmary" and a seven-minute version of "Do Right Woman" which featured singer Viola Wills in a lead vocal duet with Cocker. [NOTE: Viola Wills was to peak at Number 2 on the *Billboard* Dance Charts in 1980 with her disco version of Gordon Lightfoot's "If You Could Read My Mind" which was a big hit on the dance floor at Studio 54.]

The *Joe Cocker* album was released by A&M in the U.S. in November of 1972, and Cube Records in the U.K. It made it to Number 30 in the U.S., Number 11 in Australia, Number 8 in France, Number 4 in Italy, Number 28 in Canada, and Number 50 in Germany.

In addition, Joe scored two more hit singles off of this his third studio album. They included his version of The Allman Brothers' song "Midnight Rider." It peaked at Number 27 in the U.S., Number 29 in Canada, and Number 49 in Australia. The next single, released in 1973, was "Woman To Woman" which hit Number 56 in the U.S., Number 29 in Canada, Number 49 in Australia, and Number 72 in France. Again, that was written by Chris Stainton and Joe.

Regarding the song "Woman To Woman," Chris Stainton explains, "What happened was while we were rehearsing we wrote this song. I started playing out this riff and it was 'Woman To Woman.' Joe made a song out of it. It was on some obscure album [*Joe Cocker* / 1972] that never really did anything. But [decades later] it got picked up by all the rappers. Everybody has sampled it. There's been about 20 different people that have sampled it. Most famously was Tupac Shakur when he did 'California Love.'" (12)

Things were not perfect on the North American leg of Joe's concert tour of 1972. At least Joe was on the road, and he was somewhat successfully repairing his career. When they were in Los Angeles, Chris Stainton married the woman he had fallen in love with, and soon he had stabilized his own personal life. It was a shame that Joe could not do the same thing.

After the American concert dates, Joe and Chris and the band returned to England where they were amongst the stars at two open air rock festivals. The first one was *Great Western* which was staged at a farm in Lincoln, sort of *Woodstock*-style. The second was *Crystal Palace* held in London. Fortunately for him, Joe had added the songs "The Letter," "Cry Me A River," and "Feelin' Alright" to his stage repertoire, so it was much more crowd-pleasing.

Throughout his career one of the most rabidly supportive fan bases of Joe Cocker was his Australian audience. Once this tour was finally up and humming nicely, what could be more perfect than a series of concert dates in New Zealand and Australia? In theory, this was a great move for Joe, and the concert dates were booked and arranged.

With a troupe of 30 people, Joe Cocker, Chris Stainton and band arrived in Sydney, Australia on October 9, 1972. The tour started out optimistically with a champagne press conference in Sydney. Reportedly, Joe drank liberally all throughout the press conference and during the concert appearances he made in both Australia and New Zealand. This was a detail which was not wasted on the press. The immediate press coverage drew headlines including: "BUBBLY FAILS TO LOOSEN JOE'S TONGUE," "CRAZY JOE," "THE WILD MAN OF ROCK," "THE MAD DOG," and "COCKER POWER FIZZLES OUT."

The tour itself started out well. Joe and band successfully performed four concerts at Sydney's Hordern Pavilion. They next moved on to Adelaide. Then things suddenly went right down the tubes. On Saturday, October 14, 1972, police arrived at The Park Royal Motel in Adelaide at 10:00 in the morning, banged on Joe's hotel room door, and searched his belongings where they found a small quantity of Indian hemp. Joe was just getting his act together, or so it seemed, and suddenly he was in the middle of a high-profile drug bust. It was the last thing he needed.

Five members of his band and Chris Stainton's new wife were all arrested and questioned. They were released on 200 Australian dollars bail. The following Monday they appeared at the Adelaide Magistrates Court. Because of the political climate in Australia at the time, Joe was made into an example to other rock stars who thought they could come to the country down under and flagrantly break the drug laws. They were each fined an additional 300 Australian dollars.

On Wednesday, October 19, deportation orders were filed and signed. Again Joe Cocker was making big headlines, but for all the wrong reasons.

"GET OUT"
"JOE COCKER PLEADS TO STAY"
"POP KING WILL BE DEPORTED"

were amongst them.

In an interview with *The Mirror* Joe was quoted as defiantly claiming, "We were nicked, and we were fined. It's as simple as that. I'm not bitter about it. How could I be? We bought a bit of grass in Sydney and if we hadn't been nicked, we'd have smoked it that night. But God, I wouldn't want to be deported. I wouldn't dream anything like that could happen." (32)

The troupe attempted to continue the tour and performed in Melbourne. Joe, as per usual, got drunk during the first show of his Melbourne run, and when he returned to the hotel they were staying at, he was asked to leave immediately.

According to him, "I'd lost my shirt and I was barefoot. I just had a pair of jeans on. I go to get in the elevator and there were two black girls with me, Viola Wills and one of the other backing singers. And I'd got a six-pack of beer to take up to the room. I was pushing the elevator button, but it wouldn't close and all of a sudden, this guy says, 'Mr. Cocker, we want you to leave the hotel.' I said, 'Alright, I'll get out of here, but let me go pack my suitcase.' He said, 'No. I mean right now!' I was so furious, and I took one of these cans of Fosters and I was going to throw it at him." (1) This was not going at all well.

Joe was later to recount, "It got to be like a complete fantasy. There was this apparently endless procession of policemen coming in and accusing me of everything from tearing their trousers to thumping them in the back. All I was trying to do was prevent them breaking my arm. One of them had it bent up behind my neck. They put me in the same cell as a bank robber and an Aborigine who was alleged to have murdered someone. The bank robber seemed a nice bloke. He said he had all my albums." (33)

Unfortunately, Joe was also charged with aggravated assault when the policemen struggled with him and he threatened to hit an officer with a can of Foster's beer. According to Cocker, "I think I may have aggravated the situation when the judge read out all the ludicrous charges, because I just commented 'rhubarb' after each one. It was all such a shame really because the tour was really going well, and the band was playing great. We had to cancel our concerts in Perth and Brisbane. I think it upset Chris Stainton more than anyone. I don't know when we'll be able to persuade him to get out on the road again." (33)

Looking back on the whole situation Chris Stainton was to recall, "We did a tour in 1972 for about a year. We went everywhere: America, Europe, and we wound up in Australia. And we got busted for grass in Sydney. Joe and I got arrested. My wife Gail got arrested, the poor thing. She had nothing to do with it." (12)

Chris also explained, "To avoid being deported out of Australia, we snuck off. We went to a 'safe house' with the manager at the time, Nigel Thomas. He got us out of Australia without being deported." (12) So much for Joe's 1972 Australian comeback tour.

That was also the end of Joe going to Australia for a while. Not only did it abort his tour with catastrophic financial consequences, but it also sent him off into another career tailspin. The worst outcome was the fact that this totally alienated Cocker from his biggest supporter and best friend, Chris Stainton.

According to Chris, "We went home and went our separate ways. I lost touch with Joe completely. He was into all sorts of drugs, acid, everything. He just disappears off the radar for a couple of years." (12)

In 2013 Joe was to explain in retrospect, "The Australians actually owned up that they set us up. Somebody wrote a book a few years ago saying it was a government thing, an election thing. We were just used as guinea pigs [pawns]. But at the time it was real scary to be down in Australia. You didn't have that communication thing you do nowadays. But I don't know if anything written has ever really bothered me." (3)

Nigel Thomas recalls, "It was a great shame . . . one of those impossible things. Gail Stainton said that she wasn't allowing her husband back on the road, and Chris said, 'O.K.' If that's the way she wanted it, then he wasn't going back on the road anymore. If that hadn't happened, I don't think a lot of things subsequently would have happened." (1) Things were about to head dangerously out-of-

128

control for Joe Cocker as this chain of unfortunate events was about to set him off into still another downward tailspin.

CHAPTER SEVEN

"From 'Bad' To 'Worse'"

I t was 1973, and Chris Stainton was officially out of the picture, but Nigel Thomas continued as Joe's manager. Thomas was to explain, "When the thing with Chris fell apart, Joe went into a depressive downturn and during that time we renegotiated his recording agreement with A&M. That was the cause of my falling out with him, because we renegotiated on what were very favorable terms. David Platz [Denny Cordell's former business partner] who was paying Joe a very low royalty, fell away, and Joe became signed directly to A&M with a greatly increased royalty. But as part of the deal, we committed with A&M that we would go into the studio very quickly, and we set up three basic formulae for recording." (1)

Step One of the new plan was to go to Nashville for six weeks to record an entire album with Bob Johnston. As a producer, Johnston had previously worked with Aretha Franklin, Bob Dylan, and The Byrds. Step Two was to go to Memphis where Joe was booked to record an album with The Staples Singers, produced by Al Bell. Then Cocker was due to go to Muscle Shoals studios with Denny Cordell producing. This three-part recording marathon was due to give A&M enough material for three separate albums.

What an amazing and ambitious plan this was. It was designed to get Joe right back on track and to make his late-1970s career very classy and high-profile. That was not to happen. The day before Joe was going to leave England for Nashville with Nigel Thomas, Joe pulled the plug on it. Joe's girlfriend Eileen refused to allow Joe to leave the country for another week. So Nigel arranged for another week's time for Joe.

Then things took another huge downturn a week later when Nigel went to pick up Cocker to go to the airport and fly to Nashville. According to him, "When I went 'round the following week to pick him up there was a furious row going on between Eileen and Joe. Things were being flung across the room and she said, 'He's not going.' So there's this huge row going on and then I have a row with both of them, and [I] say that it's grossly unfair to sign a deal with a record company—and after all they've paid a substantial advance to Joe—and then to just not go into the studio." (1)

Joe was later to confess, "What had happened—I'd started taking smack [heroin]. I was living in this flat in London that Eileen owned, and, like anybody who's ever been involved in the stuff, you tend to think that nothing really matters. I said to Nigel Thomas, 'I just want to get rid of you.'" (1)

What ended up happening was that A&M Records had paid Joe $400,000 as an advance for the next three albums. When Joe told Nigel Thomas he wanted to get rid of him as his manager, Nigel told him it would cost him $400,000. This is how Joe Cocker plotted his career. He would get pissed off at his managers, pay them a fortune to "go away," and again he would be broke. He had done it with Dee Anthony, and now he did it again with Nigel Thomas while strung out on heroin no less! That was Joe.

For several months of 1973 Joe did one of his famous disappearing acts. He was signed to A&M Records, and they were expecting new material from him for his next three albums. Instead, he was "off the radar," and no one knew where he was.

Jerry Moss came to London a couple of times and attempted to contact Joe, to no avail. Finally, on one of his subsequent trips, Jerry arranged to have Joe and Eileen come to have dinner with him in his suite at The Dorchester Hotel. They were to be joined by Abe Somer who was A&M's attorney. At one point Joe and Eileen excused themselves and went to the bathroom. As Abe and Jerry listened to some music, they heard some odd sounds from the bathroom.

"Then we heard some glass shattering, and pretty soon we walked in there," Moss explained. "There was blood coming down Joe's head, and it looked like it was coming out at a pretty pace. There was blood on the carpet, and the mirror was busted, and the lamp was torn." (1)

Jerry offered to call for medical attention, which Joe declined. "I said, 'Joe, I gotta call somebody. You may be hurt.' But he said, 'No. We're just gonna go home now.' I said, 'You can't go home, you've gonna get fixed up.'" (1) Again they declined, and Eileen suddenly ran for a staircase leading to the roof. Jerry had to talk them down, and they made a hasty exit. Clearly, he was not yet out of the woods from his drug consumption.

Somehow, in the summer of 1973 Joe and Eileen went away to Cornwall and came back bright eyed and optimistic. According to Joe at the time, "I'm on my own now. I'm not looking for a manager. Not right away, anyway. I have a record contract to fulfill, and I want to start on a new album." (1)

Jim Price was one of the horn players on the *Mad Dogs & Englishmen* tour. Price wanted to get Joe back in the recording studio with him as the producer. As Cocker was to recall, "I didn't know where I was by the time Jim Price came around to my house asking if I'd be interested in making another record, which turned out to be 'You Are So Beautiful.'" (5) Price had literally dropped in to pay Joe a visit, and after he played Cocker this one song, Joe was suddenly inspired. They went into the studio and he was up and running again.

According to Joe, it was the album's musical engineer, Rob Fraboni, who is to be credited for getting the ultimate version of the song out of him. Said Cocker, "'You Are So Beautiful'—from when I was very dangerous to myself. I did about six passes and the producer, Rob Fraboni, said, 'Give us one more.' Because it was the last one, I did that *[sings broken croak]* 'to me' on the end, the little teardrop sound. And everybody in the control booth lit up . . . It's tough when you're recording because that performance, it's going to last forever, and sometimes you don't know why you're not nailing it and you have to hope that some higher spark comes through." (6)

One of the things that Jim did to make the outcome even better was to reach out to his circle of musician singer-songwriter friends. This distinguished list of songwriters included Billy Preston, Alan Toussaint, Harry Nilsson, Randy Newman, and Jimmy Webb. It was Preston's "You Are So Beautiful" that kicked off the recording sessions, and they were progressing. However, they were not without their glitches along the way. Although he was optimistic and finished riding the heroin horse, Joe went back to heavy drinking. The drinking had escalated to the point where Joe drank so much, he would vomit, and start drinking again.

Half of the tracks were recorded at various studios in London, and the other half were done at Village Recorders in West Hollywood, California. It was there that Joe worked with a group of famed session musicians who had their own albums and called themselves Stuff. They included Richard Tee, Cornell Dupree, Eric Gale, Gordon Edwards, Chris Parker, and Steve Gadd. It also introduced him to the members of the 1980s group Toto: Jeff Porcaro, David Paich, and Steve Lukathur. On this album Tee, Dupree, and Porcaro appear with Joe for the first time.

Two of the best moments on the album are provided by the piano playing of the songwriters themselves. These include Randy Newman's "Guilty" and Jimmy Webb's "The Moon's A Harsh Mistress." One of the most amusing-yet-tragic moments of Cocker's recording career took place the day he met Webb.

According to Jimmy Webb, "Jim Price, a Texan, was a trumpet player with The Rolling Stones for a while and then started producing. One of the first projects he took on was an album with Joe Cocker [*I Can Stand A Little Rain*]. I had just written a folk song at the time that had received a cover [recording] from Judy Collins. Imagine my surprise when I got a call from Jim asking if I would like to come down to the studio and help out on a Joe Cocker session. Joe would be pleased to sing 'The Moon Is A Harsh Mistress' if I would play the piano. I drove down to the studio a little confused as to what I was getting into. 'Joe Cocker, the giant, gesticulating, rough-textured, hard-drinking hero of *Woodstock*?' Where would we go with 'Moon?' I paused at the studio door and knocked gently, hearing no raucous rock & roll, no noise at all. Jim swung the door wide [open], announcing like a ringmaster: 'And now, ladies and gentlemen, meet Joooooooe COCKER!' I stepped into the room and the first thing I saw were two stout legs with size 15s [shoes] extending out from under the desk." (34) In other words, under the influence and passed-out cold under the recording console, there was Joe!

In fact, the entire *I Can Stand A Little Rain* album had to be cobbled together. Joe could not seem to get through a whole song without either losing his place, losing his mind, losing his voice, or all of the above. Jerry Moss was exceedingly amazed about how well Jim Price kept the album on track. According to Moss, "[Price] made this record which was a tremendous record. When you think of all the splicing that had to be done under the most amazing set of circumstances . . . I went to the studio in LA. The musicians that Jim picked were so great that on the second or third take they were there, but Joe would forget the lyrics! So I went out to see him, and I put a lead sheet together. I said, 'Joe, you know it would make it a lot easier on everyone, including yourself, if you just read the lyrics off.' He said, 'WE DON'T DO THAT!'" (1) In other words, dealing with drunken Joe was akin to dealing with a three-year-old child.

And speaking of drunken, Joe was at the height of his alcohol abuse. At one point Jim Price had to call for medical advice as Cocker had passed out on the studio floor and was vomiting blood. After a medical examination, the findings were bizarre and alarming. Price explained, "The doctor called me about two days later and he said, 'He's got a circumstance within his system where if he does a tremendous amount of alcohol, he has a tendency of throwing it up.' I said, 'Really, doctor. Well, how long can a man live with a condition like this?' And he said, 'He can live to be 98 years old!'" (1) Joe simply had the ability to drink, throw up, and continue drinking more. This was a routine that was going to go on for years and years.

Although the album had to be pieced together, *I Can Stand A Little Rain* received several of his best reviews in years. Industry bible, *Billboard*, gave it a rave, declaring: "After almost a two-year layoff, Joe Cocker is back with what may well be his most consistently excellent singing since his heyday nearly five years back and perhaps the most entertaining variety of songs he has ever come up with. The powerful, bluesy vocals of Cocker stand better than ever, and he can still belt with the best, but he has also picked up the ability to control his vocals on the softer side." (35)

The successful sound of the album made A&M Records thrilled to let the world know that Cocker was truly back, healthy, and making great music. To celebrate this fact what he needed was a big, exciting event to show the world that he was again serious about his career.

Anxious to show off the fact that "Cocker is back!" with the full support of A&M and Jerry Moss, in June of 1974, Joe was booked at The Roxy rock & roll nightclub on the famed Sunset Strip in Los Angeles for a special album preview. It was going to be a truly big deal. The audience was full of rock critics, rock stars, and industry insiders. To add excitement to the event, Jimmy Webb was set to be the piano player on the gig so that he could perform "The Moon's

A Harsh Mistress" with Cocker. Even Diana Ross, Marc Bolan, and Cher were set to be in the audience. This should have been a high point in Joe's career, however, by his own hand, he turned it into his biggest high-profile disaster of his entire career.

As Joe was to explain, "After we finished the album, Jim booked The Roxy for me in LA. Everyone was there. Somebody should have kept an eye on me, but some dealer found me backstage and filled me up with cocaine. I hadn't performed live in a couple of years. I drank a whole bottle of brandy and then went out there and got through about two songs, and then I sat down on stage with a total mental block to all the words. It was rather embarrassing. Everyone just sort of closed the curtain and said, 'Good night.' That was supposed to be my return." (5)

That was Joe's big return to form. Unfortunately, the form he was in was a near-fetal position collapsed on the stage. Everyone in the audience was horrified, saddened, and shocked as Joe tried to mumble his way through a song and then sank to the floor of the stage like a heap of dirty laundry.

Jacoba Atlas in *Melody Maker* wrote of The Roxy embarrassment: "The audience, most of whom were on tabs from the record company, responded with disbelief at the display of agony and finally descended into conversation. The final blow came at the end of the show when Cocker seemed incapable of leaving the stage. The Roxy finally turned off the lights and someone came out and led Cocker away. Surely, he deserves better than this." (36)

Jerry Moss was later to recall of The Roxy disaster, "After the first song, Joe ended up not being in such great shape. I couldn't get our guys excited about working with him again after that show." (13) Indeed, after that horrifying display, the staff at A&M Records basically wrote Joe Cocker off as a hopeless drug addict.

Joe could have been so much more productive had he stayed away from the drugs in the 1970s. Surmises Chris Stainton, "I think most definitely. He was a very constant guy. He would have kept doing albums and tours. It's a great shame. But then he did his famous thing where he completely blew it on some gig someplace in Los Angeles where he collapsed and laid down on stage. It was the most embarrassing time of his life." (12)

When *I Can Stand A Little Rain* was released in August of 1974, it actually did well on the charts, hitting Number 11 in both the U.S. and in Australia. It hit Number 9 in Canada, and Number 12 in Italy. It failed to chart in the U.K.

The big treat and biggest prize from this album was the single release of the song "You Are So Beautiful." It was an off-the-wall choice for Joe, and it was to become one of the most successful songs of his career. It hit Number 5 in the U.S. and Number 4 in Canada. Although it did not chart in the U.K., it remains one of his signature songs.

With the idea of getting himself back together to support the new album, Joe found a new manager, Reg Lock, and he set about putting together a new band. Joe located a real estate agent to rent him a house in Buellton, California, approximately 40 miles from Santa Barbara. It was a horse ranch which had been sitting vacant.

One of the musicians, Mick Weaver, recalls, "We were supposed to rehearse, but to get everybody sober enough at any one time proved impossible. It was summertime and everybody just sat out on the lawn, drinking Tequila Sunrise until the sun went down, and by then nobody was in a fit state to rehearse." (1)

Somehow, by August Joe took the show on the road. The reviews were horrible and really reflected the state of Cocker's health and lack of sobriety.

In *Melody Maker*, critic Chris Charlesworth wrote, "Joe Cocker is a shadow of his former self. The once great voice that thrilled thousands seems to have succumbed to the punishment Joe has been enjoying during long layoffs. On stage at The Academy Of Music [in New York City] he came over as a stumbling drunk." (37)

Somehow Joe and his new Cock & Bull Band as they were named made it through two tours both disastrous. Meanwhile, wanting to capitalize on the success of "You Are So Beautiful," A&M Records in April of 1975 released his next album, cobbled together from previously done recordings and leftovers. The album, entitled *Jamaica Say You Will* had mainly been recorded over a year ago and did less well on the charts than his previous releases had. It made it to Number 42 in the U.S.

Highlights on the album include Randy Newman's "I Think It's Gonna Rain Today." This was the first Newman song to appear on a Cocker album, and Joe's voice and delivery was perfect for Randy's characteristically quirky story-songs.

One of the songs on the album was the tune "It's All Over But The Shoutin'." According to Joe, "I hated it. I could never finish the song because we put the track down when I was drunk underneath the piano and I'd put it in too high a key. It was real hard work for me to get through it. I still think I made a bit of a hash of it." (1)

The critics generally liked *Jamaica Say You Will*. According to *Record World*, "Cocker's ability to vocally reach out and grab your head is unfaded." (38)

In 1975 Joe and his Cock & Bull Band played dates in the U.S. and then took off for Australia. It was to be Cocker's first visit "down under" since he had been forced to leave the country in 1972. The Cock & Bull Band was an eclectic one including Richard Tee on keyboards, Cornell Dupree on guitar, Gordon Edwards on bass, Pete Gavin on drums, and the legendary guitar wizard Albert Lee. Trying to "keep it together," Joe made it through the tour without legal incident.

On the way back to the States, Joe and the band did a single concert in Hawaii and then returned to California. At the time Joe was renting a house in Paradise Cove in Malibu, and Albert Lee and his wife Karen were living there with him. According to the Lees Joe's old girlfriend Eileen would come to the house often. The last time Eileen had split up with Joe, she had gotten married to the owner of a shop in Hollywood, and she now had a baby.

Karen Lee recalls, "She used to come to the house all the time. She'd arrive in a cab from Hollywood and move in for a while with the baby. Joe would take her in. She caused him some wild times. She seemed very resentful of his fame as if she should have had some of it. She was always in competition for attention." (1) Eileen and Joe had some crazy times during this era. While attending an Elkie Brooks show at The Roxy, a drunken Eileen stripped naked backstage, much to the embarrassment of Joe. It sounded like Joe now had another reason to stay clear of The Roxy.

It was a shame that things fell apart so badly during this era. Joe had made such a name for himself. His presence on the music charts confirmed his talent. And he had made a great impression on his peers. In 1973 *Rolling Stone* magazine reporter Ben Fong-Torres interviewed Joe's idol Ray Charles. Ben asked Ray if Joe Cocker could authentically sing the blues. According to Charles, "Look, I think that if a man has had the kicking around and the abuse and the scorn, I think that if he has talent, he can put that some way or another so that people can hear him. I remember one time a guy asked me, 'Hey man, do you think a white cat could ever sing the blues?' which is a legitimate question. It didn't hurt my feelings. I feel that anybody, if you ever have the blues bad enough, with the background that dictates to the horror and the sufferin' of the blues, I don't give a damn if he's green, purple—he can give it to ya." (39) By his own hand, Joe had earned the right to sing the blues at this point!

In 1975 Joe went to Kingston, Jamaica to record his next and final album for A&M Records. Entitled *Stingray*, the album was produced by Rob Fraboni, who had been one of the musical engineers on Joe's most recent pair of albums that Jim Price had recorded. Fraboni had also gone on tour with Joe as a soundman, so it seemed like a logical fit for Cocker to work with him.

It was impressive that Joe could easily go into the studio to record this album with the group Stuff, Albert Lee, and several other friends. The nice surprise on the album was the song, "Worrier," which featured a guitar solo by Eric Clapton and an impressive background vocal turn from Bonnie Bramlett. He also covered two songs by Bob Dylan: "Catfish" and "The Man In Me." In a very interesting move, Cocker recorded a Leon Russell song for the first time since *Mad Dogs & Englishmen*. He covered Russell's most famous song, "A Song For You," on this album. It was a track that Leon had originally played for Cocker in 1969, and Joe does a great version of it here.

Something else unique appears on this album, the song "The Jealous Kind" which was written by Bobby Charles. Ray Charles was so taken by Joe's singing of this song that he was subsequently inspired to record his own version. Here was Joe, totally inspired by Charles as a teenager, now inspiring his childhood idol.

It was Richard Tee who challenged Joe to write a new song for this album. Tee apparently put Joe through his paces on the song "Born Through Indifference." Tee had challenged Joe to come up with the lyrics of the song which they were writing together. According to Cocker, "I don't know if you heard the last record I made, but there's a song on it that got nicknamed 'Born Thru Indifference,' and I must have sung that 40 times trying to think of different words. After doing about 40 or 50 overdubs we ended up using the first take I did." (40)

As Joe explained, it was not an easy process: "Yes, me and Richard were brothers. I only wrote one—well, I just made a mess of one. He just gave me a chord sequence, and I rambled over the top of it." (41)

Regarding Rob Fabroni, *Stingray*, and how he ended up with Eric Clapton on his album, Joe confessed, "I don't know Eric that well, except that I stayed in Miami in the same room he slept in. But I managed to make a bigger piss stain on the floor than he did. And the guy says to me, 'I see you're working with Cornell Dupree—I'm not good enough for you, is that it?' Come on, Eric. So the man helped me out; he gave me a solo." (41)

And as to how he came about the obscure Bob Dylan song, "Catfish," Cocker claimed, "Rob Fraboni knows Mr. Zimmerman very well, and he said, like, 'You got a song for Joe?' And Bob said, 'Well, I've got this song here.'" (41).

While recording part of the album at The Record Plant in Sausalito, California, Joe was to recount a crazy story about Sly Stone, drug dealers, and nearly getting busted. According to him, "We were in San Francisco—ridiculous, over the water, you know. You go over the bridge, and you're into the village. I was trying to remember the words to the song, 'Jealous Kind.' That's one of my favorites, if I've got any, and a lot of what we do—we got ourselves in trouble. Sly Stone, he likes a bit of poker, a lot of the cops they gave us a right hard time. I was standing in this studio, and you know, Rob goes walking out of the place, everyone leaves the studio, and I'm left in there with a dealer. I'm saying, 'What the hell's going on here?' And this black cop puts his head through the door and says, 'There's two of them in here.' 'Two of what?' 'Shut up.' I go out in the lobby and they've got everyone face down, right, shotguns everywhere. And they'd chased some kids into the studio, who had apparently got a dozen pounds of whatever it is, and I had to just sort of try and cool them all out. But it worked. Amazing." (41)

The one person who was totally unimpressed with the recordings for *Stingray* was Jerry Moss. He found it to be a boring collection of garbage. As Joe was to recall, "He was appalled. He was saying, 'What do I do with it?' And I said, 'Well, do what you do with most of 'em—try and sell it.' He was saying, 'But there's nothing in this. There's nothing in it I can work.'" (1)

Unfortunately, the 1976 record buying public was to agree with Jerry Moss. *Stingray* was now the poorest-selling album of Joe Cocker's A&M Records career. It made it to Number 70 in the U.S., Number 35 in Australia, and Number 21 in Canada. It failed to chart in the U.K.

When the album came out, Joe went back on the road with the group Stuff as his band. Reportedly, Joe looked and sounded like hell personified. Reviewing his New York City appearance in May of 1976, *Melody Maker* reported, "The wisest thing Cocker could do is take a year's holiday on a health farm." (42)

Having gotten acquainted with the studio recording group, Stuff, both on his *I Can Stand A Little Rain* and *Stingray* albums, Joe felt quite friendly and comfortable with them. There was a little nightclub located at 97th Street and Columbus Avenue in New York City called Mikell's. It was famous for playing host to dozens of established and up-and-coming performers. Whitney Houston used to play there with her mother, Cissy Houston, before she became a superstar, as well as pop/jazz chanteuse Phyllis Hyman, and the group Stuff as well.

Joe had taken to hanging out there whenever Stuff was headlining. Occasionally Joe would get up on stage and sing an impromptu song or two. "I'd just go and sit in the audience," Cocker explained. "They'd start a number I knew, and I'd jump out of the crowd and climb on stage." (40)

On October 2, 1976, one of the most memorable events in Joe's career happened in New York City. The event was the live broadcast of Cocker as the musical guest on the irreverently amusing comedy variety TV show, *Saturday Night Live*.

The memorable segment from that show featured John Belushi appearing—apparently to much surprise—alongside Cocker as the

British singing star performed the song "Feelin' Alright." Dressed in an identical white suit and Stuff tee-shirt, Joe's in blue, John's in black, and doing a spot on impersonation of Cocker, Belushi paid tribute to Joe, mimicked Joe, and simultaneously poked fun at Joe. This crazy segment of the show was hysterical.

The funny thing was that crazy comedian John Belushi had been doing his Joe Cocker impersonations for quite some time. In 1973 John had previously done a parody of Cocker in the *National Lampoon's Lemmings* live-on-stage show. However, this 1976 version, singing alongside Cocker was nothing short of classic comedy.

Actually, Joe Cocker was impressed and amused by the comic tribute to him by Belushi. According to him, "During the time of 'You Are So Beautiful,' I was working at Village Recorders in Los Angeles, and someone comes into the studio and says, 'Joe, we've got this video to show you that you're not going to like.' I don't know how long *Saturday Night Live* had been on the air because I never watched much TV, but when I saw this video of John Belushi doing me being spastic and pouring beer, I became hysterical. Everyone said, 'Joe, you're not supposed to find this amusing. You're supposed to find this gross and offensive.' I said, 'Oh, come on. You can't not laugh at this.' I didn't even know who Belushi was." (5)

Cocker further explained, "By then, it was pretty well documented back in the '70s I was pretty well out of it. I was pretty heavily drinking. And I remember this producer Geordie Hormel in LA asks me, 'Did you see this guy Belushi doing an impersonation of you? It's disgusting.' And I hadn't seen it. But pretty soon everybody was coming up to me being real negative and saying how bad it was. Well, I finally saw it. And that's what impersonation is, isn't it? I thought he did a great job. But I really didn't know what to expect when they brought me up to rehearsal. And John [Belushi] was actually quite shy. He was reticent. He just watched everything I did. I had a sore throat, so he took me to his own doctor, watched the doctor put that lollipop stick down my throat and all that. Whenever he was around me, he wasn't a comedian at all; he was actually very quiet. He made me tea!" (17)

In 2012 Cocker looked back on this event and claimed, "I always found it quite amusing. But you have to understand I was a bit of a wreck at the time he was doing all that stuff. He [Belushi] was quite shy really whenever we did any gigs together. He was almost like a schoolboy. He'd come in the dressing room; just watch everything I was doing." (15)

People were always amazed that Cocker was more flattered than insulted by Belushi. According to Joe, "John Belushi told me he practiced so hard at home that he scared his mother to death. He'd stand in front of the mirror doing all my hand movements, and his mother thought he'd gone over the top." (2)

Meanwhile, back in 1976, although he got along great with the members of Stuff, Joe simply could not afford them on a regular basis. There was and is a Musician's Union scale amount of pay that most professional musicians earn. With the status of Stuff in the business, they were to be paid triple scale. That proved too pricey for Cocker at the time, and they had to part ways.

As Cocker explained, "We get on great musically, but they know I've got no bread to chuck around." (40)

During the end of the year Joe went back to Sheffield, England, to his parents' home for the holidays. Once there he looked up his pal, Alan Spenner. It seemed that Alan and Neil Hubbard had become members of a new band called Kokomo. They had a couple of local university and club gigs lined up, and Joe accompanied them and got up on stage for a song or two. This blossomed into a promoter proposing booking Joe and Kokomo for a New Year's Day 1977 appearance at Bingley Hall in Birmingham.

Having played some of the biggest and most famous gigs throughout the decade, this turned out to be quite the letdown for

Joe. Bingley Hall, which holds several thousand spectators, had only sold a few hundred tickets. Joe was paid very little for this show.

When he spoke to a reporter for *New Musical Express*, they asked why he had accepted the gig at all. According to writer Tony Stewart, "He says that he only came to Britain to see his parents over Christmas and jammed with Kokomo due to his long relationship with Alan Spenner. He eventually agreed to perform a contracted and publicized booking with the band because: 'I need the money right now.'" (40) How sad is that? To have his dirty laundry on the pages of *The New Musical Express*; that marked a new low point for Joe.

According to Cocker at the time, "I've been panned rather heavily over the last couple of years for singing off-key and stuff like that. People were saying I did bad shows, and I always put it down to that old Stanley Holloway thing: 'Eee tha' does look queer.' If enough people say it t'yer, you can start feeling something is wrong wi'yer. I've always been very self-critical. I know when I'm in bad shape. I'm just glad to say that I'm fitter now than I have been in ages." (40)

In his article, writer Tony Stewart likened overweight Cocker to drunken 1930s movie star W.C. Fields. Both were rotund in stature, slightly disheveled, perpetually drunk, and somewhat surly. Said Stewart, "In fact, he failed to show for our meeting arranged an hour earlier at the Holiday Inn just down the street, and instead was to be busily oiling his larynx in the bar. When we're introduced, he's affable and feels no need to apologize." (40)

According to the article Stewart claimed, "Most astonishing of all, though, are his attitudes. He seems unconcerned that the attendance for this concert is so poor, and he expresses only mild bewilderment that his last studio album, *Stingray*, sold around 9,000 copies. Nine albums notched on his mic stand, a handful of hit singles of which the last was the U.S. Top Tenner, 'You Are So Beautiful,' back in 1975, and again Joe's broke. His recording career has a consistency that refutes the dramatized legend. Commercially he should have more to show than a modest house in LA and some small change in his pocket." According to what he learned from the singer, "Joe claims that he received something like $850 for the two-month *Mad Dogs* escapade. Aside from a small sum saved from the Chris Stainton All Stars Tour of '72/'73, his only reliable source of income is record royalties." (40)

As Joe explained it, "I've had so many screwed-up management situations that I asked [Bob] Dylan's old manager, Albert Grossman, for his advice. He said that, first of all, I'd got to find somebody who really digs me and has my affairs at heart. That was the end for me, because I'd tried hard enough to find somebody that showed that sort of concern. And obviously, by saying that, he [Albert Grossman] didn't want the job." (40)

Joe's latest manager, Reg Lock, seemed unable to help Joe, due to Cocker's spotty reputation with record labels, managers, and concert promoters. According to Cocker, "The idea of having a manager is, I won't say t'cover yr . . . but he's supposed to protect your interests. But they start messing around. I mean, you want to get down to working with the music and a lot of those guys, you know, are frustrated rock & roll musicians. They'd love to be you up there singing." (40)

Joe admitted that a large segment came to hear the music, and another large segment came to see if he was going to have a melt down on stage. As he put it, "When it came around to people digging to see me screw-up rather than have a good performance it really did something to my head. It turned me off music for quite a while." (40)

He also freely complained about his record deal. According to Cocker, "The only knock I get is to see Jerry Moss, head of A&M. He'll say, 'Can't you give us a few more rockers?' I try to explain that because of the state of my mind at the time that's the way I was singing. And he still couldn't dig it. They want hits, you know. But what constitutes a hit I don't bother to think about because I didn't do any rock & roll tunes to have hits. I don't go for all that fuss anyway." (40)

The reality was that, although Stuff would have loved to record with Joe, they were paid top dollar to appear on other people's albums, and Joe simply could not afford their price. This was especially a problem due to Joe's usual long-and-drawn-out recording process due to his drug and alcohol excesses. Denny Cordell would have loved to have worked with Joe and Stuff together. However, it came with a stipulation.

As Joe explained, "But he's also suggested that we make a hit record, put it as plainly as that, and then all share a taste of the goodies that come from it. Rather than them wanting this lump sum when I'm in schtuck [sic] at the time, Denny suggested that rather than use the whole band we should just split up the album and get in to play on the particular songs they're suited to. That's if they want to know." (40)

Reviewing Cocker's act in Birmingham, England at The Bingley Hall on January 1, 1977, Tony Stewart found, "Cocker's not only podgy, but decidedly unsteady on his feet. He staggers forward to the mic with the full complement of Kokomo playing behind to erupt into their opening piece, 'I Broke Down.'" (40)

Looking back on the last ten years, Joe explained why he took this gig with his pals Spenner and Hubbard. According to him, "I just wanted to get together with some talented guys all with the same purpose or just with the same musical leanings to rock & roll. I used to have problems with Alan [Spenner] and Neil [Hubbard], you know. Ego battles. I used to try and calm down the 'star' bit of 'avin' me name out front and convince them it was never me desire to be like that. I've got over it now. I don't give a shit to be honest. I don't mind if they do put my name up front. Because when it comes down to it, it's the music you kick out that counts." (40)

When he was asked about his relationship with Alan and Neil, Joe compared his position in The Grease Band to what Rod Stewart had been with the group Faces. Said Cocker, "Basically, it's because I always dreamt of playing the guitar or something. Like with The Grease Band I didn't want to be me and The Grease Band; I just wanted it to be The Grease Band with me in there. Take Rod Stewart for instance. For a while he could handle it, right? It was just The Faces. Then suddenly they lifted him out of that and made it his deal, so the line-up of the group starts changing and The Faces could be anybody. Now it ain't The Faces anymore at all." (40)

With regard to his health at the time, Joe explained, "I just went to see this doctor and he said I'm suffering from alcohol fatigue. But I'm convinced, because I've been having these spewing bouts every day, that most of it is just because of the state my life is in, not particularly down to this," and with that he drained his beaker full of beer. "But a lot of it is illusionary. It's just that people get this idea of what you are and everything. I'm just an overweight rocker who smokes too much." (40)

As 1977 started, Joe Cocker had A&M Records very unhappy with his last record and his continuing drunken behavior on stage. He was now between managers and was finding that most managers found him to be unmanageable. And the worst part of it all, he was flat broke again. The only way he could go was up from here because he was truly at rock bottom at this point.

CHAPTER EIGHT

"Many Rivers To Cross"

After his 1976 *Stingray* album bombed, Joe's first priority was to solve his management issue. He needed to find someone he trusted, who could not only line up gigs and a better recording label situation but could control him as well. Cocker knew he was in bad shape, and he wisely realized that he needed help. In spite of all of his other crazy behavior, he did have sense enough to know to ask for help instead of wallowing in self-induced misery.

In the last ten years, one of the people he trusted the most was Michael Lang, one of the organizers of the *Woodstock Music Festival* in 1969. It was Lang, along with his business partners, who pulled off the insanely successful *Woodstock*. He was able to book the stars and keep the whole thing running.

Joe had enlisted the assistance of a music business lawyer by the name of Michael Rosenfeld. It was Rosenfeld's idea to reach out to Michael Lang. He had heard that Lang was currently putting together a jazz festival to be held in the south of France. Rosenfeld contacted Michael and asked him if he would be interested in booking Joe as he was currently on tour with the jazz/funk/rock group Stuff. Lang was intrigued, and he agreed to add Joe and Stuff to the bill.

The performance in France came off nicely, and the musical style of Stuff worked well with the rest of the jazz program. Joe, however, was a total mess at the time. Michael Lang was shocked to see the deterioration of Cocker at this point.

"He was in really bad shape," recalled Lang. "That tour with Stuff was a rough one for him. He wasn't well, and they were really tough to be on the road with. Great musicians, and he loved their music, but very hard guys to get along with. He was drinking an awful lot, throwing up a lot on stage. I think that tour probably clinched his demise in terms of a career at that point. It just wiped out his career." (1)

Not long after the jazz festival in France, Michael Lang saw Joe performing again. Joe was booked at The Beacon Theater on the Upper West Side of Manhattan, and he was clearly a drunken mess on stage. According to Lang, "It was a really sad point in his career." (1)

What stunned Michael even more was to witness the amount of liquor Joe would drink. According to him, "In the late morning, Joe would down a bottle of Scotch and sleep under the piano in the afternoon and do it again at night. It was pretty brutal." (13)

It was a couple of days following The Beacon Theater gig that Lang again heard from Michael Rosenfeld. He asked Lang if he would consider becoming Joe's manager. After all, it was Lang's *Woodstock* festival that had really launched Joe's career into the stratosphere to begin with. At the time, Lang had just finished a six-month trial of managing Billy Joel. Lang passed on working further with Billy Joel. He now knew what it was like to work with an artist who really liked to drink, and here was Rosenfeld offering him the chance to manage a real major-league alcohol hound.

In the beginning of 1977 Joe and Michael Lang started discussions about a management deal. According to Lang, he said to Cocker, "Listen, if you want to do this, if you really want to get up and put it back together and pick up the pieces that are rightfully yours, then I'll do it with you." (1) When Joe concurred, Lang agreed to become his manager. It was to become one of the best decisions Joe could make.

One of the first things that Michael Lang did after agreeing to take over Joe's career was to visit him at his house in Los Angeles to get a feel for Cocker's life, circa 1977. He was horrified at what he discovered. First of all, there was Joe Cocker himself, the king of regular "day drinking." He was heavily liquored up, and his house was a hippie den for every parasitic "hanger on" in Los Angeles. He was a soft touch who was supporting a sea of freeloaders who were living with him for the drugs and non-stop party vibe.

Cocker himself admitted, "That place got a bit scary. There were about nine or ten dealers there in no time with it being so close to Hollywood." (1)

Meanwhile, Joe was quite unhappy with his relationship with A&M Records. They wanted him to create hits they could release, and he wanted to do whatever he wanted with his recordings. At the same time, A&M was getting weary of Cocker's antics.

According to Jerry Moss, "Joe had become very unwieldly as an artist to promote. It got down to, if he did two shows at The Winterland in San Francisco, the first night when the press was there, he'd throw up on stage." (1) During this era in Joe's career, it was common knowledge that he hit the stage drunk, continued drinking, and would vomit at least once while on stage and then continue singing and drinking. It was hard to take on many levels.

With this atmosphere, Michael Lang was able to talk Jerry Moss into "cutting his losses" and letting Joe out of his contract. Based on what Joe was doing with his life and career, A&M must have been confident at the time that they now owned the music from the best and the most focused recordings of his singing career. And they may have had a right to feel that way.

The next two tasks were stabilizing Joe and getting him back on tour. Joe had a major league drinking problem, and there was no pretending anything different. According to Michael Lang, "We sat down and made an agreement that he would not go on stage drunk. I said, 'I'll cancel the shows if you do.'" (1) He had Joe between a rock and a hard place, and he knew it. Joe agreed to the terms. No more doing shows while drunk.

At the *Woodstock Music Festival* that Lang produced in 1969 one of the lesser known acts to perform there was a band called Quill. They were managed by a man by the name of Dan Cole. Circa 1977, one of the new aspiring bands Cole was working with was called The American Standard Band. They were basically a New England bar band. They were proficient and had been together for years. Michael Lang and Joe went to a nightclub in Massachusetts one night to see if they might be the right fit for a new and inexpensive band for Joe to tour with. They fit the bill, and Michael Lang hired them for Joe. However, since it was Joe Cocker they would be backing, Lang knew that he had to hire a couple more musicians, who were more of the caliber of Cocker. With that in mind he lined up veteran rockers Bobby Keys and Nicky Hopkins. That way Joe wouldn't feel that he was just touring with a bar band from New England.

Joe explained at the time, "I've got a band, The American Standard. They're great kids in their 20s, and they jump all over the piano and all over the fucking drum kit. Love 'em, love 'em to death." (41) The American Standard, consisted of Kevin Falvey, Cliff Goodwin, Howie Hersh, Deric Dyer, and John Riley.

The one major market that Joe still sold records in was Australia. It seemed like the perfect place to book Joe to try out his act with The American Standard Band. On the flight to Australia in 1977 Joe got so drunk on the flight that there was no controlling him. He got hold of the stewardess' microphone and started making announcements all his own. The flight stopped off in Fiji, dumped Joe and Bobby Keys off the plane and continued on to its destination. It is one thing to be "86'd" from a bar for drunken behavior but to be thrown off of an international plane voyage mid-trip, that was pretty bad.

Since this was to be Joe's big return to concert tours of Australia, the press was watching him very closely. Two of the headlines he created were "MAD DOG COCKER TAKEN OFF PLANE" and "ROCK STAR ORDERED OFF." Joe had a reputation as a drunken mess to uphold, and he was holding it up very nicely already.

While in Australia, Joe was interviewed by *The Sydney Morning Herald*, and he confessed to them, "I just have to watch the drinking habit before performances. I know when I do a bad show it hurts me, so I drink another gallon of beer to try to forget it." (43) That's our Joe!

Reportedly, all of the 14 shows Joe did with his new band went off well. The one incident came when they arrived in Perth, only to have Joe exit the plane and promptly vomit on the tarmac. Old habits die hard.

He apparently got along great with his new band and his two seasoned drinking buddies. According to Nicky Hopkins, "It was like the blind leading the blind. This is why I can't recall too much about the tour. But it was a great time. Jesus, he could sing!" (1)

Joe was in great voice during the Australian leg of this tour. Next, they headed to South America for concerts in Brazil and Argentina then to Mexico where they played a bizarrely disperse number of gigs including one in a bull fighting ring and another in a school gymnasium.

Meanwhile, now that Joe had officially left the label, in 1977 A&M Records released the album *Joe Cocker's Greatest Hits* in the United States, Canada, Australia, and New Zealand only. According to Joe, "Jerry Moss chose the tracks. I was so chuffed at the fact that he'd even bothered to get out of bed and select them, you know." (41) The album made it to Number 2 in New Zealand, Number 88 in

Canada, and only to Number 118 in the U.S. At this point, Joe was pretty much off-the-radar in the music business.

While all of this was going on, Michael Lang was working on securing Joe a new recording contract that would put his career back on track. While Joe had been on tour in Australia, Lang came to Los Angeles where he negotiated a deal with Elektra/Asylum Records. As he recalls, "I took three days and flew from Australia into LA and back again in the middle of the tour. I brought the tapes with me, and I sat down with Joe Smith and Steve Wax, played 'em the songs and made a deal, a really good deal. Then I flew back and finished the tour and when we came home, we started to try and approach putting the album together, the *Luxury You Can Afford* album." (1)

There were several different ideas bantered around. One thought was to have Chris Stainton come back to "Team Cocker," but it was not meant to happen yet. When Joe was asked by British rock writer John Tobler about Chris, Joe claimed, "I haven't seen Chris for a couple of years. I'm still trying to locate him to see what he's up to." (41)

Another idea was to have Joe reunite with Denny Cordell. The night that Joe went to the recording studio to meet with Denny he promptly curled up under the piano and fell asleep in a drunken haze. He had reportedly only been in the studio ten minutes before he was unconscious. That did not impress Cordell one bit. Back to the drawing board.

The next plan was to approach Allen Toussaint, the famed New Orleans producer who gave LaBelle their huge Number 1 hit "Lady Marmalade." To everyone's delight, he agreed, and *Luxury You Can Afford* looked like it was on track. They had Toussaint aboard and lined up the guys from Stuff as the musicians. Apparently, the guys from Stuff ended up costing a fortune, and the costs for the album started to get out of control. Then Toussaint backed out of the project with it only two-thirds completed. To finish the album, The American Standard Band was brought in as they would musically accompany Joe in the recording studio for a lot less money than Stuff.

It seemed that everyone had their own ideas of what songs Joe should be recording on the Elektra Records album. One inspired choice was the Procol Harum hit, "Whiter Shade Of Pale." Joe wasn't totally convinced at first. According to him, "I felt a bit embarrassed about that track for a while, because I go into the office at Asylum and there's my manager Michael Lang and Steve Wax, who's the president of the board [of Elektra Records] or whatever it is. And I'll tell you, the guy who sings 'Tie A Yellow Ribbon Round The Old Oak Tree,' Tony Orlando, comes waltzing in, and they say, 'Joe, we need you to sing "Hold On I'm Coming."' I said, 'Man, you've got to understand I'm part of the soul elite, right?' I said, 'I never used to sing that shit even in its heyday. I'm a Ray Charles freak, right? Alright.' But what's wrong, what can be wrong? And Michael jumps up and says, 'We want a guarantee.' I said, 'You're supposed to be on my side, you're managing me.' There's the office, all I know. 'What song can you hear Joe singing?' And Michael comes up with this 'Whiter Shade Of Pale,' and I said, 'It won't hurt,' so we just put it down." (41)

Phil Driscoll wrote three songs for this album including "Boogie Baby," "Southern Lady," and "Wasted Years." According to Joe at the time, "Phil's a beautiful guy. I've just written a couple of songs with him, and one of them is a little too obvious. But I mean, I respect his writing. I found him through my manager once more, and the song 'Wasted Years' is supposed to sum up my career. Anyway, we've been messing around with these songs. He works in Jacksonville, Florida." (41)

With regard to the song "Lady Put The Light Out" Joe explained, "I got the song through Frankie Valli, care of the management, but I did talk to Frankie on the phone, and he said, 'Joe, you can handle this one.' I didn't realize that David Clayton-Thomas had done it." (41)

Luxury You Can Afford should have a been a classy "return to form" album for Joe and in many ways it was. He had a lot of star musicians on it, including Billy Preston, Rick Danko of The Band, and Dr. John. Unfortunately, the album did not find a huge audience and cost a lot of money to produce.

The *Luxury You Can Afford* album only sold approximately 300,000 copies, stalled at Number 76 in the U.S., which at one time was his biggest market. However, the album did make it to Number 12 in Australia, and Number 25 in New Zealand. Still, it was not a good sign, as it made no noise in the U.K. at all.

On top of that, the reviews for the album were semi-horrible at best. *The Los Angeles Herald Examiner* called it "uneven and hopelessly boring." The music industry had changed, and Joe had not. That same review pointed out, "Too much has happened since 'Delta Lady.' Everything might have sounded right for those times, but our era is different now. Joe Cocker may indeed be alive and well, but the majority of the music he associates himself with is dead and gone." (44)

Joe had gone down to Muscle Shoals studio to record a couple of the tracks for the album, did not keep records of expenses, and Elektra ended up suing him for the money which he could not prove were legitimate expenses. Then it came to light during this era, that in the previous ten years of being a recording artist, Joe had never paid British Income Tax. So they sued him for that. Then Elektra, unhappy with how the album did, dropped Cocker from their roster, and once more he was without a record deal and the advance money it would have paid. Again, Joe Cocker was broke.

Then there was Joe's complicated personal life. To get away from the craziness of Hollywood, with Michael Lang's encouragement, Joe moved to the Los Angeles suburb Woodland Hills. Eileen came back in his life for several months, but that proved a real disaster. They got into a fight, and Joe took off and wandered the streets for two days. On the second morning of his "runaway" event he slept on a bench, and a good Samaritan came up to him and offered to buy him a cup of coffee like he was a street bum. It was raining, and Joe certainly legitimately looked like a homeless person.

According to Joe, "It doesn't rain in LA, but it started pissing it down, and I found like a bus stop. I was curled up in there, and this guy came up and said, 'Hey, come here. D'ya want a cup of coffee?' He thought I was a wino, a vagrant, but what it was, I was waiting for my lawyer's office to open on the Monday morning, so I could go in and get some money." (1)

Clearly, things had to change with Eileen. Cocker explained, "We were still together and then she said she couldn't take the States anymore, so she went back home. She asked me to buy her this house in Sheffield, which I did." (1)

In the summer of 1978 it was time for Joe to make a new move away from Los Angeles. What ended up happening was that Jane Fonda had a ranch she owned, north of Santa Barbara, and she was renting it out. The last tenant had been Cat Stevens, who had just moved out. Joe had a terrible reputation for trashing houses. Ultimately a deal was made for him to take out a special insurance policy and to pay $1,500 a month rent.

He said at the time, "I'm staying at this house of Jane Fonda's; she's my landlady. Who could ask for a more delicious landlady than that?" (41)

In reality, the only reason that Joe was able to get the house was that the director of one of the local charitable children's summer camps, who also used a piece of Jane's property, was a big Joe Cocker fan who took pity on his situation. Her name was Pam Baker, and she became, in time, the most important person in Joe's life.

According to Pam, "He didn't have all that great a reputation at that time. In fact, there was a lawsuit against him for a house where he had been staying in Malibu that got trashed, totally trashed. But you know, I was a fan of Joe's. I just really wanted to meet him, so I pushed for it. And I was the one speaking with his management at the time, and I said, 'Well, maybe if he put up a really large security deposit, we could work something out.' He was just very dear. He was really, really very sweet, a really nice man. And over the course of the next six months or so we just became better friends and started going out to dinner, and yeah, dating a little bit, and then he would be off, and he'd be gone, for six, eight, ten weeks while he was on the road. Then he'd come back, and we'd start to see each other again. So it went on like that for quite a few years, actually." (45)

Baker was to recall, "I think Joe felt real comfortable being there because nobody hassled him, and they left him alone, and we were able to protect him because there was a private gate into the ranch. To get to Joe's house you had to drive past all the other cottages and houses on the ranch, so we'd immediately find out a lot of people that used to just drop in and, eventually, they just stopped coming around." (1)

Joe moved into the Santa Barbara ranch in October of 1978 and then went out on a 28-date concert tour with The American Standard Band. He played a few of his chart hits, but mainly he was promoting the *Luxury You Can Afford* album. Although the tour was mainly colleges and club dates, on November 3 he did headline Carnegie Hall in New York City.

As Joe Cocker was to explain at the time, "I moved up to Santa Barbara about 1980. I spent time in LA, but I found it too heavy. Imagine spending five years in Hollywood in the '70s, when everything was so crazy. I'm happy to be out of that." (2)

In the summer of 1979 Michael Lang put together a ten year anniversary event for *Woodstock* by staging *Woodstock In Europe*. He booked Arlo Guthrie, Richie Havens, Country Joe, and, of course, Joe Cocker. There were four open-air shows planned in Germany, and at one of them someone slipped Cocker LSD, and he took it right before the show. Michael Lang went ballistic when he found out.

Without the tour dates, Joe would have no income at all. Somehow adhering to Lang's edict, Cocker did his shows without being drunk, and all went smoothly for a while. The following summer Joe played in front of 20,000 people in Central Park. The event was recorded as *Joe Cocker: Live In Central Park*, for an Australia / New Zealand only record label.

That year a new tour manager was brought into the Joe Cocker camp. His name was Tom Sullivan. The previous one, Hobie Cook, had had enough of the backstage nonsense that was rife at a Cocker appearance. One of the first things that Sullivan noted was that Joe was now playing in odd gigs and dive clubs where he should not have been booked, according to the stature of his name. However, Joe had a spotty reputation at best, and he often had to take whatever gigs he was given.

Early on Tom Sullivan noticed that there was the odd bunch of sketchy characters who would come to see Joe and would try to get backstage. According to Sullivan, "Just a lot of people kept showing up. I didn't know who they were, but I soon got to learn. I started seeing these people coming from every direction. They came with their pockets out and expected them to be filled when they left, having had a good time. Joe feels sorry for people. He's easily taken in by people who make themselves sound so down for the count. I learned from a lot of bad experiences. I don't want to make it sound like it was everybody Joe associated with in the past. It's not all horror stories; there are a lot of nice people out there. But some of the others . . . I've had arguments with people. I've had screaming, yelling matches. There was a girl in San Francisco. I didn't know who she was, but she seemed a little off-center. I wouldn't let her get to Joe and Joe didn't want her around anyway. She went up and down the hall screaming that she was gonna kill me. She was gonna find Joe. She was knocking on all the doors. Things like that. I had to call security for them to fetch the police to get her out. I didn't know what she was capable of. She was somebody from the [Joe's] past, that's all I knew about her." (1) This was typical of the kind of craziness that Joe's concert tours would attract. It did not make for an easy-going atmosphere, to say the least.

In the autumn of 1980 Joe was back in Europe for concerts in Holland, Germany, France, and Italy. One of his concerts in Germany was taped as *Rockpalast 1980* and became a popular television event which was repeated several times and helped let the world know that Joe was still out there working.

This was an odd era for Joe. He had previously had the confidence of knowing there was a record company behind him and looking out for him. That was not the case for Cocker in 1980. According to Michael Lang, it was frustrating not having an American record deal for Joe. He claimed, "I think we were without a deal for about two and a half years during which time we did some touring, did a lot of work out of the country. And Joe really started to come back, his life started to come back. We just really concentrated on that area, but I think that time was well spent. We started to build his career back up in Australia and in Europe to lay some groundwork for what's ultimately come to be." (1)

One of the strangest bookings from this era was a gig booked in Tarrytown, New York, at what was then called The Dick Clark Theater. It was Joe Cocker and Leon Russell on the same bill. Although the two men who were once the stars of *Mad Dogs & Englishmen* never made personal contact backstage, it was a shaky moment. Joe didn't want to open the show for Leon, and Leon didn't want to open the show for Cocker. Leon ultimately went on first, and Joe, determined to give his all, delivered a reportedly stellar and exciting set.

The 1981 tour included dates in Australia and Japan which went quite well. He ended up going back to Sheffield for Christmas with his parents and brother Vic, and it seemed that Joe was really getting his life back together.

That year also ended up with a great performance by Joe on record. It was not, however, part of his own record deal or a "Joe Cocker" record at all. It was a pair of guest duets with The Crusaders [aka The Jazz Crusaders] for their album *Standing Tall*. Joe Sample, who was the keyboard player for the group, sent Joe a couple of songs he was convinced would be great for Cocker to record with The Crusaders. The songs were "This Old World's Too Funky For Me" and "I'm So Glad I'm Standing Here Today."

Joe recorded the two songs, and everyone was amazed at the results. The one song "I'm So Glad I'm Standing Here Today" really hit a chord with Cocker. It was about survival against all odds. According to him, "I got quite emotional when we recorded that one." (1)

When the two songs with the Cocker vocals were released as a single in 1981, it got a lot of attention. In fact, at the beginning of 1982 it was announced that "I'm So Glad I'm Standing Here Today" was nominated for a Grammy Award in the category of Best Gospel Recording. To celebrate it, The Crusaders and Joe were invited to perform the song on the telecast of *The Grammy Awards* live from The Shrine Auditorium in Los Angeles.

Given the mess Joe had made of his appearance at The Roxy, the memory of that disastrous Los Angeles event was still in the minds of many. Could Joe Cocker take the pressure of a live broadcast and not screw it up? Joe and Michael Lang flew into LA and everything leading up to his performance went without a problem. When the big moment came, Cocker amazed everyone and gave one of the most emotional performances of his career.

Ultimately, the song "I'm So Glad I'm Standing Here Today," was one of the highlights of the international telecast, but it did not end up winning a Grammy Award. However, it set off a chain of reactions that was going to lead up to one of the biggest and most lasting commercial successes of his entire career.

CHAPTER NINE

"Up Where I Belong"

The interesting thing about appearing on a huge television special like the 1982 *Grammy Awards* telecast is the fact that while you are on camera you have no idea who is in front of their home TV screen watching you. That is basically what happened when Joe Cocker performed the heartfelt song, "I'm So Glad I'm Standing Here Today." While he was at The Shrine Auditorium singing the song, Joe had no clue that singer Jennifer Warnes was watching the telecast, and she was deeply touched. No one suspected at the time, but that very event was going to turn Cocker's career around in a very big way.

As a performer and recording artist, Jennifer Warnes was something of an exact opposite to Joe Cocker. Joe grew up wanting to be a big, bawdy, blues and rock singer who fully embraced the drug & booze lifestyle that rock & roll seemed to personify. Warnes on the other hand was comparatively conservative and known for her lovely ballads like the hit "Right Time Of The Night" which reached Number 1 on the U.S. Adult Contemporary singles chart and Number 6 on the pop charts in 1976. She had so many chart hits that she had already released her *Jennifer Warnes' Greatest Hits* album in 1981.

When Jennifer saw Joe on the 1982 *Grammy Awards* it left quite an impression on her. According Warnes, "Joe walked onto the stage in his day clothes, no tie, no coat, in front of The Crusaders and sang 'I'm So Glad I'm Standing Here Today.' He stilled everybody, and he stirred everybody, and he just sliced through all the pomposity and brought me to life again." (1)

At this point in her career, Warnes had recorded two songs that had been included in movies, each of which was nominated for Academy Awards. The first one was the song "It Goes Like It Goes" for the 1979 film *Norma Rae*. It ended up winning an Oscar as the Best Song from a motion picture. The second one was the Randy Newman song "One More Hour" from the 1981 film *Ragtime*. Although nominated, it did not win that year. However, to have two Oscar nominated songs to her credit, made film producers think of her when it came time to put music to their movies.

According to Warnes, "Paramount called and asked me to pick a movie. I did some homework and said, '*An Officer And A Gentleman*' just before, I'd seen Joe sing on the Grammies." (46)

The song "Up Where We Belong" itself was a very inspiring song which had come about in a very odd way. It had been written in parts by Buffy Saint-Marie, Will Jennings, and Jack Nitzsche, and it seemed like the perfect song for a ballad treatment.

With regard to the telecast of *The Grammy Awards*, Jennifer claims, "I thought they were generally embarrassing, crass and plastic. Joe came on in a tee-shirt and cut through mountains of bullshit. He didn't pander to the plastic; he sang from the heart. I knew then that he wasn't dead, that his heart was intact. So many people go dead in this business, but Joe still makes singing honorable; he's kept his dignity. People that survive have strong spirits. Joe still has the passion to continue. Inside he's still a child and afraid." (46)

She approached the song very intellectually. According to her, "I wanted a song of yearning, not a love song. People don't see me with a man or Joe with a woman. My singing was learnt as a form of prayer. Joe learnt in the raunchy, physical blues tradition. I lend myself to this project as a sauce or a spice. It's not what I do best, but I would do just about anything to see the best shame the worst. I know this has helped Joe though he'd be too proud to say it, and it's helped me to pick and choose my new contract. When we sing together, it's real. Somebody said when we came off at *Live At Her Majesty's*, the singing felt like church. I'm not passionate about self-destruction. I'm passionate about love, understanding and helping one another." (46)

Jennifer Warnes explained, "The film was great, and one should never underestimate having a major film behind your song. The song was truly wonderful, but I always thought that the pairing had a strong ring of truth to it. It was so unlikely because Joe has this well-known, very raw, masculine energy. I was less well-known and had this very vulnerable, quintessential female energy, and we were very polarized as men and women often are these days. But we met in the middle. Potentially, it was full of potholes, but it worked." (1)

With regard to this "odd couple" pairing, Jennifer further mused, "Everyone told me we were the weirdest combination. My boyfriend said we're like Guinevere and the troll who lives under the bridge. To me, we're like raw meat and apricot mousse. Strange enough to work. It was just a wild idea of mine that we should sing together. This success just shows that if your intuition is strong enough, you should follow it. I'm the complement to Joe's voice, I bring out its full flavor. If he sang with Aretha Franklin it would be like two steaks together. As it is, I'm the horseradish sauce." (46)

Joe Cocker remembered, "I absolutely hated 'Up Where We Belong' when I first heard it. But I could tell as we were putting the track down that it was going to be a big record." (3)

Michael Lang was to remember, "I got a call about a film called *An Officer And A Gentleman*, and they wanted Joe to do a title song. We were on tour and Joe wasn't that excited about stopping the tour and going to record." (45)

Chris Stainton also echoed Cocker's impression of the project by saying, "Actually, he hated it when he was asked to do it." (45)

According to Cocker, "It was odd because, you know, the movie scene was a little different back then. And people—I remember when we did 'Up Where We Belong' like the whole theme of the movie was designed around that song. And Stewart Levine, the producer [of the song], said, 'Joe, I can hear you sing it.' And I hated the demo they sent me. 'You know,' I said, 'I just don't want to do this. It's not my thing, you know?' And Stewart persisted. He said, 'I know we could have a massive record if you did this.' And so I relented, and then in the end I kind of could hear as I was singing it that he was turning it into something special, you know?" (47)

The song was recorded in May of 1982, and the single version of "Up Where We Belong" was due to be released on July 22, 1982. It was quite ironic, because in the interim, Joe was enjoying being signed to Island Records at the same time, and he had been working on the tracks for the resulting album, *Sheffield Steel,* during this era. Although completely different projects, *Sheffield Steel* and "Up Where We Belong" were oddly intertwined.

The road to *Sheffield Steel* had begun in 1981 in another roundabout turn of events. The American Standard Band landed a recording deal with Island Records apart from Joe. Guitarist for the group, Cliff Goodwin, explained, "I went down on holiday to the Bahamas. I went up to see Alex Sadkin who was producing a Grace Jones album at Compass Point [recording studio] and also to visit Robert Palmer whose album, *Secrets*, I played on . . . just to visit friends. And Chris Blackwell said, 'How you doing? You still with Joe?' I said, 'Yeah.' He said, 'How is he?' I said, 'He's fine.' He said, 'Is he still drinking?' I said, 'Of course he's still drinking. He will never stop drinking. That's the way he is.' And I think he was struck, to a point, by the honesty, that I didn't try to bullshit, I didn't say, 'Oh yeah, he's great man.'" (1)

Through that one conversation, Blackwell got into contact with Lang, and Joe was signed for one album to Island Records. The bulk of the resulting *Sheffield Steel* album was recorded at Compass Point in the Bahamas between March and May 1982.

While working on a story for *Musician* magazine, writer Fred Schruers described the scene surrounding Joe Cocker who was amidst recording his *Sheffield Steel* album in Nassau. According to Schruers, "The noonday sun has come and gone over the town of Nassau, the Bahamas, and Joe Cocker's afternoon boating party which left port as proper Englishmen has come back more like mad dogs, the result of Schlitzes [beers] and screwdrivers served on the four-hour cruise. Mike Lang, who helped organize *The Woodstock Festival* and now manages Joe, is steering our crammed rental car through a traffic jam. Alex Sadkin, who's been producing Cocker's *Sheffield Steel* album with Chris Blackwell at Compass Point Studios, is sitting up front. Guitarist and solo artist Barry Reynolds has been shanghaied off to a bar by Marianne Faithfull. And Cocker, parched from an interview, swigs from a beer, looking over a pair of American-grown, longhaired retro-hippies weaving through the traffic on foot." (48)

This perfectly describes the scenario surrounding Cocker for the recording of his eighth studio album, *Sheffield Steel*. It was meant to be a disc that would shake up his career and put him back on track with the record-buying public. It was to be a departure for Joe, and indeed it was. It was Chris Blackwell's idea to change things up a bit for this album. One of the main things was to turn their backs on the female gospel background vocals that so many of his recordings had. This time around the background vocals were all going to be male, and the record had more of a "rock & roll meets reggae" feel to it.

"Chris [Blackwell] woke me up to new ideas," Cocker optimistically said while working on the album. "At the same time, I was saying to him, 'Hold back. I do love my black girls, you know?' Maybe it's a little too bare." (48)

Sheffield Steel record co-producer, Alex Sadkin, said at the time, "What we're doing is featuring Joe, letting everybody really hear his voice, with all that gravel and whines and scars. With interesting instrumental tracks, 'yes,' without any female backing vocals. It would have been easy; it's such a comfortable thing to have these girls sing along on every chorus. But Chris [Blackwell] wanted something fresh. It's risky. But it's Joe." (48)

According to Joe, "Chris petrified [me] with his first invite. He said he could hear me singing country & western with these guys. Robbie Shakespeare is an amazin' bass player. When we first went in and were doin' this Jim Webb song, 'Just Like Always,'[synthesizer player] Wally [Badarou] took me aside and said, 'Joe, I adore these guys, but I don't know if they can deal with this tune.' But we got them introduced to the slower stuff, and they were great. I mean, Robbie - it's not like a G7th means much to him, but he would, whoomp, just slide up there and find it." (48)

He complained, "Y'know, the bio that they put out on me from the Island [Records] says in one part, 'Joe was in one of his usual depressions.' So every writer, especially from the dailies, just would stay on this. I mean, What are 'these depressions?' Wow! *Just like everybody else gets*, y'know?" (49)

"We kicked off [recording sessions] in '81 in the spring," Cocker explained. "And, well, I'll never know the full story, but we got six tracks done with Chris [Blackwell] being there, and Alex Sadkin. They're the producers. Whether Chris fell out of love with the project, I don't know. But Bob Marley'd died, and he was very close to Bob, discovered him, more or less, coming from Jamaica. So he sort of left me to do my work, and he went and did a film called *Country Man*. We did a few tracks while he was away. We got some different musicians in, but we shelved them because we picked up the threads again just after Christmas and got the same band together." (49)

When it was suggested that the resulting *Sheffield Steel* album was a bit subdued compared to some of Joe's previous rock & roll-dominated albums, Joe explained, "Maybe it has something to do with the islands. When we were there we were really there for business, and it's pretty much of a nightlife. We don't see much of the sunshine. But I was really pleased with it. I've gotten a little uptight in the past working in studios especially putting on the vocal tracks with people walking in and out, it's sort of distracting. You start upsetting people, and everyone thinks you're a male *prima donna.* You can understand. You're standing in a booth looking through a glass screen, and people are saying, 'Hey, what time does the food arrive?' or something. And you're trying to hit the big note of this album. But for some reason, down in Nassau, people just know. They leave the doors open half the time. And that attitude helps. I had a problem with my voice because of the humidity, though. They keep the studio really cold, air conditioned. I'd sing full belt for a couple of hours, and I'd just have to cut out." (49)

Joe's *Sheffield Steel* album was released on May 22, 1982. That was the same month and year that he went to Los Angeles to record "Up Where We Belong" with Jennifer Warnes. They were completely opposing projects equally competing for attention on the record charts.

When Joe was interviewed by J. Kordosh of *Creem* magazine in Livonia, Michigan, the writer found Cocker to look like an overweight slob as opposed to a sleek rock star. According to Kordosh's description of the singer: "Well, his hair, what's left of it, is frazzled and thin. He's got a decent paunch. While I interviewed him, he was barefoot and wearing a pair of lawn-green pants that were too short to have ever been in style, unless he used to be in [the rock group] Slade and I missed it. Despite the heat, he was wearing a sweater that was truly and extremely ugly." (49) Especially in the 1960s, 1970s, and 1980s, Joe still failed to grasp the concept behind the phrase, "Dress for success."

When *Sheffield Steel* was released it was a critical hit. It featured a new "stripped down" sound throughout, all with a decidedly reggae feel to the tracks. "His best work in years" claimed *The Vancouver Sun*. And "A fine Cocker album" wrote *The Los Angeles Times*. On the charts it made it up to an impressive Number 14 in Australia, Number 10 in France, Number 14 in New Zealand, and Number 15 in the Netherlands. However, it did not chart in the U.K., and it only made it to Number 105 in the U.S.

There were four singles released off of *Sheffield Steel*: "Many Rivers To Cross," "Ruby Lee," "Sweet Li'l Woman" and "Talking Back To The Night." Only "Many Rivers To Cross" became a big success, peaking at Number 38 in France. Because he was signed to Island Records at the time, the song "Up Where We Belong" was to be released by that label. Chris Blackwell reportedly hated that song and only reluctantly released it. How ironic is that?

To cut to the chase, the Joe Cocker / Jennifer Warnes song "Up Where We Belong" was to have the distinction of becoming the biggest selling Number 1 song of Joe's entire career. It not only became his first and only Number 1 hit in the U.S., it also topped the charts in Australia, Canada, and South Africa. It was in the Top Ten in the U.K., Sweden, Spain, New Zealand, Ireland, and West Germany.

During this era, Joe paid a visit to one of his *Mad Dogs* co-stars, Rita Coolidge. She recalled, "I heard such horror stories it was breaking my heart. I have had conversations with Joe over the years where he would get loaded and I'd have no idea what he said. I'd get bits and snatches here and there. And then about 1982, he played in Los Angeles, and he came over to the house afterwards. We sat in the kitchen and talked until about six o'clock in the morning, and I understood every word he said. I was just so amazed at the clarity of his memory about things that went on. He would tell me stories

I had totally forgotten and quote word-for-word what someone had said to him and what I'd said. It was then I knew he was gonna be all right." (1)

It had now been 12 years since the famed *Mad Dogs & Englishmen* tour, movie, and album that had defined Joe's career. Now in 1982 he had it much more in perspective. "Those were amazing times," he said. "We all stayed up at Leon's house in LA and ran around naked all day with these girls from Oklahoma lookin' after us. They were a lot hipper than me to California life, but in the space of a day, literally, they just whispered it all together." (48)

With regard to the drugs on that tour and the conflicts that occurred, Joe explained, "It wasn't a drug outing, particularly. Leon had that religious element, organizing meals everyone would attend and singing 'Will The Circle Be Unbroken.' I'm not as cynical as I was. Everyone says he [Leon] was a bully towards me, but it was all part of the music. There were a lot of fights. I kept well out of it. I went down to about 130 pounds tryin' to prove a human being could live on fresh air alone." (48)

Speaking of the financial mess that followed *Mad Dogs & Englishmen*, Joe claimed, "I'd been offered 85 percent of the gross, and I felt fantastic. I didn't know I had to pay all the costs. The movie company still claims I owe 'em money." (48) Finally, he was able to put all of that behind him and move forward into the 1980s.

In February of 1983 the song "Up Where We Belong" won a Grammy Award as "Best Pop Vocal By A Duo Or Group." And when *The Academy Awards* were televised, Joe and Jennifer were on hand to sing the song and to see it win an Oscar as the "Best Song" of the year. Joe Cocker had never had such a runaway hit in his entire career, and he was enjoying it to the fullest. This was to become one of the most centered and calm eras of Cocker's career so far. With a successful new album and his huge Number 1 hit it was time for him to reflect upon where he was in his life.

In 1983 Motown soul singer Marvin Gaye was shot and killed by his own father. It was quite a shocking scandal to say the least. Joe really admired Marvin, and the night that Gaye's death was announced at his concert in Cologne, Germany, Cocker paid tribute to him. According to Joe, "He was one of the greatest to me. A tough character, but O.K. He didn't receive enough appreciation for his music. His *What's Going On* album meant very much to me. He was a milestone in black music though in the music business he was a black sheep. Maybe people understand now what a great talent has been lost." (1) That night Joe sang Marvin's "Inner City Blues" and dedicated it to Gaye.

After all the attention that he garnered because of "Up Where We Belong" Joe was suddenly a relevant hit-maker again. It was as if he had been brought back from the dead. Now what was he going to do with his new-found and revitalized fame? One of the first things that occurred was one that flattered him to no end. He found himself invited to take part in a tribute to his lifelong idol, Ray Charles, in a unique way.

Being invited to be one of the guest stars on the TV special entitled *Ray Charles: A Man & His Soul* was an amazing treat for Joe Cocker. As a teenager he longed to sing like Ray Charles, and now he was going to have the rare opportunity as an adult to sing WITH Ray Charles.

On Ray's TV special, the two men were shown talking to each other and having a dialogue in front of the camera. According to Joe, "Well, Ray's been called 'a genius.' That word's been slung around a lot. I mean, you know, he's a god to me, but I mean, a 'genius' he certainly is."

Charles laughingly said, "Always hitting at me: 'Don't you think he sounds like you?' And I say, 'Well if he does, he sounds like he's the best replica in the whole world.' And I mean that."

Joe then commented to his idol: "God bless you for it!" (45)

The other participants on the hour-long program were Lou Rawls, Smokey Robinson, Barbara Mandrell, Glen Campbell, Dick Clark, Englebert Humperdinck, Quincy Jones, Dottie West, Mickey Gilley, and Stevie Wonder. Joe was thrilled to be asked to sing the song, "You Are So Beautiful," with the legendary Ray Charles. It was like a dream come true for Cocker.

Looking back at that experience of being on Ray Charles' TV special, Joe proclaimed, "It is quite a mindblower to me. I never dreamed in my wildest days that I'd sit in a dressing room chatting with him. It's especially strange after you've idolized somebody to find out how weird they can be. Ray can be very weird. He's not with me, but he's very cranky with the people around him and with his musicians. We keep threatening to make a record together, but it's tough finding songs for two guys like us to sing." (2)

In the summer of 1983 Joe was in Germany to be one of the stars of a massive televised rock concert event called *Rockpalast '83*. Also on the bill were The Steve Miller Band, U2, Dave Edmunds, and The Stray Cats. There was not only a massive live crowd in attendance, but the event was also due to be telecast to a potential audience of millions.

Of this high-profile performance Joe was to recall, "The worst feeling in the world is to lose your voice before a concert. Happened to me in Germany. We were doing this show for, like, 90,000 people, televised all across Europe, and that morning I wake up with no voice. So I go to this doctor, and he gives me a shot so powerful I thought he'd turned me into a woman. It was that big a dose. That night I opened my mouth, and I couldn't believe it. I sang like a bird. I was so scared of the power coming out of me that I realized why people are so afraid of drugs." (5)

In early May of 1984 Joe got himself into hot water in Vienna, Austria. He was accused of being too drunk to perform at a concert that he was booked to perform, and for once it was not exactly true.

Apparently, the promoter failed to provide the promised equipment and instruments needed for the gig. Joe was to pay the price for it, at least in the terms of bad headlines. The concert promoter chose to hide his errors by claiming Joe was too drunk to make the concert. It seemed like a believable enough alibi, knowing Cocker's past. It ended up with Joe getting arrested and later being cleared of any charges. Still the press coverage damage was done.

During this era Joe recorded a new album of music with two distinctly different sides to it done by different musicians and different producers. The first half was made at Village Recorders in LA with producer Gary Katz who is best known for his work with Steely Dan. For his sessions he essentially used the group Toto—Jeff Porcaro, Steve Lukather, and David Paitch—as the accompanying musicians. The other half of the tracks were done in Nashville with Stewart Levine as producer. They recorded with some of the cream of Nashville studio musicians including Reggie Young, Larrie Londin, and David Briggs. Joe ultimately entitled the album *Civilized Man*.

Similar to when Chris Blackwell first heard "Up Where We Belong" when he heard the tapes for *Civilized Man* he hated them. In fact, he hated them so much he and Joe agreed to part ways.

According to Joe, "Blackwell hated it, so we had a gentleman's agreement and packed up the deal at Island, and I went to Capitol." (1) Essentially, that was what happened. When his Island Records contract ended after only one album, Joe signed a deal with Capitol Records and for the first time since his days at A&M Records, he had a long-term record deal.

Now, at the age of 40, Joe knew that he was an act from the early 1970s who was struggling to keep himself relevant for new generations of music fans. During this era Cocker claimed, "I get called 'a fossil,' which is O.K. when I start thinking of some of the musicians I've known who are dead. People talk with morbid fascination about who is most likely to die next. I'm sure I've been talked about as the next potential dead candidate." (5)

The *Civilized Man* album was released by Capitol Records in 1984, and it was well received in several markets. Overall it was quite an entertaining album, and it featured several notable guest musicians throughout. The song, "Hold On (I Feel Our Love Is Changing)," was given to Joe by his friend Joe Sample of The Crusaders. Randy Brecker plays trumpet on one of the tracks; his old friend Jim Keltner plays drums on one song, and Cissy Houston provides background vocals to two of the numbers.

It was the biggest chart hit in Germany (Number 7) and the Netherlands (Number 8). It hit Number 17 in Australia, Number 20 in Sweden, and Number 30 in New Zealand. In the U.K. it made it to Number 100 and in the U.S. Number 133.

In October of 1984 Joe brought his new love, Pam Baker, back to Sheffield to meet his parents and to see where he grew up.

Joe's brother Vic was to recall, "The first time we ever met her I was just totally surprised at the sort of person she was. You know, so organized and together, compared to a lot of the people he'd been with. I'd never quite seen Joe ever having that sort of partner, but it was what he needed." (45)

Pam got along great with his mom and dad and with his brother. Unfortunately, two months after Pam's visit to Tasker Road, Madge Cocker died. It was very sad. Throughout her life she had been Joe's biggest fan. Thankfully Pam had gotten the opportunity to meet Madge Cocker.

Michael Lang was confident that the work he was putting Joe through during the 1980s were gigs which were going to create a strong and devoted foundation audience of music fans for him to build upon. According to Lang, "The *Rockpalast* shows in 1980 and 1983 were milestones, but they didn't really clinch it. What clinched it was being out there working all those cities all those times. We built it from the roots; that's what did it. It evolved his following. People started to love him. We did our own shows, small halls, 3,000-seaters, and the tours just grew in size. There was a certain market, and we built on that." (1)

Significant changes were underfoot in 1984. That year was bigger and glitzier than ever in the music business. Prince was at the top of his game, but it was definitely the Year Of Michael Jackson and his *Thriller* album. Madonna burst forth in 1984 with her *Like A Virgin*, and Tina Turner suddenly went from a cult figure to become a bona fide superstar with the success of her *Private Dancer* album and the song, "What's Love Got To Do With It."

Of special note in relationship to Joe Cocker was the breakthrough of Tina. For years, through the 1960s and 1970s, she had been half of The Ike & Tina Turner Revue. She had also been the target of Ike's physical abuses. When she broke loose of Ike in the mid 70's she went through a catharsis to find her inner strength. She also embraced the teachings of Buddha. However, she had an uphill struggle launching herself to solo stardom. That was up until she signed a management deal with Roger Davies, and suddenly she was reborn, bigger, hotter, and better than ever. Clearly, this was the kind of treatment that Joe Cocker could use.

Since Tina Turner had found record-selling success by creating albums featuring several different producers and teams of musicians, for Joe's 1986 album, *Cocker*, he employed the services of five different producers or teams of producers: Terry Manning, Albert Hammond & Diane Warren, Ron Nevison, Richie Zito, and Bernard Edwards of Chic. Additionally, the album was dedicated to the memory of Joe's mother. On the record charts, *Cocker* hit Number 2 in Italy, Number 4 in Germany, Number 9 in Australia, and Number 50 in the U.S. The album opens with a high powered track called "Shelter Me" and features Joe's dynamic tribute to Marvin Gaye on "Inner City Blues."

Based on the fact that Joe was now associated with movie theme songs via "Up Where We Belong," he was suddenly on the 'A' list of singers to think of when movie producers went looking towards film music. Joe's music appeared in seven more films during the 1980s:

Teachers / "Edge Of A Dream" (1983)
Wildcats / "We Are Alone" (1986)
9 1/2 Weeks / "You Can Leave Your Hat On" (1986)
Zabou / "Now That You're Gone" (1987)
Harry And The Henderson's / "Love Lives On" (1987)
Bull Durham / "When A Man Loves A Woman" (1988)
An Innocent Man / "When The Night Comes" (1989).

The most memorable one came in the 1986 film *9 1/2 Weeks* where Joe's singing of the song, "You Can Leave Your Hat On," during a strip tease scene. "That was quite a departure," Joe claimed. "I mean, that was almost like a comedy song. You know, it's become like the strippers' theme, you know what I mean." (47)

In 1987 it seemed like Joe Cocker could do no wrong in Europe and especially in Germany where he gave several of his best and most well-attended concert events in recent years. He was no longer performing in little clubs and bars; he was now doing concerts like the one he did in Nürburgring in West Germany before 100,000 people, followed by a concert in Stuttgart. The next day he sang as part of the *Rock In Münster* music fest. He continued to tour from one end of Europe to another including an appearance at The Glastonbury Festival where Cocker headlined on the third day of the festivities.

That fall he took part in television specials to commemorate the anniversaries of the famed Apollo Theater in Harlem, and Bill Graham's rock Mecca clubs: The Fillmore West and The Fillmore East. He also took part in a TV special all-star tribute, *James Brown & Friends*. Joe was in the fine company of several stars and idols, including Aretha Franklin, Wilson Pickett, and Robert Palmer.

At the time, the prime celebrity photographer for *The Detroit News* was Linda Solomon. She had become quite friendly with Aretha Franklin in the 1980s, and they remained close until Aretha's death in 2018. Because of Linda's close relationship with Aretha, she was asked to come to the event and the dress rehearsal beforehand to photograph Aretha, James, Joe, and the other stars.

As Solomon explains, "This was a special that was done for Cinemax. It was a James Brown special billed as *James Brown & Friends*, but he wanted Aretha, and Aretha insisted that it be done in Detroit. At that time, she was not traveling, and she was deathly afraid of airplanes, so if they wanted her, they had to do it in Detroit. She insisted that everything she did was to be done in Detroit, from accepting her American Music Award to appearing on television. It was a wonderful experience, and it was taped on stage at a very small club in Detroit, called Club Taboo. She was friendly with the owners of Club Taboo, and she selected it as the venue. She then asked me if I would come along with her to photograph the rehearsal, and I agreed. I was the only one who was allowed to take photos that day because she trusted me." (50)

For Linda, it was the rehearsal that was the most fun to witness, as everyone was relaxed and interacting. According to her, "It was really fun to watch everyone together with their scripts. Aretha was wearing her tennis shoes and red leather pants. And Joe Cocker was wearing what looked like one of those colorful Australian Coogi sweaters that were so popular in the 1980s. He was wearing one of those. It was wonderful to watch the dynamic between the performers. It seemed like everyone was intimidated by Aretha, including James Brown. James was fully dressed up for the rehearsal, compared to everyone else. He had driving gloves on, red shades, and a suit. Aretha had no make-up on, very casual, and Joe Cocker had his bright colorful sweater on." (50)

With regard to Cocker, Solomon recalls, "I photographed Joe who was seated with Aretha. When they were actually doing the taping, there was a Green Room, or a small backstage area, and they were seated together on the couch. There was Aretha, her boyfriend Willie Wilkerson, Robert Palmer, and Joe Cocker all seated together before they went on stage for the taping. I remember that Joe was very pleasant, and I found that he was actually a bit quiet when he was around Aretha. He was definitely in awe of her. Joe seemed more comfortable around Billy Vera and Robert Palmer because these were his peers. He was definitely in awe of Aretha, you could just tell." (50)

Linda remembers, "I was doing a story about the show for *The Detroit News* at the time. And Joe did pose for a couple of photos for me, and he was extremely nice. And he was really nice to me. When you think about all of those famous performers on stage together, it was really a historical experience. It was the first time The Queen Of Soul and James Brown, The Godfather Of Soul, performed together, and with Joe Cocker, Wilson Pickett, Billy Vera, Robert Palmer, and Dan Hartman, it was quite amazing." (50)

Regarding Joe, Linda found him very pleasant and centered. Said Solomon, "During that one event, I found Joe Cocker to be easy-going. He was quiet, respectful, and for me, it was a great thrill to see him with Aretha. It was special for me to see that side of him because he was so very respectful to her, and I loved seeing that." (50)

For his next album, 1987's *Unchain My Heart*, Joe turned to producers Dan Hartman and Charlie Midnight. Both men were also vocalists. Dan Hartman is best known for his Number 1 disco hits,

"Relight My Fire" and "Instant Replay." And The Charlie Midnight Band once opened for Joe in the early 1980s in Texas and Oklahoma.

According to Cocker at the time, "Charlie's a singer, and it's the first time I've ever had a producer who's been a vocalist, who has a vocal-backed nature. So he understands what pains I go through when I'm out there. If I sing off tune, they tell me in a second, and a lot of people don't. But what they like about my singing is that I can do four takes pretty much identical on my phrasing, because that's the kind of singer I am, and most singers these days do like twenty-odd takes, or they just build them a phrase at a time." (1)

When it was released in 1987, the album, *Unchain My Heart,* did well internationally, hitting Number 2 in Germany, Number 14 in the Netherlands, Number 14 in Italy, and Number 15 in Sweden. In the U.S. it made it to Number 89 and Number 24 in Australia. The single, "Unchain My Heart," hit Number 46 in the U.K., Number 17 in Australia, and Number 15 in Switzerland.

More touring filled Joe's year in 1987 as he returned to Europe and West Germany especially. He was also a pre-taped part of Island Records 25th Anniversary which was a live television event in Britain on July 4.

On October 11, 1987, Joe Cocker married Pam Baker. Over the previous nine years since they had met, they had fallen in love, and finally he had someone in his life who was a stabilizing influence.

Pam amusingly recalled, "Joe had a terrible habit and it was partly, I guess, the English upbringing, but he would always introduce me as his 'old lady.' And I just hated that, as you can imagine. And I said, 'You know, call me your "partner," call me your "significant anything."' And so it ended up he started doing it just more as a joke to make me mad than anything else. But I'll never forget when he did ask me to marry him. We were down in Australia and he goes, 'I guess I'll have to marry you if I can't call you my "old lady."' So he says, 'Then I can call you "my wife."' That was really sweet." (45)

As the new Mrs. Joe Cocker was to explain, "We had a very small wedding, the actual ceremony, about 20 to 25 people, at home in Santa Barbara. A friend of Joe's, our local plumber who's also a minister, performed the ceremony. Then we had a reception for about three or four hundred people at a hotel, which was real fun." (1)

According to Michael Lang, Joe's marriage to Pam was good for him. "After a number of years, he was back as a person and getting back his confidence, and it was like watching someone come back to life, frankly, someone you kind of knew was heading the other way." (45)

By 1988 the world was turning in a political fashion as the fall of the U.S.S.R. was suddenly underway, causing the Berlin Wall to come down, and a new era for Germany was about to begin. Divided into East Germany and West Germany since the end of World War II, suddenly Germany was one whole country again. And by an interesting set of events, Joe Cocker was in the middle of it.

Once again, as he had done with *Woodstock*, Michael Lang got involved and pulled off an amazing event. According to him, "I started thinking about the 20th Anniversary for *Woodstock*, and what I'd sort of come up with was doing a show at The Berlin Wall, actually, over The Berlin Wall." (45)

Joe Cocker's two open air concerts in East Germany drew 100,000 people. And on June 2, 1988, he was in Dresden, East Germany, where the crowd totaled 85,000 people. Joe was the first international performer to hold a concert in East Germany in years, and to commemorate the event, the field that concert was held in is now officially called, "Cocker Meadow," and a historical marker commemorates the event.

With regard to the concerts in Berlin and Dresden, Ray Neapolitan, Joe's personal assistant, claims, "It was the cornerstone of Joe's European success. Joe gave everything for that two hours on stage." (45)

On June 6, Joe took part in the massively covered 1988 *Prince's Trust Concert*, performed before Princess Diana and Prince Charles. The event was held at London's prestigious Albert Hall. Also on the bill were The Bee Gees, Eric Clapton, Peter Gabriel, Phil Collins, and Mark Knopfler,

Then, on June 11, Joe took part in the 70th birthday celebration of Nelson Mandella, which was held at Wembley Stadium. The event drew over 80,000 people and was televised. For his number in the show, Joe performed his current hit, "Unchain My Heart."

In a form of bizarre déjà vu, one of the people who came backstage to see Joe at Wembley Stadium was his original musical idol, Lonnie Donegan. He was absolutely blown away to see Lonnie who had nothing but great things to say about Joe. When Cocker asked Lonnie what he was doing, Donegan confessed that things were getting difficult for him with the exception of a sporadic show or two here-and-there. Although Joe never publicly discussed it in relationship to seeing Lonnie Donegan that day, it must have strengthened Cocker's resolve to continue recording new material and remaining relevant in the business.

During the winter of 1988 into 1989 Joe worked on his next album from Capitol Records which became entitled *One Night Of Sin*. Again the producer was Charlie Midnight with Dan Hartman and Michael Lang serving as executive producers. The really big news about this album was the fact that it marked the return of one of the most important men in Joe's entire life, Chris Stainton!

It had been years since Chris had seen Joe, let alone worked with him. In the interim, Stainton had some good years and some bad years. For a while he had toured and played with Eric Clapton and for other streaks he did less-well. One gig he had for a while was as the keyboard player on the show *Starlight Express* which was playing on The West End in London. According to Chris, "I was broke, down the Jobcentre, filling out Social Security forms. I was desperate, then a friend of mine said I should go down there, they always need deps [sic] for holidays and such. So I went down, got introduced to the keyboard player, sat through the show, and I learned it through the headphones. You're supposed to be able to read music but I couldn't. I was pretending, having learned it by ear." (1)

Joe was thrilled to have Chris back in his life. According to Cocker, "We were always so close, and it's been a pretty emotional thing getting back together. And the whole band has such a high regard for him. Musicians being what they are, they soon sensed that Chris is extraordinary. I've worked with some marvelous players, but he's something else." (1)

Chris Stainton found that it was great to be back together with Joe in the late 1980s and throughout the early 1990s. He recalled, "We did all the old stuff, which I enjoyed, but we also did the new stuff like 'Up Where We Belong' and 'You Are So Beautiful' which I got to play, and it was great. But we had two keyboard players. We also had a guy called Jeff Levine from New York." (12)

The *One Night Of Sin* album opens with the Bryan Adams' song, "When The Night Comes." Hit-maker Adams also played rhythm guitar on that particular track. According to Cocker, "Yeah, he has a special way of doing it. He was a little bit reluctant to give me the tune at first because he probably could have made it a hit himself, but I was grateful." (1)

The album made it to Number 2 in Germany, Number 4 in Italy, Number 34 in Australia, and Number 52 in the U.S. And the single, "When The Night Comes," became the biggest selling single he had in a while since "Up Where We Belong," in fact! It made it to Number 65 in the U.K., Number 11 in the U.S., Number 23 in Canada, Number 25 in Germany, Number 50 in Australia, Number 9 in Austria, and Number 7 in Switzerland.

In early 1989 Joe was invited to play at an inauguration concert for incoming American President, George Bush. Cocker was to explain, "I'm not really a politician, but if I had any leanings I'd probably be more of a Democrat. Most of the neighbors on the mountain in Santa Barbara were surprised I did it, but to me it was an honor, I supposed, being asked by the President to perform for him. Trouble was I ended up singing so much at the rehearsals I had no voice when it came to doing the show. But he [George Bush] came along and he looked me in the eye and said, 'Weeell?' And I said, 'Congratulations, Mr. President,' and he went, 'Alright!'" (1)

He further explained, "It was strange for me because I lost my voice. I remember seeing the old George Bush bringing in Barbara, his wife. They're very tall. And I get up there and I go [croaks] 'You are so beautiful.' I tried my best to sing but I could not get a note out. I'd been singing all night the night before with Sam Moore at rehearsals. We'd just been singing the blues." (3)

During the summer of 1989 Joe found himself back in Europe for 80 concert dates, playing stadiums, bullrings, and even a beach concert for 50,000 at DePanne in Belgium. He also played a massive concert in Salzburg, Austria. Joe was to proudly recall, "Mozart's hometown. There was a huge thunderstorm, a bit like *Woodstock*, marvelous colors in the sky. The Town Hall couldn't agree who to let play in their Town Square for the first time, and they chose me. It was a big kind of family deal, a lot of fun." (1) While on tour in the U.S., one of the Cocker shows in Lowell, Massachusetts, was recorded for the 1990 Capitol Records album, *Joe Cocker Live*. Throughout the album it was great to hear Chris Stainton on keyboards, along with The Memphis Horns, and Joe's touring band. Michael Lang was listed as the live album's producer. The resulting CD of the album had two bonus studio tracks, including Joe's rendition of Diane Warren's "What Are You Doing With A Fool Like Me."

Joe's concert tour of 1989 ended up with Joe returning to his old hometown of Sheffield, England, for a show at the City Hall.

Although his father, Harold Cocker, was in town and in fine health, he did not attend the concert of his youngest son. He told *The Sheffield Star*, "It's not really my kind of music." (51)

According to Harold at the time, "People sometimes ring me, and they think I'm kidding when I say I haven't heard from him for so long. He'll ring me occasionally from Australia or Germany or somewhere, and then he'll suddenly appear. I don't hear a lot from him because he's not much of a one for either writing or telephoning. But I always used to say where our John's concerned, no news is good news! So I never worry myself unduly when I don't hear from him." (51)

As the decade of the 1990s began, Joe was comfortably living in Santa Barbara with his wife, Pam. They were enjoying their quiet lifestyle there. Unfortunately, while Joe was in Philadelphia, disaster loomed nearby as a huge firestorm moved close to the California house where they lived. As Joe was later to comment, "I remember feeling helpless, turning on the TV and it blowing my mind when I saw 'Painted Cave.' And when we went home, being amazed at just how close to the house it actually came. It was literally feet; it melted the satellite dish!" (1)

In 1990 Joe did not tour in Europe, although he made a quick trip to Liverpool to be part of a TV tribute to John Lennon. It was a show that was organized by Lennon's widow, Yoko Ono. Later that year Joe toured in the United States with blues guitar wizard, Stevie Ray Vaughn.

It was reportedly quite a great tour for Joe. According to his personal assistant, Ray Neapolitan, "To this day, that was one of the strongest match ups for Joe. It was such a good feeling, that whole tour." (1)

Like Joe, Stevie Ray had an alcohol problem and had just recently sobered up. According to Joe at the time, "We talked about doing 'Take Me To The River,' the Al Green song, but we never got it together. He was going straight after a bad drinking problem, and we were all chugging away, and we were kinda warned to keep off him. I talked to him a bit; he was a cool kinda guy, a brilliant player." (1)

Not long after Stevie Ray's last 1990 gigs with Joe, he was killed in a horrific helicopter crash in Wisconsin. It was a huge loss and such a shame, in light of the fact that he had just kicked alcohol and was getting his life and his career on track.

The dawning of 1990 officially marked the 20-year anniversary of Joe's historic *Mad Dogs & Englishmen* tour. How did he feel about that, did it make him nostalgic? Not exactly. According to Cocker from this two-decades-later perspective, "Jim Gordon ended up murdering his mother, incarcerated for life. Jesse Ed Davis committed suicide. After the tour I was in The Sunset Marquis in Los Angeles having lost a lot of weight, thinking, 'Is this what it's all about?' It's one of those things I'll never quite understand." (29) For Joe, a lot of unresolved emotions still remained.

One of the big films of 1991 was the drama with music: *The Commitments.* It was about a scruffy bunch of Irish teenagers who accomplish great success singing American rhythm & blues classics from the songbooks of Motown, Stax Records, and the blues. It kind of mimicked what Cocker had done by fashioning his singing after Ray Charles. This was especially true of actor Andrew Strong, who played a white boy singing the blues. According to Joe at the time, "I was amazed when I saw the film *The Commitments* because it reminded me so much [of] playing the smoke-filled rooms and pubs. I feel sorry for Andrew Strong because, talking about him, they always drop my name. It seems a terrible blight on the kid. He's got his own style, and I can see him developing. He's only young. I got my thing from Ray Charles, and it took years before it started to evolve into my own. With this new interest in soul and blues, there's hope for me!" (29)

At the time Joe was happy that he had "With A Little Help From My Friends" to sing over-and-over again. According to him, that year "We end up just about every show with that 'cause it's really one of the anthems. I try to do a few old songs and mix them in with some new ones. I'm 47 now, so I try to find songs, lyrics that suit me mentally at this age. I can hardly sing 'Da Ya Think I'm Sexy?' Rod Stewart doesn't even spend much time doing that now." (2)

It was in 1991 when Joe decided to make some changes in his career, particularly with regard to his management and business deal with Michael Lang. According to Derik Dyer of Joe's band, "We were somewhere in Europe, and I think Michael added some extra [tour] dates in, moved things around and Joe didn't want to do it. And he'd really had enough, and he just decided to make a move when the tour was done and change management." (45)

Much to everyone's surprise, Joe suddenly fired Michael. As Lang explained, "I got a letter from a lawyer. That was it. I would have expected him to have been the one to pick up the phone and say something, but once it was done, I think he just went on. I love him as an artist and as a person. It certainly went on further than business. You don't go through the things we went through for all those years just as a business. He could be very emotional about certain things, and other times he could be very cold about things. Especially relationships. So it was hard to really know him, to really know him, know his heart." (45)

Joe was later to recall, "The thing with Michael was getting to the point where it was almost like a hobby, and I felt that I'd still got a lot of drive if only it was handled right. It had been on my mind all that summer, and when we got back after that tour of the States and Europe, all over the place, I was so worked up about it. So instead of waiting, having a week to settle down, I just thought, 'I'll do something about it.' And I wrote him." (1)

To say that Lang was hurt was an understatement. According to him, "It was the way it was done that hurt. If the guy had spoken to me, said, 'Let's have a meeting,' but he just sent a note. You know I never really wanted to go into management in the first place. I just did it for him." (1)

Ray Neapolitan claimed that Joe owed Michael Lang a lot and, in fact, was alive because of Lang's efforts to keep his life on track all these years. According to him, "When he left Michael Lang, he never talked to Michael again. And I saw that with band members and with other people that were close to Joe. Once he closed the door, that was it." (45)

This was often how Joe did business. When he decided it was time to make a decisive move in his career, he would simply go ahead and do it. Often, he would fire band members, or in Michael Lang's case, he would also get rid of managers whenever he was displeased. Indeed, Lang had most likely saved Joe's career, and in many ways, his life. But as far as Lang was concerned, Joe's relationship with him was done, and he never spoke to Michael Lang again.

CHAPTER TEN

"Straightening Out"

When Joe came to the decision about firing Michael Lang, he had thought for a while and pondered what he would do if he went through with such a plan. One of the people he considered asking to be his new manager was concert promoter Bill Graham. Joe actually had a meeting with Graham, but they didn't seem to be on the same page with regard to the direction Cocker should go.

What Joe most liked seeing was how Tina Turner had turned her life and career around, all thanks to the management efforts of Roger Davies. Tina always had the talent and the drive, but she needed someone behind her with a vision and the resources to put plans into action. Davies seemed to be the perfect candidate for the job of being the driving force behind Cocker's career.

According to Davies, "Managing Joe came about almost by accident. I was invited to The Greek Theater in Los Angeles. I hadn't seen him play live for a long time and I sat there and just loved the show, really enjoyed it. I immediately saw things as a manager that I thought I would have done differently—the lights and staging and the way the band looked—but I didn't go there thinking I was going to manage Joe." (1)

Not long after seeing him at The Greek Theater, Roger Davies was invited up to Santa Barbara to have a meeting with Joe and just see what ideas he had and what thoughts the meeting might spark. Roger was to recall, "I went up to Santa Barbara. I didn't know what to expect, but I had a good time with him. I really didn't want to take on any more clients, but I just felt that he needed someone to look after him, and he was such a talent. I felt like I wanted to hug him, to help him. I didn't know much about him, really." (1)

Roger made it very clear to Joe that he would want to make some sweeping changes in Cocker's career. He wanted to be involved in Joe's new music, the look of his stage show, and how Joe dressed when he was performing. Davies told Cocker, "Well, my management style is, I have pretty strong ideas and if you don't listen to me then there'd [be] no point [in] me being your manager." (1)

Davies continued, "The problem at the time was that he'd just almost finished an album, *Night Calls*, and I like to be involved. So he said, 'I understand that and maybe on the next record you can get more involved.'" (1)

Indeed, Joe had already recorded most of the music for the 1991 *Night Calls* album. This time he used Jeff Lynne, the driving force behind the group ELO, as the producer of the title track. Then the other 11 songs were done either with David Tickle or with Danny Kortchmar. Joe did some great rock & roll cover tunes on *Night Calls*, including Steve Winwood's "Can't Find My Way Home," Elton John's "Don't Let The Sun Go Down On Me," and a return to The Beatles' songbook on "You've Got To Hide Your Love Away."

Joe had sent out the word that he was looking for material for this album, and several friends in the business responded. One of the songs was "Please No More" which Joe explained, "[is] a beautiful ballad that Dave Edmunds sent me. Through various weirdnesses, I ended up doing the track with another producer, even though Dave wanted to produce it. He was very upset and sent me a very nasty letter." (29)

Then Prince also sent Cocker two of his tunes to consider. One of them was the song, "Five Women." According to Joe, "He played instruments on the tape. He sent me two songs, one of which was very strange, all falsetto and a little too obscure for me. I couldn't hear myself even rearranging it. As I get older, I find it tougher finding songs that suit me. At my age 'I want to stick it to you baby' would be silly." (29) Ultimately, Prince's "Five Woman" ended up being one of the most interesting tracks on Cocker's *Night Falls* album.

Once Roger took over as Joe's manager, a lot of changes had to be made, and Cocker was game to let the changes occur. One of the main things was that Joe had to start dressing like an adult rock star. Davies didn't want Joe looking like the tee-shirt clad mess that he often was in public. He wanted Joe in shirts and jackets that made him look like a more dignified rock & roll adult.

According to Joe's personal assistant, Ray Neapolitan, "So here we are with Roger, and Roger had been with Tina Turner now and had brought her back from almost obscurity, back into the view of the world, basically, as an international artist. So we followed in that track. We cleaned—I say cleaned Joe up. We dressed him now with more flashy clothes, and we had more production. And it brought everything up another level, which supported Joe into finding his way to being this international artist." (45)

One of the first things that Roger Davies set out to do was to return Joe to the record charts in his native England. Joe was a huge star in Germany and Italy, but he couldn't seem to get noticed in the U.K.

Joe claimed at the time, "I've often wondered if I'm just a bit primal for the English scene, a bit jungle-like. When I think of Cliff [Richards] and Kylie [Minogue], it's still a very pop-oriented country in its tastes, isn't it? But I was surprised to find out that Eric [Clapton] really doesn't do that well in Germany. We've been selling out 10,000-seater halls and bigger. Eric doesn't do that much.

Fortunately, the Germans always bought my records even when I was pretty whacked out on drugs and stuff in the '70s. In Britain, I'm just going to have to get grassroots again, do the rounds a few times." (29)

Ultimately, Joe's 1991 *Night Calls* album did well in several countries. In New Zealand it made it to Number 3, in Germany to Number 6, and in Italy to Number 9. In the U.K. it went to Number 25 and in the U.S. it only hit Number 111. The single version of the song "Night Calls" hit Number 37 in Germany and Number 11 in France.

One of the biggest changes to occur during this era was Cocker's move from California to somewhere more relaxed and out of the mainstream. The state of Colorado became something of fascination to Joe and Pam. In 1991, while in Colorado for an event, they had some time off to look at property.

A friend and real estate agent they knew took them around rural Colorado to take a look. Joe was to explain, "Pam and I just said, 'Wouldn't it be nice to have somewhere to come for the summer, to have a bit of land?' We went up to combine a holiday and look 'round, and we looked everywhere from Aspen to Grand Junction to the whole of what we call the North Fort Valley, the West Slope. We'd seen a few things we almost kind of liked, but not enough, then [the agent] said, 'Well, how remote are you talking about?' The whole point was to get somewhere out of the way, and he said, 'I got one place you might like.'" (1)

Where they ended up is Crawford, Colorado. It is located 70 miles southwest of Aspen, about 150 miles northeast of Telluride, and about 90 miles to the southeast of Grand Junction. It is a distinctive piece of property—160 acres of it, dotted with mountain peaks jutting upward in the background. It seemed like a perfect and tranquil place for Joe and Pam, so they bought it. Look out Colorado. Here come the Cockers!

While all of these changes were underway, Joe was off on his 1992 world tour. He started out the year in London with rehearsals at The Hammersmith Odeon Theater with his current touring band. It included his best friend, Chris Stainton on keyboards, hit-maker John Miles on guitar and keyboards, Phil Grande, Derik Dyer, and their new drummer, Dan Hickey.

Although he was used to playing the 20,000 capacity arenas in mainland Europe, there was now a concentrated effort to reinstate Joe's stature in England and Scotland. This would take a series of bookings at 2,000-seat theaters in smaller towns throughout the British Isles. There was also a concert at the Sheffield City Hall that year to welcome back its native son. The show that evening was particularly successful, garnering headlines like: "JUMPIN' JOE'S STILL COCKER THE NORTH." This was an interesting tour for sure, as on the road with him this time was not only his wife, Pam, but her mother, Ruby, came along for select dates as well. You could say that Joe had certainly come a long way from his more raucous days on the road. This time around he had his mother-in-law in tow for part of it.

In *The Observer* music critic Jasper Rees claimed, "Like that lone forelock on his head, a scrap of hair bravely hanging on in an area of deep recession, Joe Cocker is still up where he belongs. The man for whom no self-abuse antic was too excessive or off-stage would be the first to admit that he is not your average pop singer. He doesn't look like one, with a body that moves to the music like an unreliable corkscrew, and by the normal method for measuring these things, he doesn't sound like one either. Singing pop songs has never looked harder; how often have they sounded better?" (52)

The tone of the shows while Pam and her mother were on tour with Joe was apparently different than the ones where they were not around. Now that Michael Lang was not looking out for him, the pattern of doing shows while under the heavy influence of liquor was back. According to Ray Neapolitan, "Joe was still drinking. He was drinking a lot. And it was really difficult for everybody involved because the shows were good, and some weren't so good. He would be drinking on stage while performing and he would go through seven, eight beers at a time on stage. I remember guys running out as soon as Joe's cup was empty. One of the roadies would run out to fill the cup with beer again. And between the lights, the stress, the heat, Joe would get sick all the time." (45)

Chris Stainton recalled, "He'd suddenly disappear in the middle of a song and run 'round the back, and some guy had a bucket for him to throw up in." (45)

Ray remembers, "We would gauge the show by how many buckets, meaning, 'How many times did Joe throw up? And the crew had to clean it up." (45)

When the show ended, the drinking continued. According to Chris, "Then after the show we'd go out to eat, and he'd start the drinking [again]. I'd be in a restaurant with him, and he'd down a bottle before the food came. Then he'd get another bottle of Bacardi [rum] and start on that." (45)

Joe claimed in 1992, "In my 20s I felt like I had boundless energy which I could never harness, but nowadays I can pace myself a lot better. On this tour I've virtually been on the night shift. After the show I'm pretty wound up with the adrenaline rush, so it's four or five in the morning before I can get to sleep. Back then I stayed up all night and all day. That period, '67 to '71, Roger Chapman of Family and I would drink a bottle of cough mixture before we went on. We were so young we didn't think we could be killed. We were out there." (29)

With regard to drinking on the road Joe explained, "On tour in the '60s there was no such thing as catering, the hotels weren't so good, weren't customized like these days. The wear and tear today is much less. But the road is still pretty grueling, and I like to hang out with the band and chug a few down. I'm still capable of getting silly, though I try not to get into that area anymore. But I don't see why I should totally abstain. A lot of AA guys can be terribly boring!" (29)

In *The Guardian* writer, John McVicar, wrote an interesting article in which he tried to define what Joe Cocker's appeal was to his audience. He surmised that the most die-hard Cocker fan was likely to be a young white man with a wild past. According to his article, McVicar claimed, "Joe reminds these men of when they were one of the lads, when they drank too much, nearly OD'd on speed or acid, smashed up cars, got busted, had punch-ups, screwed around but occasionally got involved with some woman who left them shattered. He sings to them of not getting about yourself, not being a phony, always helping someone down on their luck, and not being too proud to accept help when you're down either. It is an ordinary message of mutual respect, punching straight from the shoulder, and not whining when things go against you. There is nothing sentimental about it—as there isn't about Joe. Emotionally it hits a genuine spot. Joe is a humanizing entertainer, an experience-tempered icon to the value of being an ordinary bloke." (53)

In June of 1992 Joe was in England to be a guest on singer Tom Jones' TV show *The Right Time*. Joe had known Tom for over 20 years, and it was a very positive reunion for the two legendary singers. Jones had his own TV show in England back in 1970, and Joe had been a guest on that program that year.

Coming forward to 1992, Tom Jones explained, "I hadn't seen Joe for a long time, then we were in Detroit. We played a place called Pine Knob, an indoor/outdoor place. We had a few drinks in the hotel and ended up in the suite, and I went to see his show the following night. We talked about some shows that I was doing for Central TV, and would he be interested in doing it, because I would like to repeat what we had done 20 years before." (1)

Joe and his band went up to Nottingham, England, to tape the show, and it was a great reunion with Tom Jones. Cocker sang his recent hit, "Unchain My Heart," then sat and chatted with Jones. They reminisced about the music-makers of the old days: Ray Charles, Lonnie Donegan, and Gene Vincent. They then did a pair of duets: "Lawdy Miss Clawdy" with Chris Stainton on piano, and then "You Got Me Running" with Cocker's full band.

While he was in his home country, he did several press interviews. He confessed to Pete Clark of the newspaper, *Mail On Sunday*, "Somehow I've neglected England. I've played every hamlet in countries like Germany since the late 1970s in a conscious effort of build up a following, and it's paid off. It would be nice to have some success in England after all these years. I feel it's something missing out of the picture." (54)

During this era Joe spoke about his relationship with his father. According to him, "There's only my dad survived. I just went to see him. He's 84 and very alert. He's never been a drinker; it was my mother's side of the family where I took up the booze. Everyone in England has a little allotment, so my dad's got his little garden. He faithfully looks after it, and I think that's what keeps him going." (2)

In 1992 a *Best Of Joe Cocker* compilation was released in the U.K. and Germany. It stitched together several of his biggest hits from the Capitol Records era, including some rarities and remixes. In fact, a 1990s version of his 1987 song, "Unchain My Heart," was released as a single and hit Number 17 in the U.K. This was his highest charting single in the U.K. in ages.

That same year Whitney Houston's movie debut in *The Bodyguard* was released. It was the height of Houston's fame, and the album from that film became one of the biggest-selling albums in the history of recorded music. To date, the album has sold over 45 million copies internationally, making it the biggest-selling movie soundtrack album in the history of recorded music. This was especially good for Joe Cocker, as he had one of the tracks on this incredibly successful album. He can be heard singing the song, "Trust In Me," as a duet with singer Sass Jordan. As this Number 1 hit album sold millions-and-millions of copies, it also filled up Cocker's bank account with royalty money. Although the Cocker song did not become a hit on its own, the money it made him over the years was quite a prize.

One of the biggest things that Joe did during this era was to finally quit smoking tobacco cigarettes. He had been a chain smoker for five decades of his life, ever since he was a kid. Admittedly, at the height of his habit, he smoked over 40 cigarettes a day, every day.

According to Joe, "As far as looking after my voice, I've never done exercises or any of that stuff. When I gave up smoking in the early 1990s, I found that a great help. It improved my breathing." (1)

In the first half of 1993, Joe was having some downtime in his new residence in Colorado. He was adjusting to a quieter lifestyle there. As his wife, Pam, was to recall, "Joe just was really crazy about it. He just loved it here in Colorado and loved the hiking, and we got our first dog which was very important for Joe. He got into gardening. That became such a passion! It was the isolation; it was the fact that he could walk out this door and walk into those mountains. He could walk for days and never see another soul. And when he did see people, he was just a neighbor. He was just 'Joe.' He could just totally forget that he was even involved in the music business when he was here." (45)

With regard to Joe's drinking habits in Colorado, Pam explained, "It was rare when Joe drank to excess here, when he was home. He knew I didn't like it for one thing. And, you know, the pressure was off. But when he started gearing up for another tour or working on a new album and the pressure would start to build, then he would tend to drink more." (45) At the time they were building a huge house on the property they had bought, and Pam and Joe spent most of their downtime in Colorado.

When Joe went out on the road again, Pam would turn over her control to Ray Neapolitan, his personal manager and tour manager. Ray explained, "It was up to me to keep Joe in line and know where he was; to make sure he was eating . . . just everything about him. You know, as Pam would say, 'His other wife.' 'Cause when we were gone, she'd say, 'You've got him now, Ray.'" (45)

Neapolitan remembers, "There were times we'd have to keep an eye on him every minute. I would have to have a key to his room. It was frightening at times. I never knew what I was gonna find when I walked in that room. And sometimes it was really bad." (45)

The drinking was always something that had to be watched out for when Cocker was out on the road. Ray was to explain, "He had the demons, you know. Joe had the demons that would come out every now and then. And he would get dark and wouldn't come out of his room or would just be by himself and just walk, or just wander, I should say. You know we always thought, 'Maybe you should go to AA [Alcoholics' Anonymous]; see a psychiatrist, you know, some help.' But Joe was totally against any of that. He says, 'No, I can control it myself. I can do it.'" (45)

These were interesting times indeed. Some rock stars died because of their excesses. Others, like Eric Clapton, were to suddenly put their lives in order and get off of the booze and drugs. Joe was determined that he could continue smoking two packs of tobacco cigarettes a day and drink like he did when he was a kid. However, the times were changing.

In 1993 Joe signed on to do a series of three concerts with Eric Clapton and several other stars. The purpose behind the concerts was to raise money for a drug recovery charity Clapton had aligned himself with. For years Clapton was dependent on booze and drugs and nearly died because of it. He wanted to give thanks to the organization that helped him out, so he began asking friends in the business to help him stage some benefit concerts, including one in Birmingham, England. Among the people he enlisted were the group ZZ Top, Jimmy Page, Bill Wyman, Charlie Watts of The Rolling Stones, and Joe Cocker.

It was a different vibe surrounding this series of concerts with Eric Clapton sober. According to Clapton, "I was a few days sober and not really that happy about being around those who weren't. But Joe was great. He turned up a bit late, but he gave it all he'd got, once he was there. He roared through his songs." (1)

According to Joe at the time, "He's a different Eric. He's very much a product of Alcoholics Anonymous. It was really weird to have him giving me looks as I poured myself a drink. I personally find it hard to totally quit drinking, especially when I'm on the road. But instead of going to Alcoholics Anonymous, I give interviews to the press. Over the years I've saved a fortune in therapy bills talking to journalists about my own drink and drug problems. I don't need to talk to therapists. A lot of AA guys become dull when the bottle's taken off 'em. I don't want that to happen to me. No, I don't think I'll ever totally give it up." (1)

For these three benefit concerts, Joe sang while being backed up by Clapton's current touring band, which featured Chris Stainton. Throughout the decade of the 1990s, Chris would go back and forth between Cocker's band and Clapton's band. That way he could work consistently.

Joe longed to try something new for his next album, so he decided to work with Rick Rubin as his new producer. Rubin had worked with The Black Crowes and The Jayhawks and had just recently brought Johnny Cash's recording career back to life with a spare and slightly rough sound to the tracks. Over a matter of several weeks Cocker went through rehearsals with several members of Tom Petty's band, The Heartbreakers. However, he was not at all happy with the resulting Rick Rubin tracks. Mid-way through the project he pulled the plug on it and bought himself out of the project.

Ray Neapolitan was to recall, "It was so raw. I still have these tapes, just like somebody turned on a mic on a cheap recording system so stripped-down it was unbelievable. We all thought, 'This is not the way Joe's going!' We bought out our contract." (1)

When Joe went back into the recording studio it was with Roger Davies and Chris Lord-Alge as producers. One of the favorite tracks on the resulting 1994 *Have A Little Faith* album was an inspired cover of The Lovin' Spoonful's "Summer In The City." Somehow that song was just made to be covered by Joe, and he did a great job with it.

Chris Lord-Alge was blown away by the experience of recording Joe. According to him, "He has the loudest voice I've ever recorded. You could hear him singing through the glass in the control room, that's how loud he was. He'd blow up microphones on me. I'd put him on an $8,000 microphone and within about five minutes he'd blow it up because he sang so loud. Get him on a stage mic and no problem. He's the raspiest singer I've ever worked with, got a great edge to his voice." (1)

Roger Davies had high hopes for the *Have A Little Faith* album. He said at the time, "I think this record is the best Joe's made in a long time. I see it as being Joe's breakthrough record, and I think he's singing the best he's sung in years." (1)

In 1994 and beyond, Joe was more than preoccupied with touring. In fact, the *Have A Little Faith World Tour*, which began that year, saw him appearing in 26 countries in 15 months. Ray Neapolitan recalls, "We were literally on the road doing 170 shows maybe a year. Really pumping it." (45)

Joe's wife, Pam, was to explain, "The '90s were when he was just touring almost non-stop. And we had moved here to Colorado by that time in '94. But it was never more than, I'd say four or five weeks, that either he didn't get to come home, or I went to visit him. But that's how it was our entire marriage, our entire 38 years that we were together." (45)

August of 1994 marked the 25th anniversary of the *Woodstock Music Festival,* and once again Michael Lang was the organizer of the event that took place. And Joe was one of the people invited back for the event. It was held the weekend of August 12 – 14 and included a line-up of original *Woodstock* alumni and a new raft of talent. Again, it took place on the site of Yasgur's farm where the original took place.

Of the performers who were at the 1969 version of the event, the list included repeat performers: Joe Cocker, Melanie, Country Joe McDonald, John Sebastian, Santana, and Crosby, Stills & Nash. The newer list of talent who performed that weekend in Saugerties, New York, included: The Red Hot Chili Peppers, Sheryl Crow, The Cranberries, Aerosmith, Nine Inch Nails, Salt-'N-Pepa, and Bob Dylan.

The big mystery of the weekend was "Would Joe Cocker encounter Michael Lang?" And "What fireworks would flare-up because of such a meeting?" It was a non-event, as it never happened.

The reality is that Joe completely missed seeing Michael Lang there that weekend, and the anticipated reunion didn't take place. According to Cocker, "I was a little nervous, not having seen him since we broke up. They said, 'He's here, he's waiting for you out there.' I got right to the stage with a guy called Bob Garcia, who I knew from years ago at A&M Records and he said, 'I've just seen Michael. He's just around the corner here, Joe.' But he wasn't there. We never met. I think at the last minute he must have been too pissed off to talk to me." (1)

The crowd that weekend was estimated at being somewhere between 235,000 and 350,000 people. Like the original event, the weekend was plagued with rain and mud. When Joe originally performed there in 1969, very few people had any idea who he was. Now, 25 years later, Cocker was a big star.

One of the treats was the fact that Chris Stainton was part of Joe's band again, so it was a reunion of many sorts for both of them. The set that Joe performed at *Woodstock '94* included: "Feelin' Alright," "Hitchcock Railway," "You Can Leave Your Hat On," "When The Night Comes," "The Simple Things," "Up Where We Belong," "Shelter Me," "Unchain My Heart," "The Letter," and "With A Little Help From My Friends." It was truly a great set of old and new Cocker classics. Three of the songs he had performed at the original *Woodstock*. The majority of the Cocker set was later issued on CD from On-stage Records, an Italian record company, as a bootleg tape. It is entitled: *Joe Cocker: Woodstock '94*.

The times had certainly changed since the 1969 original festival. This was *Woodstock* with portable cash machines and other amenities. Joe later commented, "The first one, there was no commercialization. Look at the film, there were no billboards, no Coca-Cola signs, even, nothing. It was literally a free festival. It was an honor to be asked to play on this one, but we were supposed to be reliving a great experience. I'm hardly The Grateful Dead, but I'm into my third generation of entertaining 15-year-olds. It was a little strange out there, the generational difference, you know. I got the vibe that they are on their way somewhere, but where, I don't know." (1)

While apartheid had ended in South Africa, there was still a segregation issue going on in that country. When Joe and his band arrived there, it was not like they had envisioned. Recalls Joe, "When we got there, it was only just after Little Steven and [the recording] '(I Ain't Gonna Play) Sun City,' so it had still got a pretty bad reputation. We were offered a lot of money and I was expecting, after all the changes, the black government and everything else. It was early Nelson Mandela times. I was expecting to see a lot of black people in the audience. I thought quite a lot of black people would come to our shows, like Capetown and Johannesburg, but the only black people I ever saw were the ones I had working behind the scenes. The audiences was all white. It's like East and West Germany. People just don't mingle overnight. We saw a lot of things in the hotels that showed it was still predominantly a white society." (1)

In 1994, both the *Woodstock '94* event and the Sun City gigs took place within a 14-day window. They returned to London in time for an upcoming evening concert at The Forum. However, when the lights went on, Joe had a slightly different band. Chris Stainton dropped out on keyboards, and C.J. Vanston replaced him.

It had seemed like Joe and Chris would be continuing to work together from now onward. That was not the case at all. According to Chris Stainton, "Why did I leave Joe? Simple—Eric [Clapton] gave me a better offer. I'd been with Joe five years and at the end of it, I was just breaking even. I was having a hard time with tax bills coming in and starting to go into the red. I've been bankrupt for eight years of my life. I didn't want to slide into bankruptcy again, and Eric was offering five times as much money as what Joe was paying me. Joe, bless his heart, he pays what he can afford, but I've got a family to support, and I need the cash. I've told him, I said, 'I'm not leaving you. I'll probably be ringing you after this is all done.'" (1)

Indeed, that was exactly what was to happen between Chris and Joe. If Eric Clapton was on tour and was paying Chris, he would gladly go with Clapton. However, if Clapton had some down time, Chris would gladly rejoin Joe. He would go back and forth throughout the rest of the decade. As Stainton explained in simple terms, "I was doing Eric and Joe for a while, all through the '90s. Inevitably, there was a clash and there were tours booked at the same time. I had to turn Joe down, unfortunately, because Eric was paying considerably more money." (12)

Joe continued to do concert dates on his *Have A Little Faith World Tour* which began in August of 1994, ran for 15 months, and found him in 26 countries.

In November of 1994 came the TV broadcast of the documentary special, *Have A Little Faith*. It traced Joe Cocker's roots from his beginnings in Sheffield up to his present album of the same name. Amongst the guests interviewed on the program were Rita Coolidge, Ray Charles, Eric Clapton, Tom Jones, and Jennifer Warnes.

For Joe, the year 1995 began with a February kick-off of his next leg of *World Tour* dates. These were to include 46 in the U.S., 75 concerts in Europe in the spring and summer, and a fall with 39 dates in Australia and New Zealand.

In November of 1995, the combined record labels, A&M and Polygram, commemorated Joe's event-filled career with a 63-track boxed-set of CDs, entitled *The Long Voyage Home*. Joe had a hand in the track listing and explained, "They sent me a list to choose from and I didn't know where to start. Basically, I still love the ones that stand out, like 'You Are So Beautiful,' that's still very special, and 'Little Help.' But I'm not heavy into nostalgia. I'd never dream of playing my own stuff once it's recorded." (1)

Joe was to explain, "I thought I was going to take all of '96 off. I did a tour with Buddy Guy in the States which kind of went pretty much un-noticed, and in the middle of that tour I got a message from the German label, saying, 'We know you don't want to go in the studio 'til March next year, but can you give us something to fill the gap?' And I never do things half-heartedly, an album's an album to me. You can't do half an album. But when they suggested Don Was [who] wanted to do a record with me and the idea of redoing some of my older songs—at first it didn't appeal too much. Then Don put it to me in a way that, when he suggested all these different musicians and actually recording live on the studio floor, it sort of rekindled the idea on me." (1)

Don Was, who is one half of the group Was (Not Was), had a huge hit in 1987 with "Walk The Dinosaur." Don had later gone into producing other people, and when he worked with Bonnie Raitt on her monumental Grammy-sweeping album, *Nick Of Time*, suddenly everyone in the music business wanted to work with him.

The resulting album, entitled *Organic*, found Joe stretching out into some new material, while revisiting and updating several of his hits from the past. Among the Cocker hits of the past that got a '90s refresh were: "Something," "Delta Lady," "Many Rivers To Cross," "You Can Leave Your Hat On," "Darling Be Home Soon," and "Bye Bye Blackbird." Of the new material, the one that everyone seemed to love instantly, was Van Morrison's "Into The Mystic."

Organic featured several big name musicians making contributions to the album. They included Billy Preston, Randy Newman, Merry Clayton, Jim Keltner, Dean Parks, and his Grease Band buddy Chris Stainton.

The *Organic* album was a popular seller for Cocker outside of the U.S. It made it to Number 5 in Germany, Number 10 in France, Number 49 in the U.K., and Number 69 in Australia. It sold over 500,000 copies and was an overall success. The one hit single from the album was the song "Don't Let Me Be Misunderstood" which hit Number 22 in Austria.

According to Joe at the time, "There were a few [that] I was skeptical about. Don talked me into doing 'Delta Lady' by playing me a Taj Mahal track that had a slower kinda groove on it, and I think it came off pretty good in the end, that one. The others—he sent me a bunch of Stevie Wonder's songs like 'You And I.' I picked that one out. The Van Morrison song 'Into The Mystic' I'd wanted to do for some time and 'Can't Find My Way Home' was suggested from Helmut Fest at EMI. 'Dignity'—I heard that on a radio station in Colorado. I hadn't done a Bob Dylan song in a while, and I've always loved his shuffles. I think, with Billy Preston on the record, it really brought everything to life. It was a shame that we couldn't get Billy on tour, but he wanted too much money." (1)

In 1997 Joe went to Los Angeles to work on his next album, *Across From Midnight*, which was to be produced by Chris Lord-Alge. At the time he remarked, "It's been tough again finding songs. I wanted to do a radio-friendly album, more up-tempo, but it hasn't really worked out that way." (1)

Somehow things worked themselves out and the results were an even bigger seller for Cocker. When *Across From Midnight* was released in September of 1997, it sold over 600,000 copies and hit the Top Five in seven European countries including France, Germany, and the Netherlands. As he toured to support the album, he presented first-time concerts in Poland, the Czech Republic, Lebanon, and Russia.

The song "N'Oubliez Jemais" was a huge hit for Joe in France where it hit Number 10, in Belgium where it made it up to Number 7, and in Austria where it hit Number 11. In France he was honored by winning one of that country's top awards: Chevalier De L'Ordre Des Arts et Des Lettres.

Not long after releasing *Across From Midnight*, came his next album: 1999's *No Ordinary World* which was Executive Produced by Joe Cocker and Roger Davies. For the actual production work there were four different producers and three locales: London, Paris, and Los Angeles. The producers included Pete Vettesse, Steve Power, Pete Smith, and Jean-Jacques Goldman.

No Ordinary World made it to Number 3 in Germany, Number 12 in France, and continued his global touring. The album also hit Number 30 in the Netherlands, Number 50 in Sweden, and Number 63 in the U.K. The only single to take off was Joe's version of Leonard Cohen's "First We Take Manhattan" which charted at Number 74 in Germany.

In September of 1998, *The Birmingham Post* in England published an article called: "Who Would You Rather Be? A Tale of Two Brothers" by Dennis Ellam and Simon Evans. They interviewed Joe's father, Harold, and the writers proclaimed of the Cocker sons: "One has become stunningly successful, famous and wealthy. The other went into show business. Born four years apart, the soberly urbane chief executive of the Severn Trent Water empire (Vic) and the raucous, sometime hell-raiser of a rock singer (Joe) have matured into middle age and still offer no clues that they are even related." (55)

Joe's mother had been gone several years at this point time. According to Harold at the time, "I'm proud of both my sons. They fulfilled their ambitions in their different fields and you couldn't ask for more than that. Victor is like me, quite a serious chap. I suppose with a job like his, he has to be. But his brother takes after Madge. He's an extrovert and an easy-going lad, who doesn't seem to worry about too many things." (55)

Harold was to explain, "Victor has worked steadily up the ladder and done well for himself. On the other hand, I admire the way John [aka Joe] has calmed down and controlled the damaging side of his life." (55)

At this point, Vic lived in a large house in Solihull with his wife, Jennifer, to whom he had been married for years. For vacations they would take holidays to the States where they would stay with Joe and Pam on their Mad Dog Ranch in Colorado. Although they had completely different personalities and interests, Vic and Joe remained close as brothers.

Speaking of large houses, by the end of the 1990s, Joe and Pam had completed construction on their dream house, and it was huge. As the royalty checks from *The Bodyguard* soundtrack album and other projects came rolling in, this put Joe in the best financial shape of his life. It enabled he and Pam to build the mansion of their dreams on their Colorado property.

From the outside, the massive house looked like "stately Wayne Manor" from the 1960s TV series, *Batman*. Breathtakingly huge, it was designed by the architectural firm of John Kelly & Associates who are located in Santa Barbara, California.

According to an article written by Kathleen M. Bush in *Western Colorado Style* magazine, the finished product was quite impressive, inside and out. Claimed the publication, "Pam and Joe Cocker live at the base of the Elk Mountains, just on the outskirts of the ranching and farming community of Crawford, Colorado. Their 160-acre spread, The Mad Dog Ranch, sprawls amidst the time-fractured slabs of rock that form laccoliths, familiarly called Needle Rock, Castle Rock, and The Cathedral. The Cockers 17,000 square-foot castle-like mansion seems to take on the mood of the clime." (56)

Joe and Pam lived there, ranch style, with outer buildings and lots of animals. Their menagerie included Ankole Watusi cattle, quarter horses, as well as two dogs and three cats. Pam revealed that Joe's passion for gardening, particularly tomatoes, had caused him to refer to himself as "Mr. Tomato Head."

With regard to his tomatoes, Joe claimed, "Well, my dad used to take me up to his allotment as a kid. I remember the smell of the tomato plants. After a couple of long Colorado winters I put up a greenhouse, and I've become quite the tomato man. I get seeds given to me all around the world. Heirloom varieties—different colors, different shapes." (6)

According to a home tour in the *Western Colorado Style* magazine article: "To call the main floor magnificent could be an understatement. Pillars, cherry wood built-in bookcases, grand windows and a grand piano highlight the downstairs. Posterity accents, such as a miniature Ray Charles, can be found throughout the house. Admittedly, Pam says that they spend most of their time in the family room, kitchen and bedroom. When they aren't reading in one of these rooms, they like to spend time fishing, walking with their dogs, Chili and Chunk, and gardening. Pam also likes to motorcycle throughout Colorado, while Joe likes to get on his horse and head for the hills." (56)

Because of Pam's background of running summer camps for disadvantaged kids for Jane Fonda when they lived in Santa Barbara, she helped to create a new charity organization called The Cocker Kids' Foundation. As Joe explained it, "Delta County is the fourth poorest county in Colorado, so we are drawn to aid youth in achieving their goals. The purpose of the Foundation is to provide a community resource that assists youth up to the age of 21 in the areas of education, recreation, the arts, athletics, medical emergencies, and other needs which provide opportunity." (56)

In addition to the foundation, they also financed The Mad Dog Ranch Fountain Café for the kids they benefit to give them somewhere to hang out and relax. According to that same *Western Colorado Style* article, "This is not the Cocker's only philanthropic endeavor. They also give generously to The Telluride AIDS Benefit and Kids Fest, out of Aspen. As you can see, not only can he (they) sing 'With A Little Help From My Friends,' but they live it and that, of course, makes the dynamic duo of the famed Mad Dog Ranch and The Mad Dog Ranch Fountain Café feel alright." (56)

For Joe, the biggest event of 1999 came on June 1 when he was the guest of opera-singing legend Luciano Pavarotti. The classic singing star was hosting a fund-raising event and recording a soundtrack album of it to raise money for the impoverished children of Guatemala and of Kosovo. The event was entitled *Pavarotti & Friends For Guatemala And Kosovo.* The concert was held in the Italian city of Modena, and the other singing stars on the bill included: Mariah Carey, Gloria Estefan, Ricky Martin, Lionel Richie, and B.B. King.

At the event Joe sang a solo version of his hit "You Can Leave Your Hat On," and then he sang a duet version of the song "You Are

So Beautiful" with Pavarotti. It was a classy event, and Joe was honored to be part of it.

According to Ray Neapolitan, "Before the rehearsal we were waiting for him in a long room with a table set up with all these sweets, pastries and cream puffs, cookies, and whip creams. When Pavorotti shows up he heads straight for the table, stuffs in a bunch of pastries and then starts talking." (1)

Cocker was to explain, "He had his MD [Musical Director] with him, a guy who's always on stage with him doing the conduct. We ran through the song with an acoustic guitar, and I could tell he was pleased; at the end a sort of smile came to his face. But all these cakes, little creampuffs, he ate them like they were going out of style. I thought I had a sweet tooth!" (1) After the concert, Ray and his wife, and Joe and Pam were the guests of Pavorotti at his own restaurant. It was a classy event and evening all around.

Joe Cocker began the year 2000 playing a concert in Atlanta. It was not something he usually did, but the money proved too good to turn down. "We told them we don't work New Year's Eve, but they wanted me to do it. They kept putting money up-and-up and in the end we gave in, said 'O.K.'" (1) For Cocker it was a great way to welcome in the New Millennium and to welcome in the sweeping list of changes to come in the 2000s.

CHAPTER ELEVEN

"Rocky Mountain High"

It was a new decade, a new century, and in the next couple of years, it was going to be a new and evolving Joe Cocker as well. The year 2000 started out like any of the recent ones with lots of concert touring. One of the most high-profile tours he did that year was to be the opening act for Tina Turner on her highly publicized and widely attended farewell tour. Roger Davies was thrilled to have his two biggest acts on the road together for three months.

Again, Chris Stainton was part of the band. Unfortunately, it was to be the last tour they were to do together. He made much more money on tour with Eric Clapton and touring in Tina Turner's band, so that was to become his prime focus over the next couple of years.

Undoubtedly, the biggest change of all in Joe's personal life came in 2001. His lifelong abuse of alcohol finally came to a breaking point. And it was his wife, Pam, who finally had to take matters in her own hands and give her husband a choice: It was the booze or her. One of them was going to be finished in Joe's life.

With regard to Joe's pattern of excessive drinking since they had moved to Colorado, Pam explained, "We'd come back here and he'd be fine, and then it was just like, 'Well, he's just a social drinker when he's here. He never really takes it to extremes.' So then you'd forget about it until the next situation." (45)

A loving but no-nonsense business woman, Pam finally had enough of having a drunken husband. She recalls very distinctly the day she finally reached the breaking point with her tobacco and liquor-addicted husband. "We had a party here," she remembers. "It was the first of March, and we were getting ready to go on tour, and he was drinking. By the time the guests arrived around six o'clock he was already pretty well drunk. And before we even sat down for dinner, I had to help him upstairs to bed." (45)

Ray Neapolitan was to explain, "Pam sort of gave Joe an ultimatum, you know. 'You either shape up or it's over.' And Joe shaped up. He called me and said, 'I'm gonna quit drinking this week. So don't schedule anything. I'm wanna try this.'" (45)

Pam herself was kind of shocked to witness that once Joe quit drinking, that was it. He quit cold turkey. According to her, "I spent about a year in disbelief, thinking, 'This is not going to last.' And then I think I spent the second year being really mad at him. Not mad that he wasn't drinking, but mad that he could do it so easily. Why hadn't that happened 15 years before? And then I finally realized, 'No, he's serious. This is it. This is the new Joe. This is our new life. This is our new relationship.' And I just was so thankful." (45)

Everyone in the "Cocker camp" was on board to support this new phase of Joe's life. Both his manager, Roger Davies, and his assistant, Ray, were going to do all they could to keep the new sober Joe on track. As Neapolitan was to explain, "Joe realized after he had stopped drinking for a while, and Roger was really instrumental in showing Joe, 'Joe if you pull this together, you can be a major international artist.' And he also realized that 'I can sing "Little Help" every night.' And that was always an indicator, 'A Little Help,' because of the little scream at the end. And I think that was a factor in Joe's sobriety. When Joe realized he couldn't hit the high note—the scream—that he had to do something." (45)

Roger Davies was to recall of Cocker's first sober concert tour, "We were out in Canada and America with The Guess Who. We were in Vancouver, the first show of the tour, and we were walking to the stage, and I said, 'How are you?' He said, 'A bit nervous.' I said, 'What do you mean?' He said, 'It's the first time in my life I've ever gone on stage without having a drink beforehand.' I went, 'Ah, you'll be fine, Mate.' He said, 'I think I'll be alright,' and that was the start of it. After that it got better and better." (1)

Joe's newfound sobriety was put to the test almost immediately. When he was on a concert tour, Cocker found that he was being offered liquor almost constantly. It was widely known that he always seemed to have a drink in his hand in the past. "We were in Russia," Joe was to recall. "They take you out to eat and they brought out the vodka. They were saying, 'Joe, you must drink.' And I flatly refused. I wouldn't say that's peer pressure, but every now and then you see somebody with a nice pint of Guinness and you don't forget what you've done for 40 years. But I must say, I don't see any reason to go back to that again." (1)

The proof was in the results when it came to Joe and his new sobriety. When a reviewer for *The Cleveland Plain Dealer* saw the show, the newspaper proclaimed of Cocker, "A music wonder . . . He didn't just warm up the crowd, he set it on fire." (46)

On September 11, 2001, Joe and Pam were in New York City the day The World Trade Center was brought down. The day before he was in the recording studio singing the song, "Now That The Magic Has Gone." He was due to have a concert in New Jersey the next night which was ultimately cancelled.

According to him, "I was lying in bed with the TV on and I'd just napped out. This is in the morning about nine o'clock, and Pam was going to go and have a look 'round town. She was in the bathroom and I just said, 'Hey, Pam, there's a thing come on TV says — "Stay in your hotel room in New York City."' And right then we just saw that bit of a trail of smoke coming out of one of the towers." (1) That made for one sad, sobering, and tragic day.

A further tragedy came in November of 2001 when Joe's father, Harold Cocker, died at the age of 94. Regarding his father, Joe was to lovingly recall, "I used to go out and dress in all the insane rock & roll clothes and he never got it until I was on *Top of the Pops*. He was quite impressed with that—that I could come into his living room without him trying." (3)

In 2002 Joe released his next album, *Respect Yourself*, which he did for Parlophone Records. He recorded five new studio albums in the new century for several different European recording labels. Each of these albums would be released internationally first, and then the following year they would find their way into the U.S. marketplace.

Respect Yourself was produced by John Shanks who wrote six of the songs on the album. The title track was Joe's take on The Staples Singers' 1970s hit, and again Joe made it all his own. Now that he was no longer drinking or smoking, the song "Respect Yourself" was something of a personal anthem.

Cocker claimed that he was very enthused about working on this album with John Shanks. According to him, "What got me buzzing to work with him was the song 'You Can't Have My Heart.' He co-wrote that with C.J. Vanston and the strange thing I found as we got into making the album was that he'd actually sent that song to me a couple of albums back and somehow it had slipped through the cracks." (1)

With regard to the song "Respect Yourself," Joe explained, "For the last year I'd been hearing it in different places, and it kept crossing my mind. You often wonder if a song's too early to resurrect, but John dropped it out as we were progressing, and I thought that's a good enough cure for me."

According to Roger Davies, finding songs for his artists to record is often challenging. He claimed, "I find it increasingly difficult for all my acts who don't write. There seems to be a drought of great songs nowadays. People I used to go to, I could always rely on for good songs. I don't know whether they've dried up, they've got older, or what, but it's harder and harder to find material. I guess these guys have made a bit of money and they're not as hungry." (1)

Pam Cocker was frustrated by the stacks of CDs and albums that Joe would go through searching for songs to cover or reinvent. She claimed at the time, "He listens to them by the hundreds when he's working on an album. Then I yell and scream because they're all over the house in different piles that nobody can possibly understand except him. And then when he's done with his research the piles just seem to stay there. When he's working on finding new material, he'll listen to music for hours every day." (1)

The *Respect Yourself* album was quite successful in the countries that were Joe's biggest lifelong supporters. It hit Number 3 in Germany, Number 13 in France, and Number 15 in Italy, Number 34 in the Netherlands, Number 51 in the U.K., and Number 84 in Australia. The single, "Never Tear Us Apart," hit Number 38 in Canada and Number 85 in the U.K.

By far the most high profile event in 2002—and one of the biggest honors—came when he was invited to be part of *Party At The Palace: The Queen's Jubilee Concert,* a gala event broadcast live from the grounds of Buckingham Palace in London. It was also billed as *The Queen's Jubilee Garden Party.* The show was organized to commemorate the 50-year reign of Queen Elizabeth II and was going to be televised and seen by millions.

Roger Davies recalled, "I watched the show from the side of the stage—That was pretty exciting—and the rehearsals the day before in the afternoon. What I thought was fantastic was Joe being surrounded by his peers—McCartney, Phil Collins, and Steve Winwood—and they were happy to be around him." (1)

Joe had known Steve Winwood and Paul McCartney since his first two albums in the 1960s. Winwood played guitar on Cocker's debut album, and McCartney had personally given him "She Came In Through The Bathroom Window" to record for his second album.

The show included a glittering "who's who" of international rock & roll talent, including Paul McCartney, Eric Clapton, Annie Lennox, Rod Stewart, Tom Jones, Brian Wilson, Queen, Ozzy Osbourne, Steve Winwood, Ricky Martin, Cliff Richard, and Joe Cocker. Also on the bill where a pair of separate class acts, Shirley Bassey and Tony Bennett. In other words, Joe was in amazing company for this event.

Ray Neapolitan was to explain, "What they wanted Joe to perform was 'A Little Help' which Joe would never perform outside of a stage performance…meaning it took Joe 19 songs to warm up in order to hit the scream at the end of it. What changed Joe's mind: the Queen. As simple as that. It's my Queen, I'm gonna do that! Joe's adrenalin was working, and I think that did it for him. Joe was so proud to be part of it. With all his peers, between Clapton, McCartney—Sir Paul, and Phil Collins. Just everybody was there. You know, Joe was very pleased, and just felt like he still had his heart in England." (45)

Joe sang his song "With A Little Help From My Friends" which came in-between Ray Davies of The Kinks performing "Lola" and Phil Collins performance of "All You Need Is Love." Both Steve Winwood and Brian May of Queen played with Joe as his guest star musicians. It was an amazing event, which was later released on DVD.

Cocker was to recall, "I got to talk to Princess Anne and had a word with Tom Jones and Paul McCartney. I told Tom I'd quit drinking. He was saying, 'But can't you imagine a pint, Joe, you must miss a pint.' His son said, 'Leave him alone!' Paul kept having a chat, asking me where we were playing. One nice thing, he said, 'I think your version of "With A Little Help" is the consummate version.' I was pleased about that." (1)

The rest of 2002 was taken in further global touring. One of the most memorable events to take place was on December 2 when Joe played Tulsa, Oklahoma, and who should be his opening act? Leon Russell!

It had been 32 years since their historic *Mad Dogs & Englishmen* tour, their bombastic success together, and their subsequent estrangement. Everyone was buzzing about "What is Joe going to do?"

Joe recalls, "I got this message saying if you want to talk to him, he's coming straight in the building, doing his set, and then in five minutes he'll be gone. I went with Deric Dyer and we sat at the back in the wings. I saw and heard his whole set. He had a band, obviously home-picked guys, and his daughter playing a weird African drum. But he had a word-prompter that he would raise by his feet and every now and then it got a bit late, so he'd play a few bars 'til the words came up. As he got up to walk to his dressing room, he came by me. At first, I don't think he recognized me, and I just said, 'Hi, Leon, how's it goin', Man?'" (1)

Leon wasn't expecting Joe to be standing there, and suddenly the recognition kicked in, and there he was face-to-face with Cocker. According to Joe, "Within seconds he was asking me stuff like we'd said 'goodbye' only yesterday. 'Do you remember me talking to you about art in Denny Cordell's house for several hours?' I didn't, but he kept throwing stuff like that at me. I was expecting all that hostility after what people had told me. So I finally got to say 'Hello' after all that time. I never said, 'You're welcome to get up [on stage with me]' or anything. I just felt it was enough to have actually spoken to him." (1)

Meanwhile, Joe and Pam were living an idyllic life in Colorado when he wasn't on the road. According to Mrs. Joe Cocker during this era, "In the last ten years, I think Joe's got real comfortable with his life and himself and his career. He takes it all totally in his stride. Moving to Colorado was a big thing. It gave him a sense of community, belonging, and real friends who are non-industry. He counts on that a lot. He's always had tremendous enthusiasm for what he does, but since he quit drinking, he's got even more. Before, there were times when alcohol would just make him be depressed and look on negatives and that's just gone. Now he's the most optimistic person I've ever met. It's inspirational. I must say when I first met Joe in 1978, I certainly wouldn't have foreseen this kind of future. We have a great marriage, and we're as happy as ever, and I just feel really glad that we found each other." (1)

Joe released his next album, *Heart & Soul,* in 2004 in Europe and 2005 in the U.S. It was produced by C.J. Vanston. Executive Producers on the project were Roger Davies, Joe Cocker, and Ray Neapolitan. At this point in his career, Joe was bouncing from one record label to the next one, and this was originally released on Next Door Records. This album featured songs by U2 ("One"), Marvin Gaye ("What's Going On"), James Taylor ("Don't Let Me Be Lonely"), Screamin' Jay Hawkins ("I Put A Spell On You"), John Lennon ("Jealous Guy"), and Joe's old pal Paul McCartney ("Maybe I'm Amazed").

While promoting the *Heart & Soul* album Joe explained, "My main thing is the singing. I just enjoy the performance. I took a bit of flak for some of the songs on this new album, like doing [Marvin Gaye's] 'What's Going On,' and people said they had already been defined so well. And it might have been a bit self-indulgent. But because of my vocal style I don't try and reinvent them. Even if the arrangement isn't that far removed from the original, I try to bend them around in a certain way that gives them a new approach. I was a little disturbed doing [U2's] 'One' because it was such a Bono tune. But it sounded very personal, and I've always had a way of converting everything into love songs, sort of man/woman songs. So I rethought it to suit a bad affair." (56)

The *Heart & Soul* album featured several guest musicians supporting Cocker, including Eric Clapton, Jeff Beck, and Jeff "Skunk" Baxter of The Doobie Brothers. According to Joe, "A lot of it has to do with the producer. I always give the producer full access, 'cause you pick the producer in the first place because you're drawn to the guy. I'm not electronically minded at all, but we were able to download the songs, and then Eric or Beck would record their guitar parts in England, and the tracks just came back to us. I was too shy to ask either of them myself, so I left that to my producer. I was in shock to get a solo from Clapton, let alone a good one, I think." (57)

When it was released, the *Heart & Soul* album did well internationally. It hit Number 14 in Germany, Number 20 in France, Number 32 in New Zealand, Number 61 in the U.S., and Number 65 in Australia. The single, "One," made it to Number 31 in Australia.

Speaking of the relationship between his music career and his idyllic and peaceful life at home during this era, Joe explained, "I live up in Colorado. When I'm off the road, that's where I am, in bear country. I kind of love it up there. But it is nice to get out and make music. I mean, 'cause I never thought after 40 I would be making music—probably. So to be still bopping is not bad at all." (47)

He continued touring during this era, and now that he was both sober and suddenly no longer a cigarette smoker his stamina was very good, and it looked like he could go on and on for a long time. Joe had arrived at a nice and productive point in his life. Every couple of years he would record a new album and truly enjoy touring.

While on tour in New Zealand in 2005, Joe explained that he was able to wander around town during the day, relatively unknown and anonymously. According to him, "In the daytime when I've got my denim jeans on and a polo shirt, I can keep a low profile. Once in a while in shops people stumble on it, but otherwise I can get around unnoticed. It's kinda nice. I think back to those days when I had a real big hit, and I couldn't go anywhere. So this is a new freedom. But when people do recognize me, they don't make a big deal, they just talk to me, which is very nice." (56)

Cocker explained at the time, "We've just done 56 shows in 18 countries in three months. I get a bit caught up in being an old rocker because I get focused on the job. And that's why I like fishing, it's such a different world. In Iceland it was very pristine with beautiful waterfalls, very New Zealand-ish actually, except in places it's barren and volcanic. So we did that, then walked around the town until we got fed up with it." (56)

Joe also had a great relationship with his musicians. According to his sax player, Deric Dyer, "He's a wonderful guy and a tremendous *artiste*, but he's also very quiet about the way he does it and very quiet about the way he deals with his musicians. He gives you a tremendous amount of leeway. But he wants players who can really take it to the edge." (1)

During this era of Joe's life, he continued to tour and make new music, and Pam would either travel with him or stay in Colorado and manage The Cocker Kids Foundation. The idea of giving back to the community that was so supportive to the Cockers became a passion for her. According to Pam at the time, "The average family income in Delta County is only $16,000, the school drop-out rate is high, and there's a high teenage pregnancy rate. The Foundation is for kids up to the age of 21. It provides sports equipment and uniforms for local sports teams; we send kids to specialized camps, some medical things, anything from buying shoes when kids are really in need to trips to Europe. We've sent a lot of kids on cultural trips who couldn't afford to go otherwise. At the moment we're giving out $150,000 a year. We did it because the people here have been really good to us, and we started the Foundation to give something back. Joe's real proud of it." (1)

Joe's next album came in 2007, and in a way, it was the first theme-based album of his long career. Entitled, *Hymn For My Soul*, every song on this unique album was based on faith, redemption, love, inspiration, and forgiveness. It was released on Fantasy Records in the U.S. Songs on the album included Joe's interpretations of Bob Dylan's "Ring Them Bells," Stevie Wonder's "You Haven't Done Nothin'," and Percy Mayfield's "River's Invitation," and several more thought-provoking songs.

There are some great musicians who back up Joe on the *Hymn For My Soul* album. They included keyboard player Mike Finnegan, Benmont Tench from Tom Petty's Heartbreakers, background singer Merry Clayton, and *Mad Dogs & Englishmen* alumni drummer Jim Keltner.

How does Joe decide who plays on his albums? According to him, "It depends on what each different producer is looking for. I worked with Ethan Johns on the last album and he said, 'I'm a bit fussy with who I work with.' And, fortunately, he brought in some of the older guys like [drummer] Jim Keltner. A lot of the newer studio guys aren't used to doing things live. Ethan says they just can't deal with recording live in the studio, you know, like being spontaneous. I like doing sessions with live players, then taking the tracks back to start doing other work on it in production. For some reason, the younger guys seem to want to build tracks out of nothing, rather than starting with live tracks. Maybe I'm just asking the wrong guys, I don't know." (17)

When it was released, *Hymn For My Soul* became the highest ranking Joe Cocker album in the U.K. in a decade, making it up to Number 9 there, and Number 8 in Germany. It also made it up to Number 29 in France, and Number 38 in the Netherlands. The song "Hymn For My Soul" charted in Germany (Number 60), Austria (Number 46), and Switzerland (Number 65). And, in the U.S., although the album was not on the regular rock charts, miraculously it peaked at Number 9 on *Billboard* magazine's "Top Christian Albums" chart. Finding "redemption" was suddenly paying off for Joe Cocker!

One of the most exciting things that happened to Joe in 2007 was that he was awarded The Order of The British Empire (OBE) for his services to charities and culture over the years. His position in the world of music had gained him the respect of his native country, and he was in a great position in his life.

And the other monumental thing that happened to Joe in 2007 was the fact that he landed an acting role in an Academy Award-nominated film! It was not a heavy dramatic role, and actually Joe's part was more of a music video than an acting assignment. It was great for him to be seen up on the big screen. And what role did he play? A street bum, singing The Beatles' "Come Together."

The film was *Across The Universe* by controversial film director Julie Taymor who was famous for off-beat films like Shakespeare's *Titus* [Andronicus] and *Frida* [Khalo]. In *Across The Universe* the premise was to take every great Beatles song and use the suggested "plots" of those songs to string together a movie, making each song a musical number. In that way you have characters like Mr. Kite ("For The Benefit Of Mr. Kite"), Jude ("Hey Jude"), Martha ("Martha My Dear"), Lucy ("Lucy In The Sky With Diamonds"), and Sadie ("Sexy Sadie"). The plot of the film involves loosely intertwining those characters, and dozens more, in a wild, loopy, colorful, and music-filled cinematic romp.

For Joe Cocker's segment of the film *Across The Universe*, he is seen singing the song "Come Together" in three different personas described as: "Bum / Pimp / Mad Hippie." That's our Joe! Since Cocker's recording of "Come Together" was included on the film soundtrack album and also appeared on his *Hymn For My Soul* album, it gave him another widely distributed recording of a Beatles' tune. It had been several decades since "With A Little Help From

My Friends" originally hit the top of the music charts, so "Come Together" again proved that Cocker was truly in his prime reinter-preting Beatles' songs.

The film was critically praised. Roger Ebert in *The Chicago Sun-Times* called the film "an audacious marriage of cutting-edge visual techniques, heart-warming performances, 1960s history and the Beatles songbook." (28) Ultimately, the film was nominated for "Best Costume Design" by The Academy Awards.

How did Joe come about accepting this role in *Across The Universe*? According to him, "I'm not too sure how that decision came together. One of my producers said Julie Taymor had approached him. It all changed in the process, though; it was supposed to be David Bowie playing the Eggman and a whole list of different people who were going to be in it. We did a lot of location shooting in New York and New Jersey, going all night until as late as six in the morn-ing. So it was like doing a video, but a lot more work." (17)

When Joe went into the studio to record the song "Come Together," it was T-Bone Burnett who was the producer. As Cocker explained, "Starting off, it was T-Bone Burnett doing the track. And I wasn't too fired up about that, because I was hoping for a lot more from the track after I left him with it. But the script was written, and Julie laid it all out for me saying, 'You're going to play the pimp, and a tramp, and a hippie.' It's strange; it was a strange, cultish kind of movie. But here in the sticks, the teens really like it. It really intro-duced them to a lot of Beatles songs, hearing them rattled off one after another." (17)

While touring in 2009, Joe Cocker was asked how he chose the bands he took on the road. He explained, "For the last few years, I've been using the same players who are not necessarily the guys that I settle down to record with. Nick Milo, who used to be with Tower of Power. Gene Black on lead guitar, he's one of those cats who has been around LA for a long time, and he knows my songs implicitly.

You know, at one time, I used to say, 'I just don't want to go out there and do the hits.' And I still throw in a few newer songs, but I kind of realized, when you've only got an hour and a half or two hours to put it over, the audience really wants to hear those [hits]. But it's not just that. I try and reinvent them every time I go out. The nature of my material is R&B, so my phrasing doesn't have to be locked in to one set motion. Once I resigned myself a few years back that the audience is going to want to hear all those same songs, I kind of get into it in a different light, and I really do enjoy performing more now. I have a lot of fun." (17)

For the last years of his life Joe was enjoying it without the destructive involvement of cigarettes and liquor. He had a great career recording albums and touring around the globe. And he was especially happy in his day-to-day life at his Mad Dog Ranch. Like his late father, Harold, Joe took up the hobby of gardening. His pet project was his tomatoes, which he took care of painstakingly. It was a whole new Joe Cocker!

To his neighbors and local friends, he was truly the personification of "everyday Joe." As Pam was to recall, "Here in Colorado, our neighbors, and people that became our friends certainly knew his history, but they weren't obsessed by it. It didn't matter to them at all. It mattered that we were good neighbors, that we were part of the community, and Joe really liked that. He liked being part of a community. He liked that his friends were the local plumber, and the electrician, and the real estate agent, and the little country lawyer. He just loved those guys. And it made Joe a better person to have that kind of support." (45)

In 2010, at the age of 66, it had been 54 years since his first public appearance as a singer in Sheffield and 41 years after he made a name for himself at *Woodstock*. Now here he was with this 21st studio album. How has he managed to survive all this time in the music business? According to him at the time, "Because music's never been a job to me. A fun life, money, and I've survived." He also admitted, "I had a real boozing problem. You know when you stop *eating*. I used to drink to feel . . . straight. Down the pub for 11:00 a.m., a bottle of rum a day." (6)

In the intervening time, Joe continued to tour and to make new music. His next album was 2011's *Hard Knocks*. Speaking about the album's creation, Joe explained, "Well, I worked with [producer] Matt Seletic. I talked with a few producers. Matt was in a band called Collective Soul." (47)

This was an album that had a specifically planned direction to it, which was something new for him. According to Cocker, "I'd been with EMI [Records] for years, and they packed up on my record deal. So Sony Germany said, 'We'd like you to make a record just for Europe that was more of a traditional Joe Cocker record.' And I didn't quite know what they meant. But sound-wise, they wanted something that would get played on radio, and Matt and I listened to like a hundred songs, you know? 'Cause that's one thing that is more difficult as you get older. People send you teeny-bopper lyrics, you know what I mean?" (47)

He also claimed that at this stage of his career, it was becoming difficult to find songs to sing that were age appropriate for him. Apparently, songwriters still approached him with songs that would be better suited to a 20-year-old, instead of a mature man. As Joe explained it, "They custom-write songs that they think you're going to fall over backwards when you hear them. And they forget, you know, that when you're 68, you don't want to sing, 'I want to see you in the steam room, baby,' you know. And that's the kind of stuff they've been sending me. So it's a long filter process now." (47)

On March 20, 2011, Joe was in New York City, where he took part in a benefit concert held at the nightclub B.B. Kings, on West 42nd Street. At that particular event, Jonathan, who worked for years with Johnny Winter, served as the stage manager.

According to Moorehead, "It was kind of a historic event. I was with Johnny Winter at B.B. Kings a lot for different things. The one I was at where Joe performed was another event. I am friendly with a promoter, David Kramer, who has done lots and lots of shows in New York. This event involved Cornell Dupree of the group Stuff. He was very well respected. So when Cornell needed a lung transplant, my friend David Kramer put together a benefit in New York City. We had Dr. John, we had Paul Shaffer, and we had Joe Cocker—a couple of luminaries. From what I understand both Joe and Dr. John did the shows for gratis, for their sheer love of Cornell. Now, Cornell passed away before we could get him the operation, but we had raised the money. It was kind of unfortunate. I had met Cornell a couple of times." (58)

Also on hand in the band that evening were several of Cornell's musician friends, including jazz keyboard player Henry Butler, Bob Malach of The Steve Miller Band, and Lew Soloff of Blood, Sweat & Tears. Paul Shaffer, who was the band leader on TV's *Late Night With David Letterman* for years, served as the evening's MC, introducing the performers as they took the stage.

Jonathan Moorehead recalls, Moorehead recalls, Moorehead recalls, "Corky Laing from Mountain was there hanging out backstage and chatting, and Donna Godchaux from The Grateful Dead was there, so it was definitely a noteworthy event. Performance-wise, it was from the end of Joe Cocker's life. The photos of him I took that night were stereotypical shots. He was older, a bit of a belly, short-haired but balding, and still doing his thing on stage. He was very pleasant backstage. He was a doll. Everyone I have heard from, who worked with Joe, loved him." (58)

"Joe was a good guy," says Moorehead of Joe's reputation in the music business. "He was not the kind of guy whose life was full of unhappy people along the way. Joe was basically a good guy with a lot of personal demons, and there were not a lot of 'skeletons in the closet' about him." (58)

Joe's touring throughout the U.S. in 2012 featured Huey Lewis as his opening act. Personally speaking, I—Mark Bego—saw Huey and Joe at Pine Knob, in Clarkston, Michigan that year, and I can attest that I was very impressed with Joe's performance. He was very centered, very engaging, and he was in great voice.

During that tour, Joe was in excellent spirits. He told one reporter, "I'm just getting to know Huey. He's quite a comic, you know, quite a character. So we're getting on quite well, and we're making some good music, I think. We're settling in. I'm not doing much new stuff. On just a couple of blues, Huey's coming up and we're doing an old Ray Charles blues [number] together." (47)

With regard to doing new material in his show, Joe explained, "I'm only doing the title track, 'Hard Knocks.' And the rest is pretty much, you know, 'When The Night Comes,' 'You Can Leave Your Hat On.' 'Cause we've only got a short set. It was designed that way—that we both do short sets. And I find in the summertime, the people, you know they prefer, their concentration level isn't quite the same. So it's best just to whack them with stuff they know, you know?" (47)

One of the venues that Joe played during the summer of 2012 was the outdoor amphitheater called Bethel Woods, which is on the site of the legendary *Woodstock Music Festival* in 1969. Talk about "déjà vu!"

Joe found the experience to be a little bit freaky, to say the least. According to him, "They asked me if I wanted to go out front and see where everybody sat and all that, and I had no desire to—or go to the museum, really. It was more a feeling. I mean, it was like the end of the '60s and it was like when Hendrix played 'The Star Spangled Banner.' It was almost like someone ringing the bell down on the times. It was, quite literally, the end of a special time." (47)

Looking back on his career from the vantage point of 2012, Joe was able to admit that he had been lucky enough to have had such appealing hit songs to sing. According to him, "So you can call it luck or whatever, but I mean, I was fortunate enough to sort of have one of those songs come along each decade. I have 'You Are So Beautiful' in the '70s, 'A Little Help [From My Friends]' in the '60s, and 'Unchain My Heart.' So these songs just by a fluke came along, and they've sort of stuck in people. You know, I think that's why I've been able to keep going so long." (47)

For his 2012 tour, it was with Dave Mason, who wrote Joe's hit "Feelin' Alright." According to a jovial Cocker mid-tour, "Whenever I see him, I tell him, 'I've helped make you a few bucks over the years off that one, haven't I?' But I'm afraid both of us have put on a bit of weight, and so whenever he comes onstage with me, it becomes a bit of a belly banging." (15)

Joe no longer did all of his greatest hits at every show. He would pick and choose them. Speaking about what songs he liked to sing in concert, Cocker explained, "I'll do like 'Bathroom Window,' The Beatles song, and 'Feelin' Alright,' which is like I know it so well that it's a part of my soul. So I have no problems going back and singing older material, but some of it doesn't. I mean, some of it travels better than others. I mean, for some reason a song like 'Feelin' Alright' sounds as fresh today as it did back in '67 when I recorded it. But some songs you try—like I do 'Delta Lady' every now and then, and it doesn't seem right. It just didn't transfer the times the way that 'Feelin' Alright' [did]. A certain rhythm—some rhythms transgress the time period, but other kind of don't. You know what I mean?" (47)

At the time, Joe was already working on his next album, to ultimately be entitled *Fire It Up*. Joe said at the time, "I've been working on another album with Matt. We've just finished a second one since *Hard Knocks* that's going to come out in Europe in September.

This one, it's called *Fire It Up*. And again, I haven't done many covers. 'Cause people say, 'How come?' They used to complain I did too many covers, and then when I don't do them, they don't understand that, either. But this, again, it was a two-record deal I made for Europe. But we sold a quarter of a million copies of the last one, in CD form in Germany." (47)

When *Fire It Up* was released, it did well in several countries, notably hitting Number 17 in the U.K., Number 5 in Germany, Number 32 in the Netherlands, and Number 128 in France. Although *Fire It Up* didn't exactly set the global charts aflame, it was still a respectable seller for Joe. Here he was, almost 70 years old, over 50 years of rocking and rolling, and still hitting the Top Ten.

During this era Joe was quite centered and happy with his life. He also gladly did all sorts of press interviews. When writer Lee Zimmerman interviewed Joe for the *New Times* in September of 2012, he found the singer to be very centered, relaxed, and comfortable with himself. As the writer reported, "Ensconced at his Mad Dog Ranch in Crawford, Colorado, located in the remote reaches of the Colorado Rockies, Cocker turned out to be surprisingly down-to-earth, willing to open up about his history, and as gracious and engaging as any musician I've ever encountered." (15)

He was asked by Michael Hann of *The Guardian* newspaper in 2013 how he managed to sleep on the road? Joe explained, "I've been taking Ambien for a while now. I have tinnitus from years of loud music and some nights it's the only way I can put it out of my mind. My wife's always trying to get me to stop. You don't dream, which is not the best thing in the world. But I know I'm going to get some sleep. I'm 69 and you know you're going to be a casualty of the rock world somewhere down the line." (3)

When Joe was asked about his trademark spastic on stage choreography, he claimed, "You mean my arm movements? I actually saw myself with Eric Clapton—you know you see all your old stuff on YouTube now—and I was horrified at myself with my arms just flailing around. I guess that came with my frustration at never having played piano or guitar. If you see me nowadays, I'm not quite so animated, but it's just a way of trying to get feeling out. I get excited and it all comes through my body." (3)

Jimmy Webb recorded an album in 2013 called *Still Within The Sound Of My Voice* on which he re-recorded some of his favorite songs which he had written in the past. This time around he did duet versions of the songs with guest performers on it including Carly Simon, Keith Urban, America, Art Garfunkel, Amy Grant, David Crosby, Graham Nash, and several other singing stars. He decided that he wanted to re-record "The Moon Is A Harsh Mistress" with Joe Cocker. So he got in contact with Joe, and they went into the studio together.

Webb recalls of Joe's recording, "He was coming off seven shows when he faithfully showed up early for our session at Emblem Studios in the [San Fernando] Valley to re-record 'The Moon' for the first time since 1974. He gave us his best shot every time we put down the button. We had a chance to talk about kindness, sobriety, and the rigors of life on the road today. It was like sitting down on a favorite couch that might be worn a little here and there but that you would never part with." (34)

In 2013 Joe appeared with Jennifer Warnes on a German awards show. They had been invited to reprise their classic chart-topping duet, "Up Where We Belong." The show also paid tribute to Joe as well. According to Jennifer, "It was like he was a little bit more vulnerable. He seemed a little tired, but very sweet. In the early days, he was a music machine, so I'm glad he found happiness." (13)

With regard to Joe's stamina, Warnes was to recall, "Joe could function really well. He was a pro, and he was very strong. People wanted to see Joe rise. They were glad he wasn't dead, because he could have been." (13)

It was somewhere along the line during Joe's 2013 *Fire It Up Tour*, things took a turn for the worse. Ray Neapolitan was amongst the first to know that something was physically wrong with Joe. According to him, "We did a wonderful show in Cologne, [Germany], and it just was spectacular. Everything went off exactly as we wanted it. It looked fabulous, Joe sang well, 16,000 there that night. But as this happened, Joe was starting to feel pains in his sides. I would come off the stage and he would say, 'Ray, my sides are killing me. I can't catch my breath.' He made it through the tour, as heroic as he can be. And bull-headed. He just fought it." (45)

Somehow Joe made it through the tour like a trouper, even though he knew that something was physically wrong. The last concert of the current tour was September 7, 2013. Pam recalls, "He came home on September 8. He just looked awful, and he was completely exhausted. I'd never seen Joe that exhausted." (45)

As Ray was to explain, "This was a Sunday, Pam takes him in on Tuesday. By Friday he's diagnosed with Stage Four small cell lung cancer. We just kept it quiet. The word was that Joe has just taken an extended vacation." (45)

His devoted wife, Pam, was amazed how well Joe did while he was at home, watching his health deteriorate. According to her, "I don't know that I would have been able to be as strong as he was. He didn't complain. He never complained. He never said, 'Why me? Why is this happening to me?' In fact, he was almost kinda like, 'Well, considering my background and my history, and smoking for all those years, and drinking for all those years, why not me?'" (45)

Knowing that Joe was not going to survive this, efforts were made to tie up all of the loose ends of his life. Ray Neapolitan explains, "We were trying to have Joe nominated for The Rock & Roll Hall Of Fame. We had lobbied them, with all of Roger's power, all the label power lobbying them. We had signatures from fans around the world." (45)

Billy Joel, who was a lifelong Joe Cocker fan, totally got into the push to get Joe into The Rock & Roll Hall Of Fame but to no avail. The list of who does and who doesn't get onto that list of honorees is very political, and, to date, Cocker has yet to be honored by that organization.

Knowing that Joe would never make it back into the recording studio again, Sony Music quickly put together the most successful concert tapes from Joe's 2013 *Fire It Up Tour* and that same year released the CD *Fire It Up Live*. It has the distinction of being the final audio record of Cocker's final tour.

Joe lasted until December 22, 2014. That was the day the final "fire" went out, and he died quietly only days before Christmas. Although Pam had watched the whole process of Joe's decline, the end still came as something of a shock to her. According to Pam, "We were looking forward to our old age." (45)

News traveled quickly, and his closest friends heard the sad news. "He could be difficult, but everybody loved him," recalled his older brother Vic. (45) Indeed, Joe Cocker was one of the most colorful singers in the history of recorded music, and now that he was suddenly gone, it was his music, his memory, and his legacy that would live onward.

CHAPTER TWELVE

"The Joe Cocker Legacy"

What an amazing career Joe Cocker had. He recorded 22 studio albums, had several live albums, most notably *Mad Dogs & Englishmen*, and many Greatest Hits packages. He won a Grammy Award, sang for Queen Elizabeth II, acted in a film, recorded an Academy Award-winning song, and entertained millions of fans around the globe. He logged 18 Top 40 songs, and *Rolling Stone* magazine has proclaimed him as one of the Top 100 singers of all time. Joe's legacy is one of excited triumph. Yet it is also one of sad tragedy.

With a talent like his, there should have been more music from him, more creativity, and more great performances by him. Fortunately, the documentaries like *Woodstock* and *Mad Dogs & Englishmen*, film performances like in *Across The Universe*, and videos like *The Ed Sullivan Show* each keep different eras and different sides of Joe and his music alive. And what an amazing wealth of recorded music he created in his long career.

How ironic and tragic is it to think that Joe Cocker drank and smoked cigarettes his entire adult life, and finally in the 2000s, he saw the light and put them all in the past. Throughout his entire life, everyone assumed that it was all the liquor he drank which would harm him the most. However, it was the cigarettes that ultimately did it. He had found redemption in giving up both vices, but, unfortunately, it was too late.

Almost immediately following the news of Joe's passing, the tributes started appearing in the media. Chris Stainton was his longest and best friend from the very beginning of Joe's career. According to Chris, "He was born to be a star, to be up front in a band. You know, that's him. What else is he gonna do? Looking like that, singing like that." (45)

Joe had not seen Chris since their last tour, 14 years earlier. "We sort of drifted apart," Stainton was to explain. "I did my last tour with him in 2000 and I never actually did see him again. We emailed a couple of times and he used to send pictures of his tomatoes. He would grow tomatoes. The next thing I found out he was gone." (12)

Graham Nash claimed of Joe, "He always seemed to be a very fragile being, as if he would shatter in an instant, especially on an emotional level. But he was a tremendously sincere singer. When he sang, you knew he believed the song and what he was doing." (13)

Longtime Cocker fan Billy Joel said, "In my opinion, no one has come even close to him as one of the great primal rock & roll vocalists of all time." (13)

Joe's original idol Lonnie Donegan declared, "Joe Cocker is the best white blues singer in the world!" (59)

Paul McCartney claimed, "I knew him through the years as a good mate and I was so sad to hear that he had been ill and really sad to hear today that he had passed away." (60)

Although Joe's two most high profile events came early in his career, *Woodstock* and *Mad Dogs & Englishmen*, Cocker perpetually astonished his public by resurrecting his career time and time again. It would have been so easy to have written him off in 1974 as a hopeless drunk who closed his own show in a drunken heap on the stage of The Roxy in Hollywood.

Who would have suspected that the rock & roll king of vomiting on stage would not only pull his personal life together, but would also sing an Academy Award-winning song, sing for the Queen, be awarded The Order of The British Empire (OBE), perform with Pavorotti, win a Grammy Award, and recorded a track on the biggest selling soundtrack album of all times?

In so many ways, Joe Cocker was the antithesis of the words "rock star." He was not a pretty boy like Elvis Presley, Fabian, or Cliff Richard. He was not a fashion plate like Robert Palmer, David Bowie, or David Byrne. He was not svelte, or in shape, or in any definition of the words physically attractive. He spent the majority of his life carrying himself dressed like he was a rock-tour roadie and not the fascinatingly unique star of the show at all.

Yet somehow when the night was right, and the mood was correct, and Joe was in the right frame of mind, from the moment he opened his mouth to sing on stage, there was no question that he was the star of the show. With unforgettable songs sung like no one else could interpret them, Joe Cocker may have been the most unlikely rock star on the planet, but he will forever be remembered as having the voice that was the heart and soul of rock & roll.

Joe Cocker Discography

NOTE: The record labels listed are for the most part the U.S. record. With regard to the chart figures, U.S. figures are mainly listed and foreign figures are used only whenever that album hit a significant mark, or specifically in the Top Ten.

THE STUDIO ALBUMS

1. *With A Little Help From My Friends* (1969 / A&M Records) [Charts: U.S. #35, U.K. #29]
2. *Joe Cocker!* (1969 / A&M Records) [U.S. #11, U.K. #29, Canada #10]
3. *Something To Say* [aka *Joe Cocker*] (1972 / A&M Records) [U.S. #30, Australia #11, France #8, Italy #4]
4. *I Can Stand A Little Rain* (1974 / A&M Records) [U.S. #11, Australia #11, France #8, Canada #9]
5. *Jamaica Say You Will* (1975 / A&M Records) [U.S. #42, Australia #39]
6. *Stingray* (1976 / A&M Records) [U.S. #70, Australia #35, Canada #21]
7. *Luxury You Can Afford* (1978 / Elektra Records) [U.S. #76, Australia #12]
8. *Sheffield Steel* (1978 / Island Records) [U.S. #105, Australia #14, France #10]
9. *Civilized Man* (1984 / Capitol Records)

[U.K. #100, U.S. #133, Australia #17, Germany #4, Italy #2]

10. *Cocker* (1986 / Capitol Records)
    [U.S. #50, Australia #9, Germany #4, Italy #2]

11. *Unchain My Heart* (1987 / Capitol Records)
    [U.S. #89, Australia #24, Germany #2]

12. *One Night Of Sin* (1989 / Capitol Records)
    [U.S. #52, Australia #34, Germany #2, Italy #4]

13. *Night Calls* (1991 / Capitol Records)
    [U.S. #111, U.K. #25, New Zealand #20, Germany #2, Italy #4]

14. *Have A Little Faith* (1994 / Capitol Records)
    [U.K. #9, France #6, Germany #3, Netherlands #2, Italy #20, Sweden #7]

15. *Organic* (1996 / Sony Music U.K.)
    [U.K. #49, France #10, Germany #5, Netherlands #15]

16. *Across From Midnight* (1997 / EMI Records U.K.)
    [U.K. #94, France #5, Germany #3, Netherlands #2]

17. *No Ordinary World* (1999 / Eagle Records U.K.)
    [U.K. #63, France #12, Germany #3]

18. *Respect Yourself* (2002 / Parlophone Records U.K.)
    [U.K. #54, France #13, Germany #3, Italy #15]

19. *Heart & Soul* (2004 U.K. / 2005 U.S. / Next Door Records U.S.)
    [U.S. #61, France #20, Germany #14, Italy #26]

20. *Hymn For My Soul* (2007 / Fantasy Records U.S.)
    [U.K. #9 / France #29 / Germany #8]

21. *Hard Knocks* (2010 U.K. / 2012 U.S. / 429 Records U.S.)
    [U.K. #61, France #34, Germany #1]

22. *Fire It Up* (2012 / Next Door Records U.S.)
    [U.K. #17, Germany #5]

SELECT LIVE ALBUMS

1. *Mad Dogs & Englishmen* (1970 / A&M Records)
   [U.S. #2, U.K. #16, Australia #3, Netherlands #9, Canada #2]
2. *Joe Cocker Live* (1990 / Capitol Records)
   [U.S. #5, Australia #17, New Zealand #2, Italy #8]
3. *Mad Dogs & Englishmen* [2-CD Deluxe Edition] (2005 / A&M Records)
4. *Live At Woodstock* [Joe's complete 1969 set] (2009 / A&M Records)
5. *Fire It Up - Live* (2013 / Next Door Records)
6. *Live At Woodstock '94* (2012 / On-stage Records / Italy)
7. *Alive In America* (2021 / Renaissance Records)

JOE COCKER PERFORMANCES ON OTHER ALBUMS

1. *Woodstock* (1970 / Atlantic Records)
2. *Woodstock / Three Days Of Peace And Music / 25th Anniversary Collection*
   (1994 / Atlantic Records)
3. *Pavatotti & Friends: For Guatemala And Kosovo* (1999 / Decca Records)
   ["You Are So Beautiful" by Luciano Pavarotti, Joe Cocker, Alex Britti]

NOTABLE GREATEST HITS RELEASES

1. *Cocker Happy* (1971 / Cube Records Germany)
   [Australia #1, New Zealand # 32, Italy #9]
2. *Joe Cocker's Greatest Hits* (1977 / A&M Records)

[New Zealand #32]

3. *The Best Of Joe Cocker* (1983 / EMI Records Australia)
[Australia #1, New Zealand #32]

4. *Joe Cocker Classics / Volume 4* (1987 / A&M Records)

5. *The Best Of Joe Cocker* (1993 / Capitol Records)
[France #1, Netherlands #12, New Zealand #10, Italy #14, Sweden #9, Germany #7]

6. *Joe Cocker: The Anthology* (1999 / A&M Records)

7. *The Best Of Joe Cocker / The Millennium Collection* (2000 / A&M Records / Universal Music)

8. *The Ultimate Collection* (2004 / A&M Records / Hippo Records / Universal Music)

9. *Classic Cocker* (2007 / Parlophane Records)
[Australia #38, New Zealand #9, U.S. #167]

10. *Joe Cocker: The Life Of A Man* (2015 / Universal Music Records)
[Australia #44, New Zealand #21, Germany #14]

Bibliography / Source Material

(1) *Joe Cocker*, book, by J.P. Bean, Virgin Books, 2003, (previous released version: *Joe Cocker: With A Little Help From My Friends*, Omnibus Press, 1990)

(2) *Interview*, magazine, "Joe Cocker," by Susan Morgan, September 1991

(3) *The Guardian*, newspaper, "Joe Cocker: 'I Took Black Acid Once . . . It Was A Very Dark Trip,'" by Michael Hann, January 31, 2013

(4) *Radio Hallam*, broadcast, Joe Cocker, broadcast interview by Ray Stuart, 1982

(5) *Off The Record*, book, by Joe Smith, Warner Books, New York City, 1988

(6) *MOJO* magazine, "Joe Cocker," by Phil Sutcliffe, November 2010

(7) *Rolling Stone*, magazine, "Joe Cocker: 'U.S.'s Only Culture Is Black,'" by Ritchie Yorke, March 1, 1969

(8) *The Sheffield Telegraph*, newspaper, "Review" of Peter Stringfellow's rock & roll event, November 1963

(9) Decca Records Press Release, "Joe Cocker," 1964

(10) Press Release, "It's A Big Gas Man," by Martin Yale, 1964

(11) *The Los Angeles Times*, newspaper "Joe Cocker: A New Blues Boy Blows In From Britain," John Mendelssohn, August 3, 1969

(12) *Rolling Stone*, magazine, "Keyboardist Chris Stainton On His Years With Eric Clapton, Joe Cocker, And The Who," by Andy Greene, March 10, 2021

(13) *Rolling Stone*, magazine, "Joe Cocker, 1944-2014," by David Browne, January 29, 2015

(14) *Melody Maker*, magazine, "Joe Cocker: Soul Sheffield Style," by Chris Welch, October 26, 1968

(15) *New Times*, newspaper, Broward-Palm Beach, Florida, "Joe Cocker On John Belushi's Impression Of Him: 'I Thought Vocally, He Did Quite A Clever Job,'" by Lee Zimmerman, September 28, 2012

(16) *Top Stars Special*, magazine, Interview with Joe Cocker, 1968

(17) *www.SoundSpike.com* (France), website, "Joe Cocker," interview by John Voket, 2009

(18) *Crawdaddy*, magazine, "Joe Cocker Got $800 For *Mad Dogs & Englishmen*, Why…and How?," by Peter McCabe, June 11, 1972

(19) *Top Stars Special*, magazine, "Joe Cocker," 1968

(20) *AZQuotes.com,* website, "Leon Russell, A - Z," 2023

(21) *Leon Russell: In His Own Words*, edited by Steve Todoroff and John Wooley, SteveTodoroffArcheves book, 2019

(22) Proposal for the unpublished version of the 1990s book *Delta Lady*, by Rita Coolidge and Mark Bego, based on Bego's in-person interviews with Rita Coolidge, 1997

(23) *Delta Lady*, a memoir by Rita Coolidge with Michael Walker, Harper Books, New York 2016

(24) *Barefoot In Babylon, The Creation Of The Woodstock Music Festival, 1969*, book, by Robert Stephen Spitz, The Viking Press, New York City, 1979

(25) Mark Bego's interview with Melanie Safka, June 16, 2023

(26) *Rolling Stone*, magazine, "Atlantic City: Pop! Goes Boardwalk," by John Lombardi, September 6, 1969

(27) *Rolling Stone* magazine, "What's Going On Here, Joe Cocker?" by Timothy Crouse, May 25, 1972

(28) *The Chicago Sun-Times*, Review of the film *Across The Universe*, by Roger Ebert, 2007

(29) *Q*, magazine, "All Together Now," by Mat Snow, May 1992

(30) *Circus*, magazine, "Joe Cocker: The Road Which Lies Ahead," by Phil Ardery, August 1970

(31) Review of Joe Cocker at Madison Square Garden, Lillian Roxon, 1972

(32) *The Mirror*, newspaper, "Joe Cocker" interview, 1972

(33) *New Musical Express*, magazine, "Joe Cocker: They Put Me In The Same Cell As A Bank Robber And A Murder Suspect," by Keith Altham, November 18, 1972

(34) *Still Within The Sound Of My Voice*, CD liner notes, by Jimmy Webb, Entertainment One Records, 2013

(35) *Billboard*, magazine, review of *I Can Stand A Little Rain*, 1974

(36) *Melody Maker*, magazine, "Cocker Dies A Death," Jacoba Atlas, June 15, 1974

(37) *Melody Maker*, magazine, review of Joe Cocker, by Chris Charlesworth, 1974

(38) *Record World*, magazine, review of the album *Jamaica Say You Will*, 1975

(39) *Rolling Stone*, magazine, "Ray Charles" Interview by Ben Fong-Torres, October 15th, 1992 [Interview first published in that publication's January 18, 1973 issue]

(40) *New Musical Express*, magazine, "Never Give A Sucker An Even Break," by Tony Stewart, January 8, 1977

(41) *Blank Space*, magazine, "Part Three Of The Joe Cocker Story," May 1979

(42) *Melody Maker*, magazine, review of Joe Cocker's stage show, 1976

(43) *The Sydney Morning Herald*, newspaper, interview with Joe Cocker, 1977

(44) *The Los Angeles Herald Examiner*, newspaper, review of the album *Luxury You Can Afford*, 1978

(45) *Mad Dog With Soul*, DVD, Eagle Rock / Eaglevision Entertainment, 2017

(46) *The Cleveland Plain Dealer*, newspaper, review of Joe Cocker and The Guess Who, 2001

(47) *Lehigh Valley Music*, Lehigh, Pennsylvania, magazine, "Jawing With Joe Cocker: Blues Rocker Tells How He Had Hits In '60s, '70s and '80s," by John J. Moser, August 5, 2012

(48) *Musician,* magazine, "Joe Cocker's Island Renaissance," by Fred Schruers, July 1982

(49) *Creem*, magazine, "Joe Cocker Visits My Hometown! Wow!," by J. Kordosh, November 1982

(50) Mark Bego's interview with Linda Solomon, June 12, 2023

(51) *The Sheffield Star*, newspaper, interview with Harold Cocker, 1989

(52) *The Observer*, newspaper, review of Joe Cocker in concert, by Jasper Rees, 1992

(53) *The Guardian*, newspaper, review of Joe Cocker, 1992

(54) *Mail On Sunday*, newspaper, interview with Joe Cocker, 1992

(55) *The Birmingham Post*, newspaper, Birmingham, England, "Who Would You Rather Be? A Tale Of Two Brothers," by Dennis Ellam and Simon Evans, September 5, 1998

(56) *Western Colorado Style*, magazine, "Feeling Alright At The Mad Dog Ranch," by Kathleen M. Bush, 1999

(57) *Blue Ridge Now / Times News*, newspaper, "What's Old Is New Again For Joe Cocker," by Marty Clear, January 27, 2005

(58) Mark Bego's interview with Jonathan Moorhead, June 21, 2023

(59) *Sounds of The Sixties*, BBC Radio broadcast, Guest D.J.: Lonnie Donegan, July 1987

(60) *BBC News*, "Joe Cocker: Sir Paul McCartney Leads Tributes To Singer," December 23, 2014

About The Author

MARK BEGO is *The New York Times* best-selling author of 68 published books on rock & roll and show business. He has over 13 million books in print in a dozen languages. He is known for his biographies of Michael Jackson, Madonna, Elton John, Billy Joel, The Doobie Brothers, Bonnie Raitt, and Patsy Cline. In 2017 he shifted gears to become a celebrity chef when he published his all-star cookbook *Eat Like a Rock Star* (2017) which became a Top Ten best-seller. Mark has collaborated on rock star biographies with Mary Wilson of The Supremes, Jimmy Greenspoon of Three Dog Night, Martha Reeves of Martha & The Vandellas, Debbie Gibson, Randy Jones of The Village People, and Micky Dolenz of The Monkees. Mark recently scored three consecutive Number 1 books in a row on the Amazon charts including: *Aretha Franklin: The Queen of Soul—Tribute Edition* (2018) and *Living The Luxe Life* [with hotelier Efrem Harkham] (2019). His third consecutive chart topper was the highly acclaimed *Supreme Glamour* (2019) written with his longtime best friend, the late Mary Wilson. In 2021 Bego worked with legendary pop and jazz singer, Freda Payne, on her autobiography, *Band Of Gold* (Yorkshire Publishing) which became a critical hit of a book. Mark chronicled his music writing career in his 2010 memoir *Paperback Writer*. He lives in Tucson, Arizona.